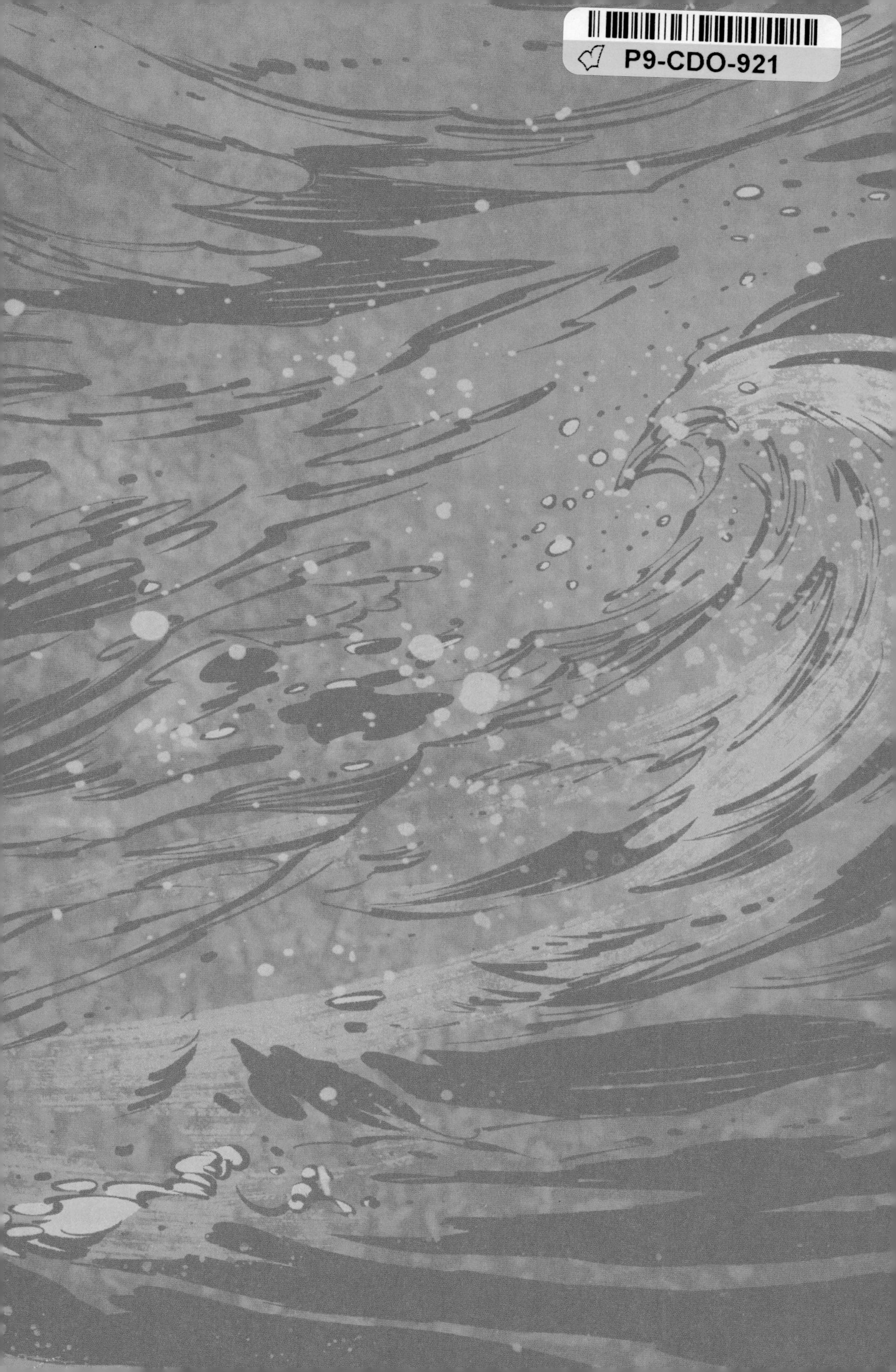

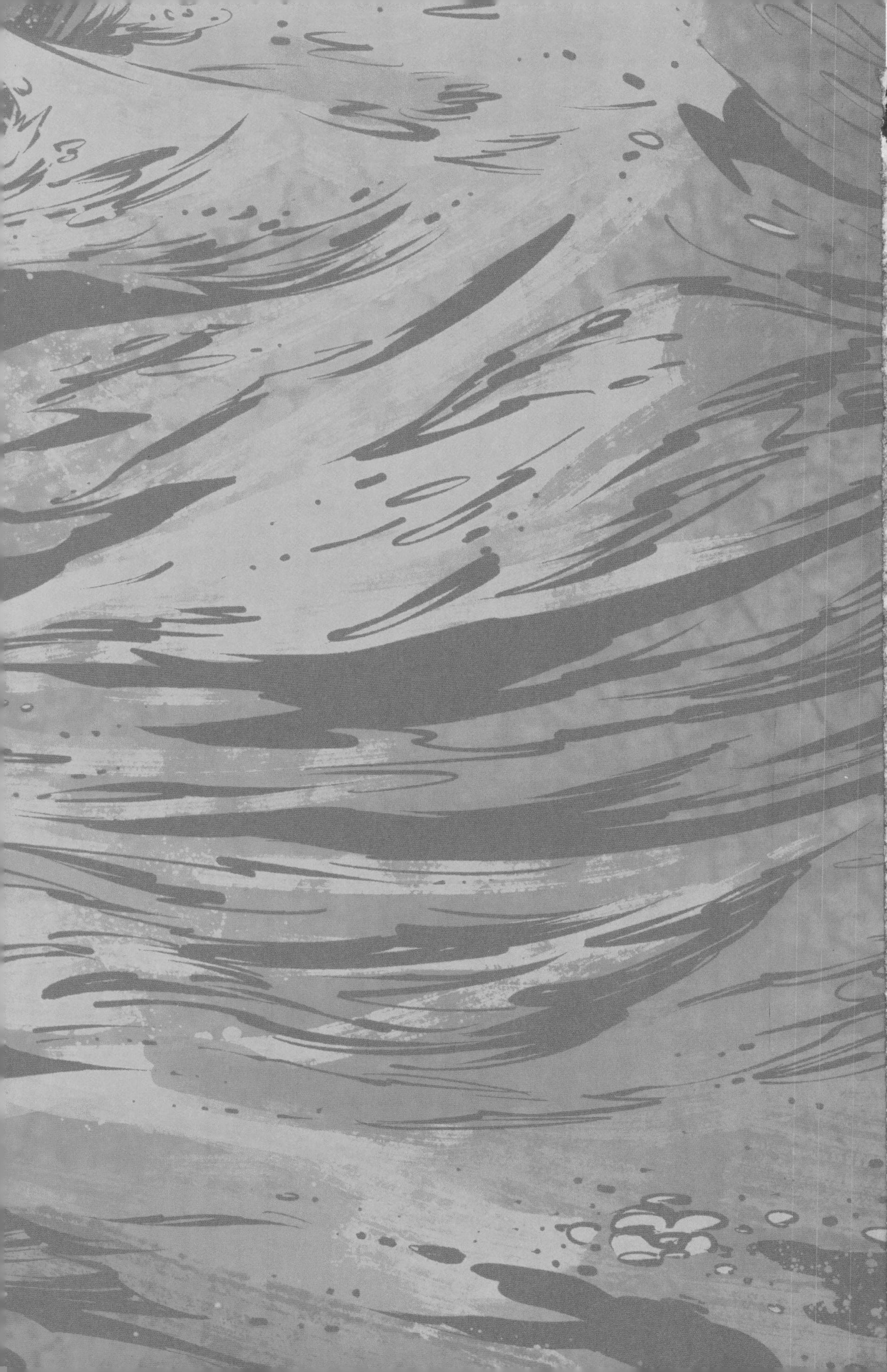

VOL. I

UNSPOKEN WATER

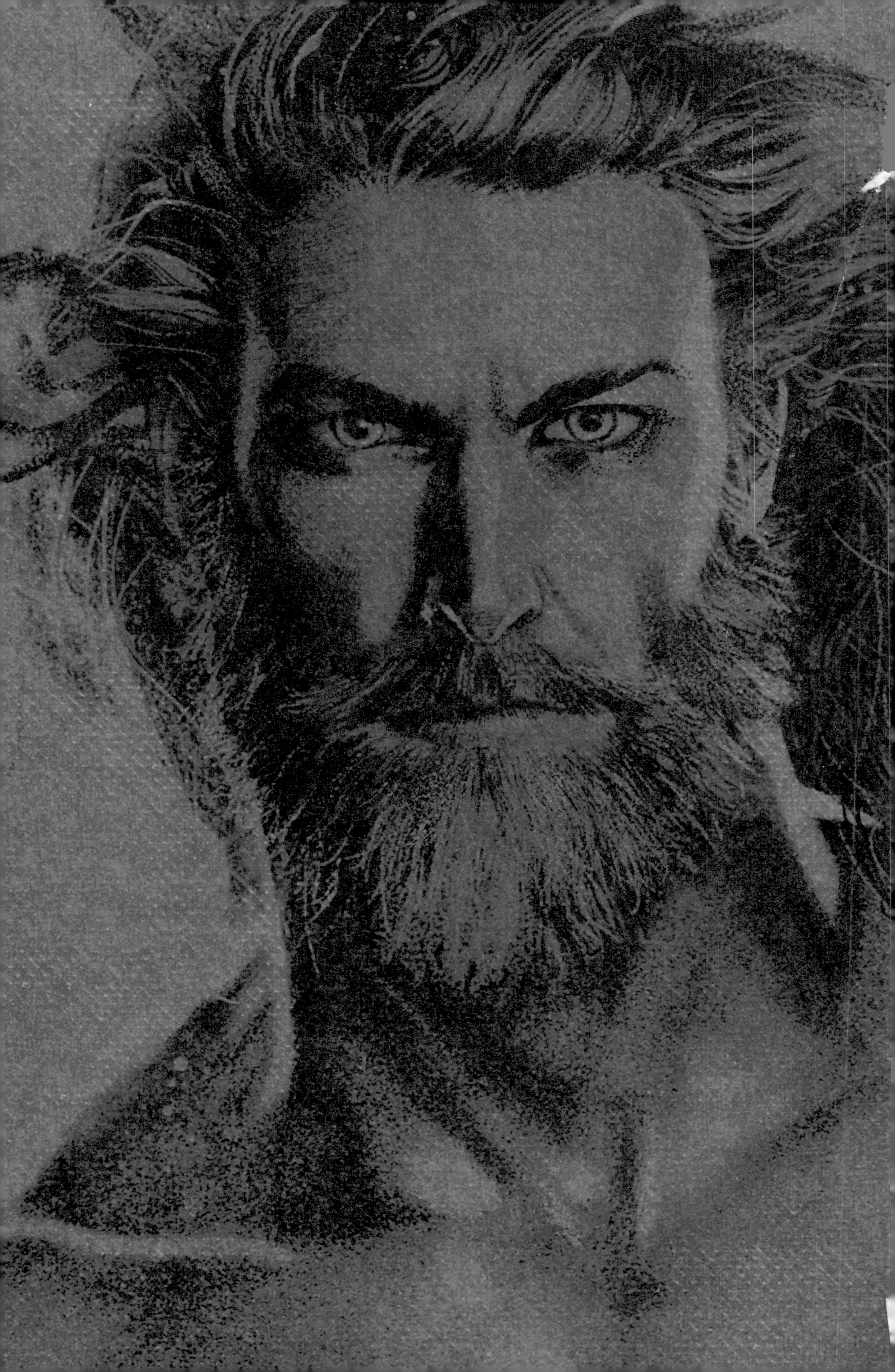

AQUAMAN

UNSPOKEN WATER

KELLY SUE DeCONNICK writer
ROBSON ROCHA penciller
DANIEL HENRIQUES inker
SUNNY GHO colorist
CLAYTON COWLES letterer
ROBSON ROCHA, DANIEL HENRIQUES
& SUNNY GHO collection cover artists

AQUAMAN CREATED BY PAUL NORRIS

VOL. I

ALEX ANTONE Editor – Original Series
ANDREA SHEA Assistant Editor – Original Series
JEB WOODARD Group Editor – Collected Editions
ROBIN WILDMAN Editor – Collected Edition
STEVE COOK Design Director – Books
LOUIS PRANDI Publication Design
KATE DURRÉ Publication Production

BOB HARRAS Senior VP – Editor-in-Chief, DC Comics
PAT McCALLUM Executive Editor, DC Comics

DAN DiDIO Publisher
JIM LEE Publisher & Chief Creative Officer
BOBBIE CHASE VP – New Publishing Initiatives & Talent Development
DON FALLETTI VP – Manufacturing Operations & Workflow Management
LAWRENCE GANEM VP – Talent Services
ALISON GILL Senior VP – Manufacturing & Operations
HANK KANALZ Senior VP – Publishing Strategy & Support Services
DAN MIRON VP – Publishing Operations
NICK J. NAPOLITANO VP – Manufacturing Administration & Design
NANCY SPEARS VP – Sales
MICHELE R. WELLS VP & Executive Editor, Young Reader

**AQUAMAN VOL. 1:
UNSPOKEN WATER**

Published by DC Comics. Compilation and all new
material Copyright © 2019 DC Comics. All Rights
Reserved. Originally published in single magazine
form in AQUAMAN 43-47. Copyright © 2018, 2019
DC Comics. All Rights Reserved. All characters,
their distinctive likenesses and related elements
featured in this publication are trademarks of
DC Comics. The stories, characters and incidents
featured in this publication are entirely fictional.
DC Comics does not read or accept unsolicited
submissions of ideas, stories or artwork.

DC Comics, 2900 West Alameda Ave.,
Burbank, CA 91505. Printed by LSC Communications,
Owensville, MO, USA. 7/5/19. First Printing.
ISBN: 978-1-4012-9247-8

Library of Congress Cataloging-in-Publication Data
is available.

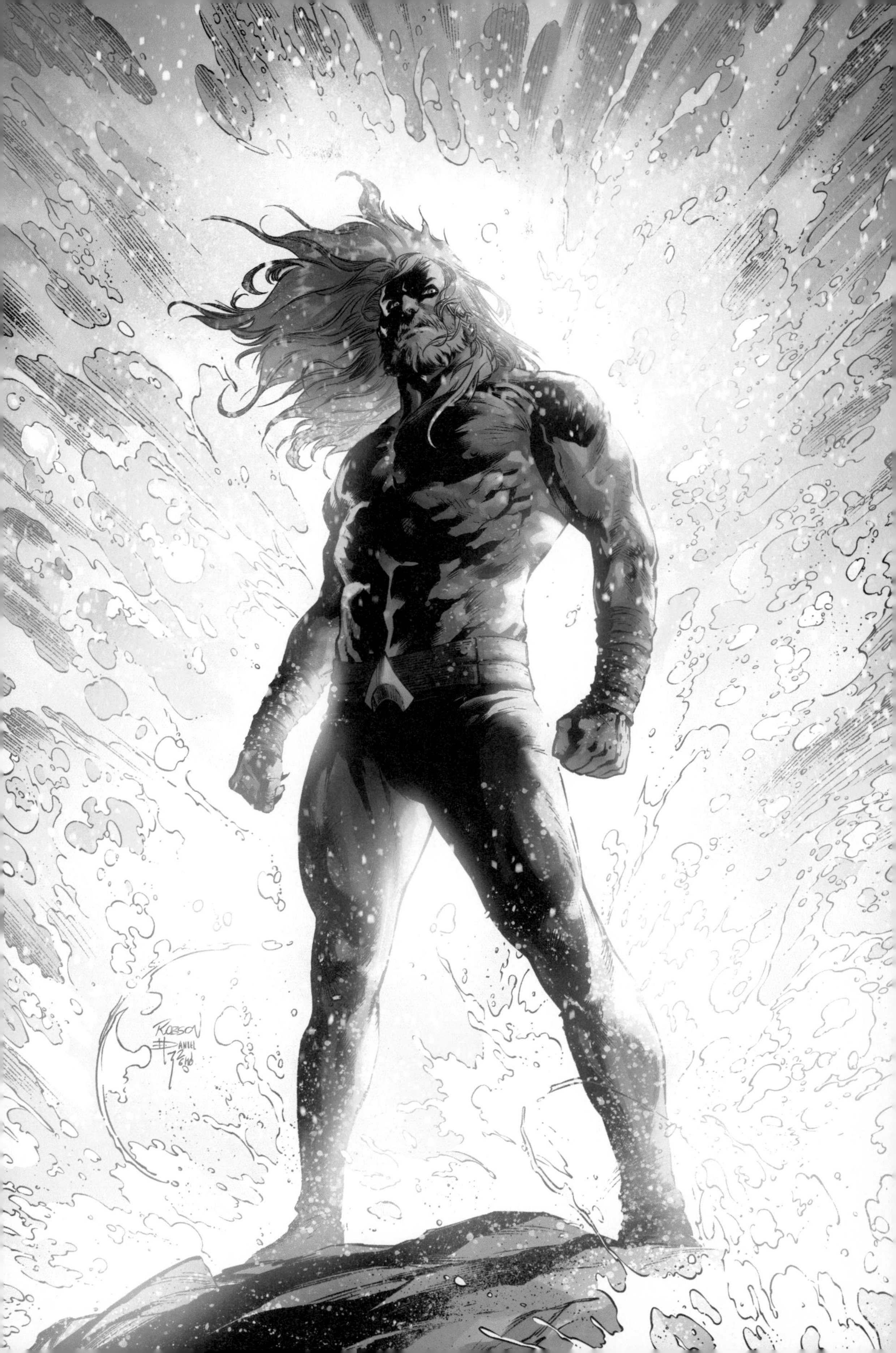

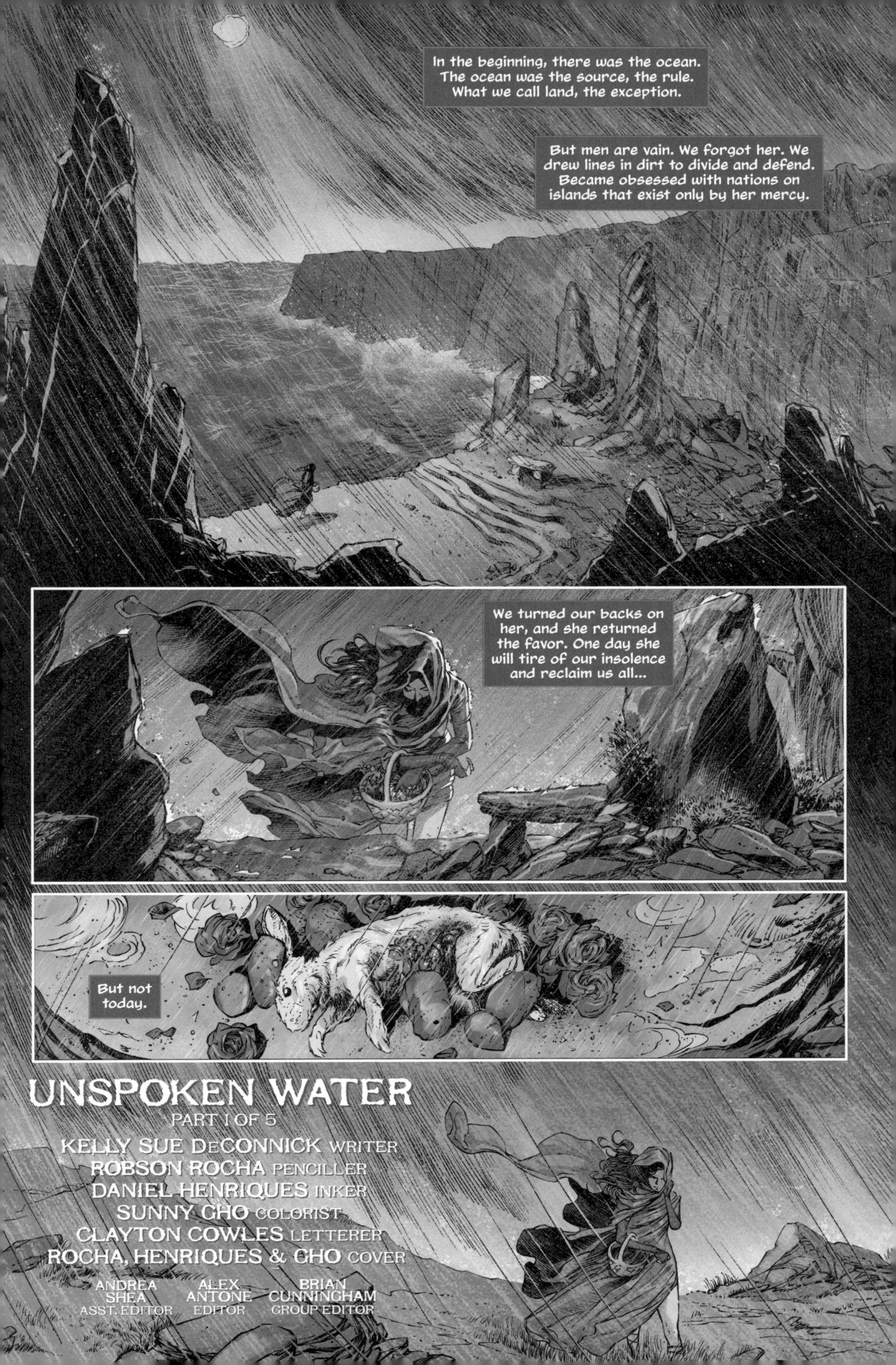
In the beginning, there was the ocean. The ocean was the source, the rule. What we call land, the exception.
But men are vain. We forgot her. We drew lines in dirt to divide and defend. Became obsessed with nations on islands that exist only by her mercy.
We turned our backs on her, and she returned the favor. One day she will tire of our insolence and reclaim us all...
But not today.
UNSPOKEN WATER
PART 1 OF 5
KELLY SUE DeCONNICK WRITER
ROBSON ROCHA PENCILLER
DANIEL HENRIQUES INKER
SUNNY CHO COLORIST
CLAYTON COWLES LETTERER
ROCHA, HENRIQUES & CHO COVER
ANDREA SHEA ASST. EDITOR
ALEX ANTONE EDITOR
BRIAN CUNNINGHAM GROUP EDITOR

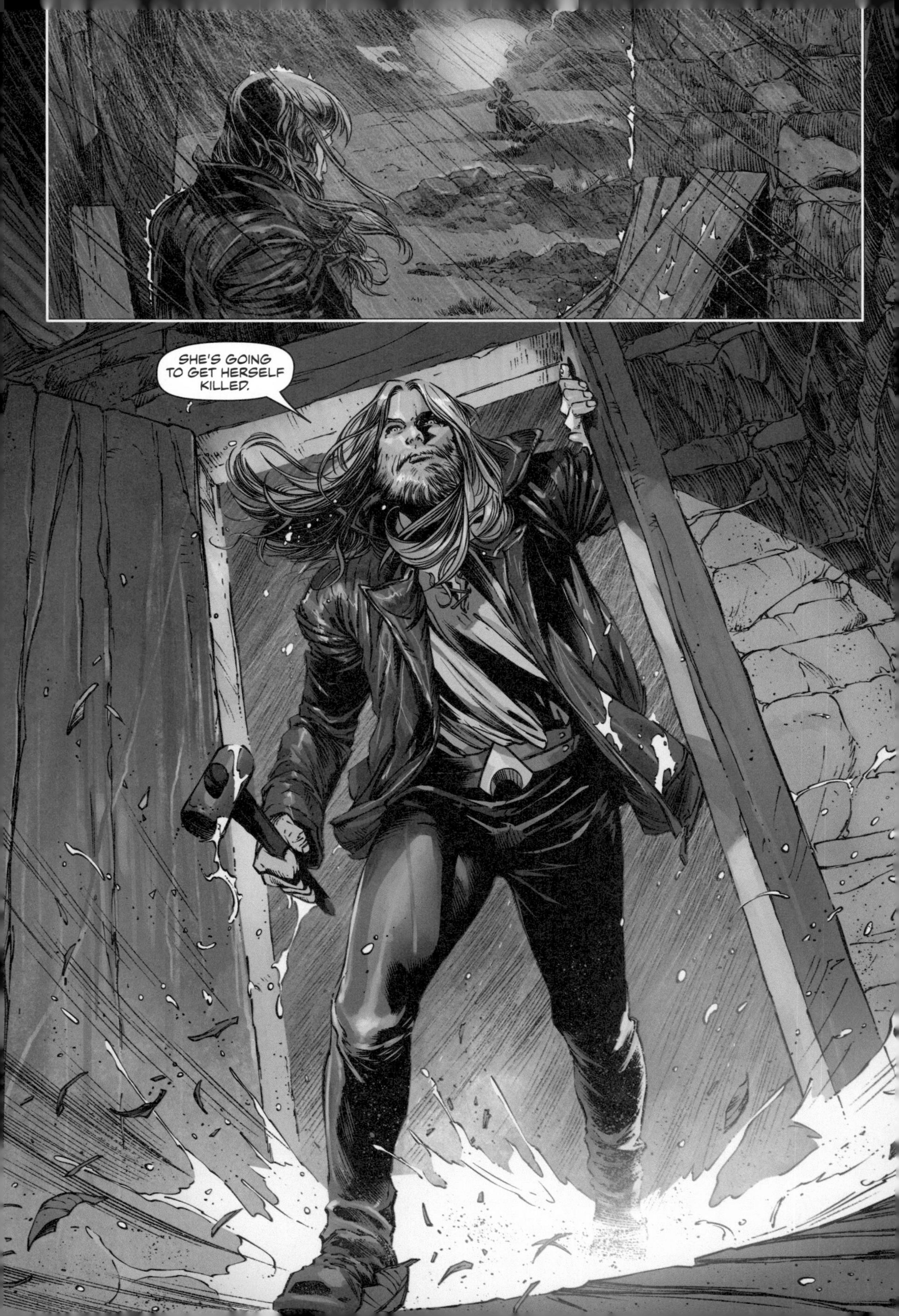
SHE'S GOING TO GET HERSELF KILLED.

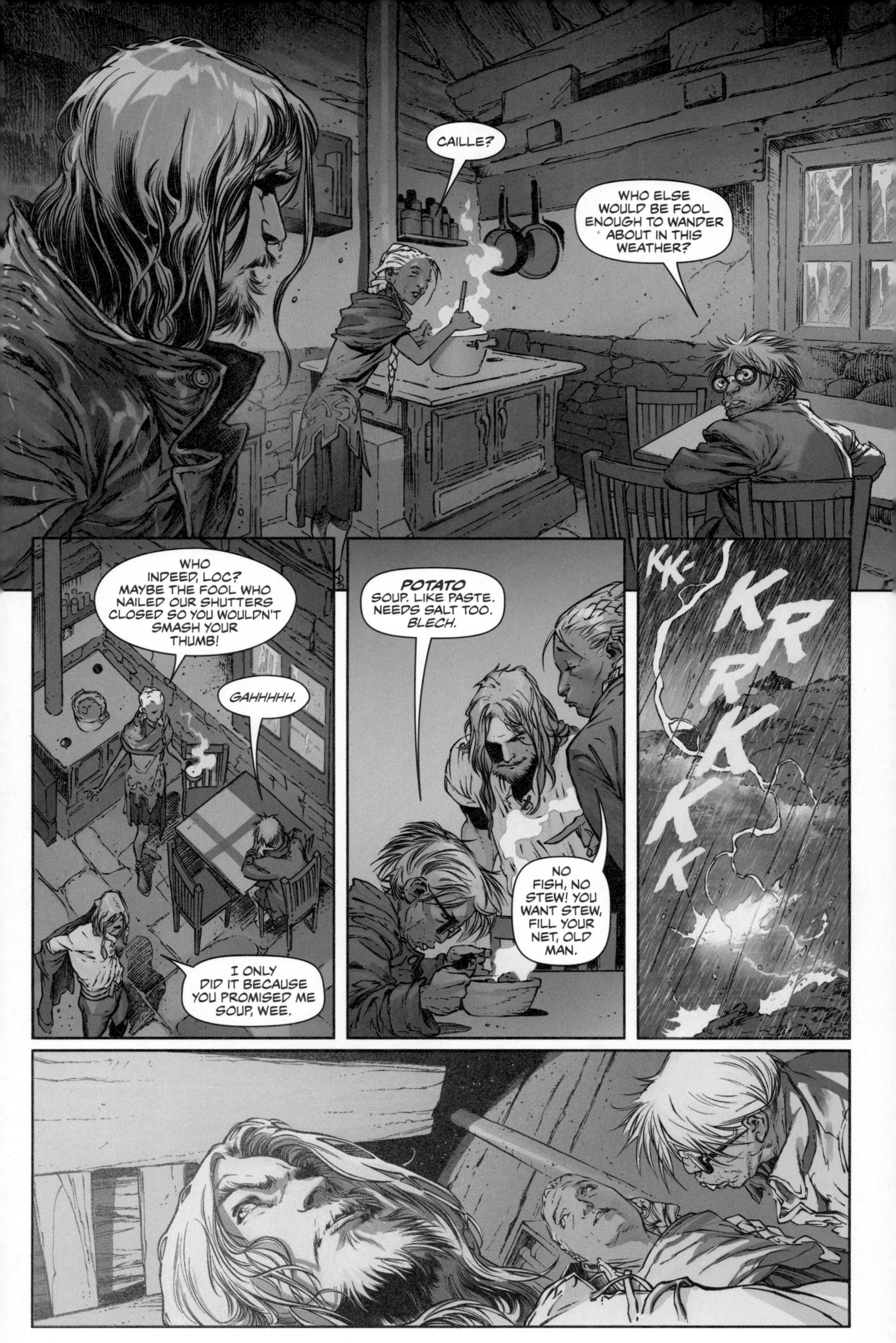
CAILLE?
WHO ELSE WOULD BE FOOL ENOUGH TO WANDER ABOUT IN THIS WEATHER?
WHO INDEED, LOC? MAYBE THE FOOL WHO NAILED OUR SHUTTERS CLOSED SO YOU WOULDN'T SMASH YOUR THUMB!
GAHHHHH.
I ONLY DID IT BECAUSE YOU PROMISED ME SOUP, WEE.
POTATO SOUP. LIKE PASTE. NEEDS SALT TOO. BLECH.
NO FISH, NO STEW! YOU WANT STEW, FILL YOUR NET, OLD MAN.
KK-KRRKKKK

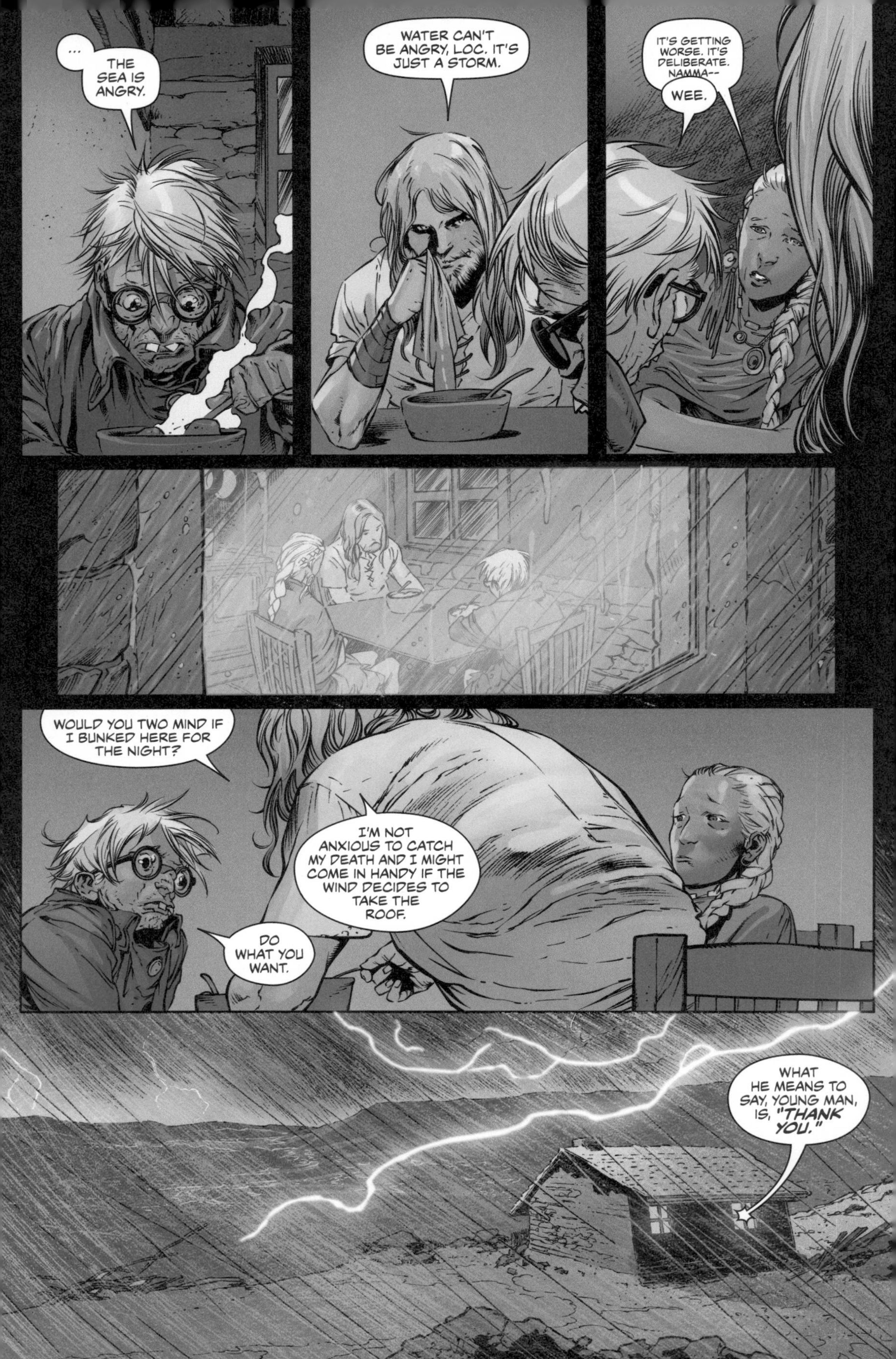
...
THE SEA IS ANGRY.
WATER CAN'T BE ANGRY, LOC. IT'S JUST A STORM.
IT'S GETTING WORSE. IT'S DELIBERATE. NAMMA--
WEE.
WOULD YOU TWO MIND IF I BUNKED HERE FOR THE NIGHT?
I'M NOT ANXIOUS TO CATCH MY DEATH AND I MIGHT COME IN HANDY IF THE WIND DECIDES TO TAKE THE ROOF.
DO WHAT YOU WANT.
WHAT HE MEANS TO SAY, YOUNG MAN, IS, "THANK YOU."

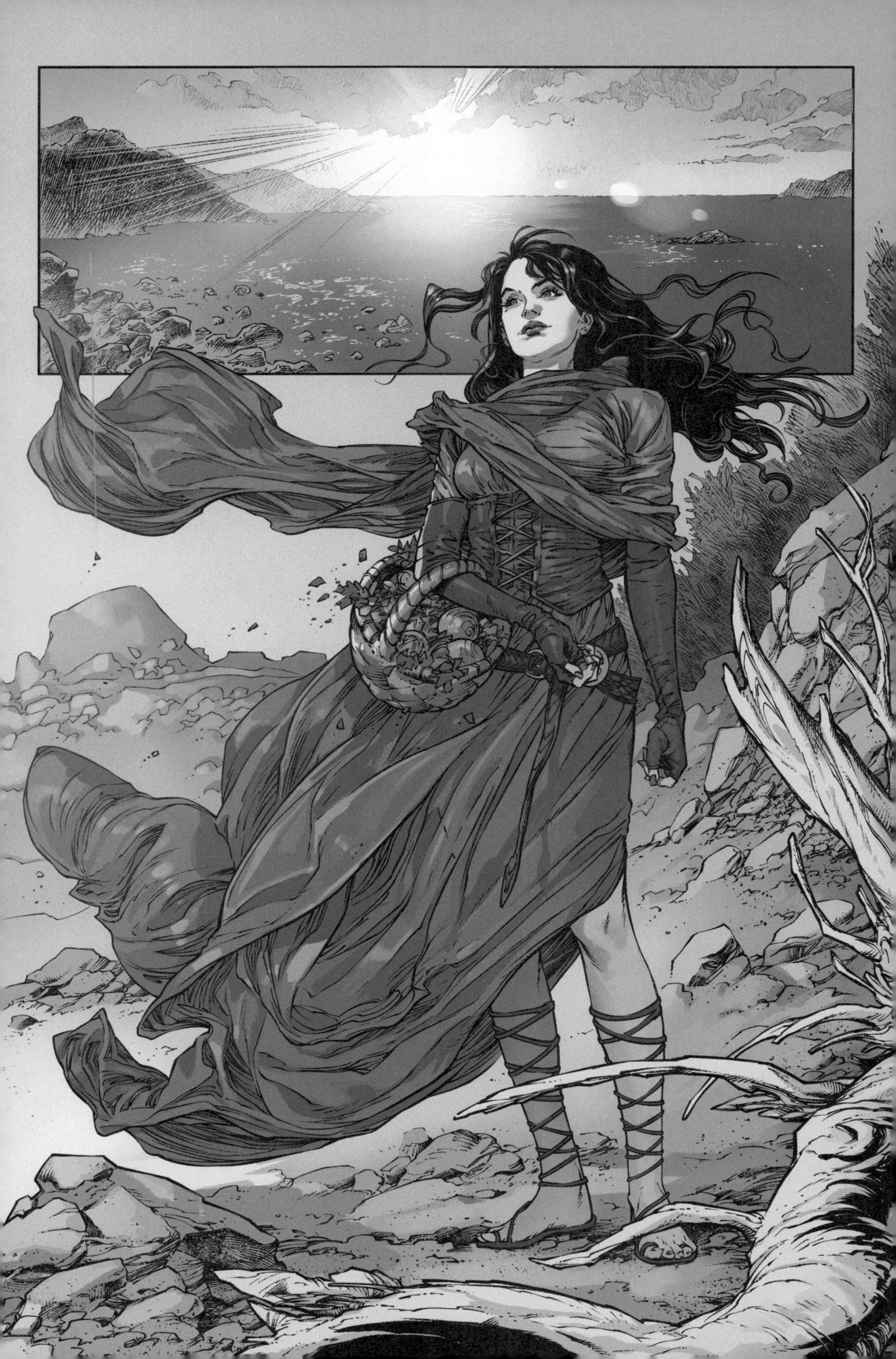

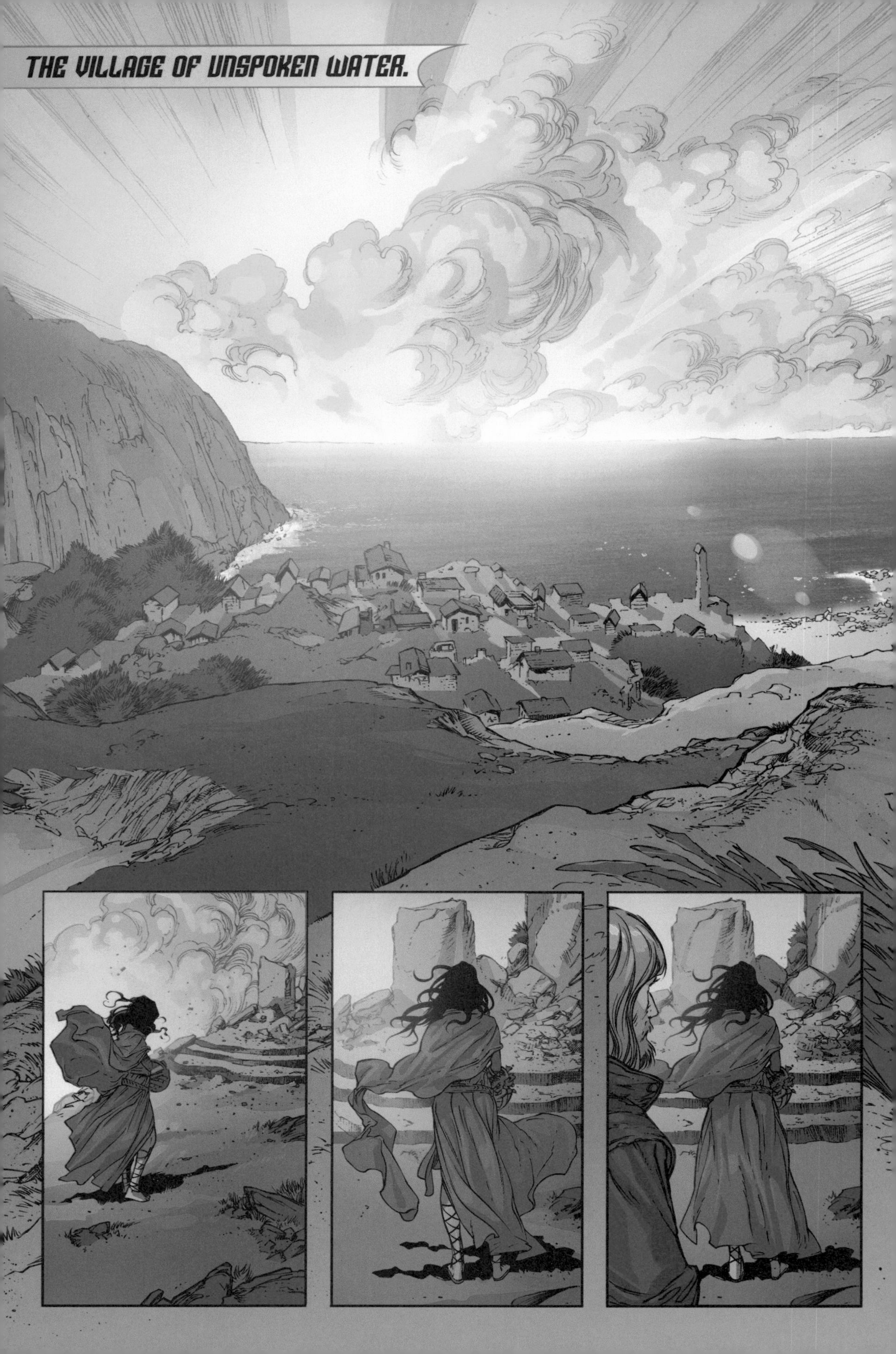
THE VILLAGE OF UNSPOKEN WATER.

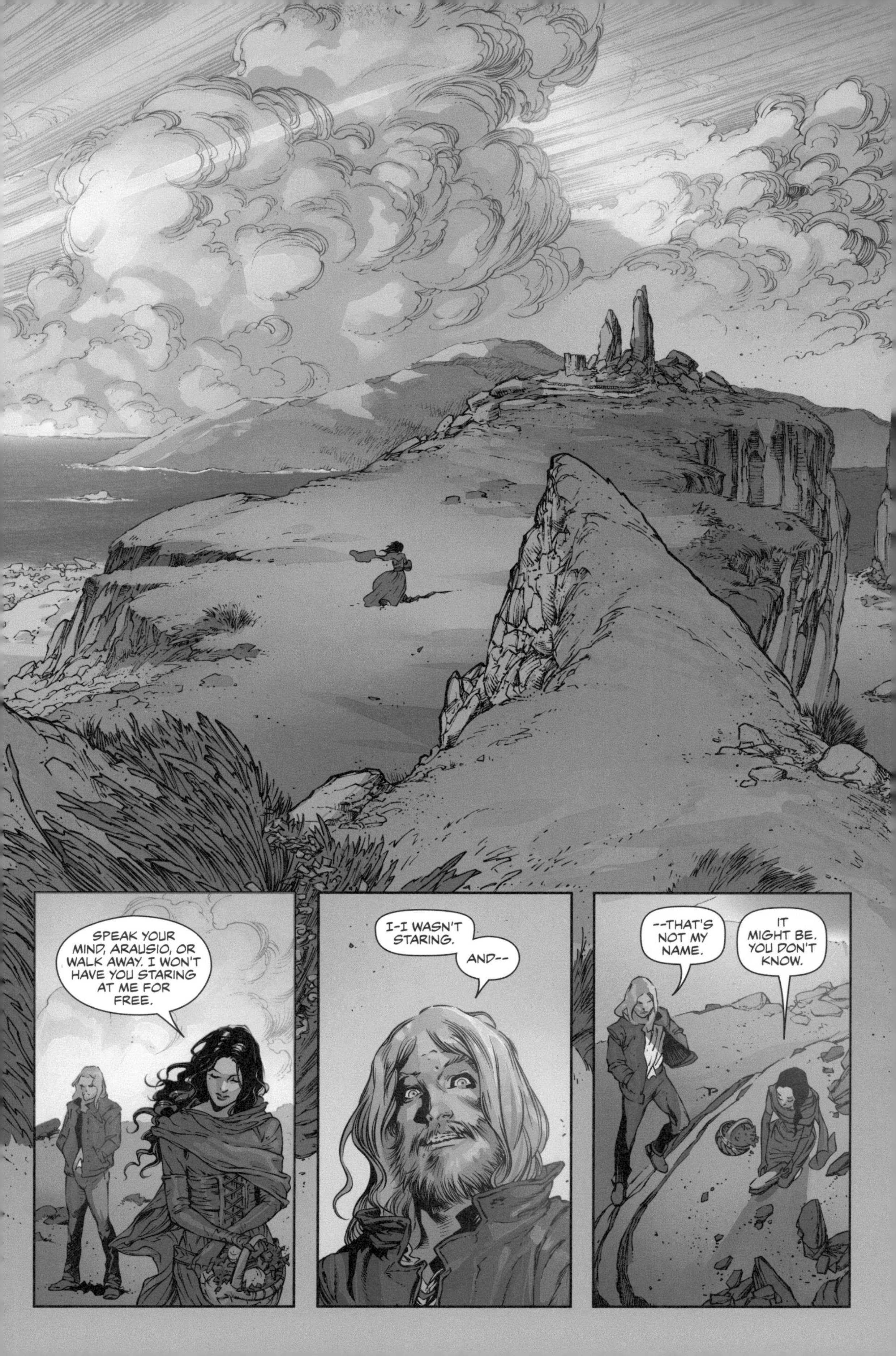
SPEAK YOUR MIND, ARAUSIO, OR WALK AWAY. I WON'T HAVE YOU STARING AT ME FOR FREE.
I-I WASN'T STARING.
AND--
--THAT'S NOT MY NAME.
IT MIGHT BE. YOU DON'T KNOW.

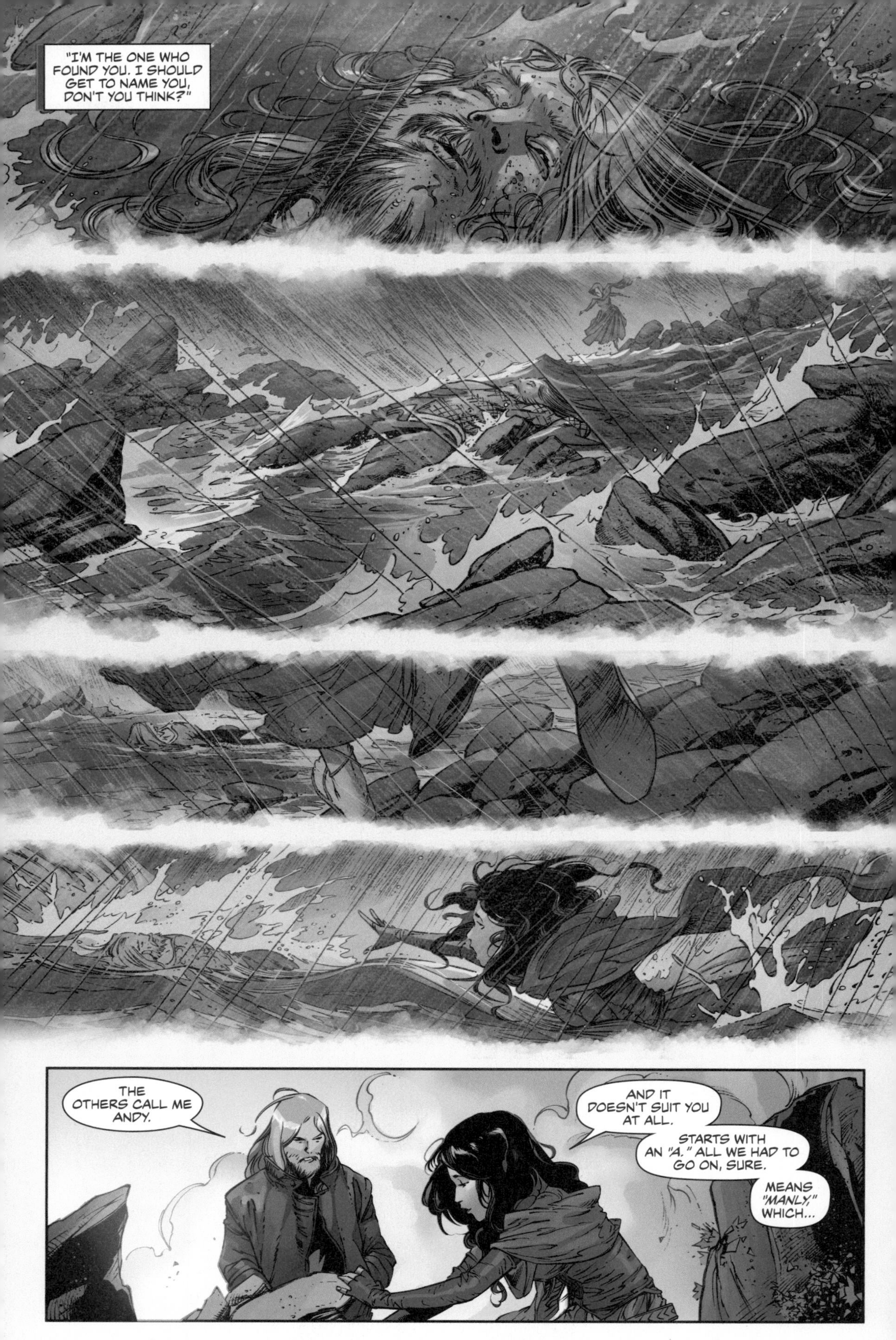
"I'M THE ONE WHO FOUND YOU. I SHOULD GET TO NAME YOU, DON'T YOU THINK?"
THE OTHERS CALL ME ANDY.
AND IT DOESN'T SUIT YOU AT ALL.
STARTS WITH AN "A." ALL WE HAD TO GO ON, SURE.
MEANS "MANLY," WHICH...

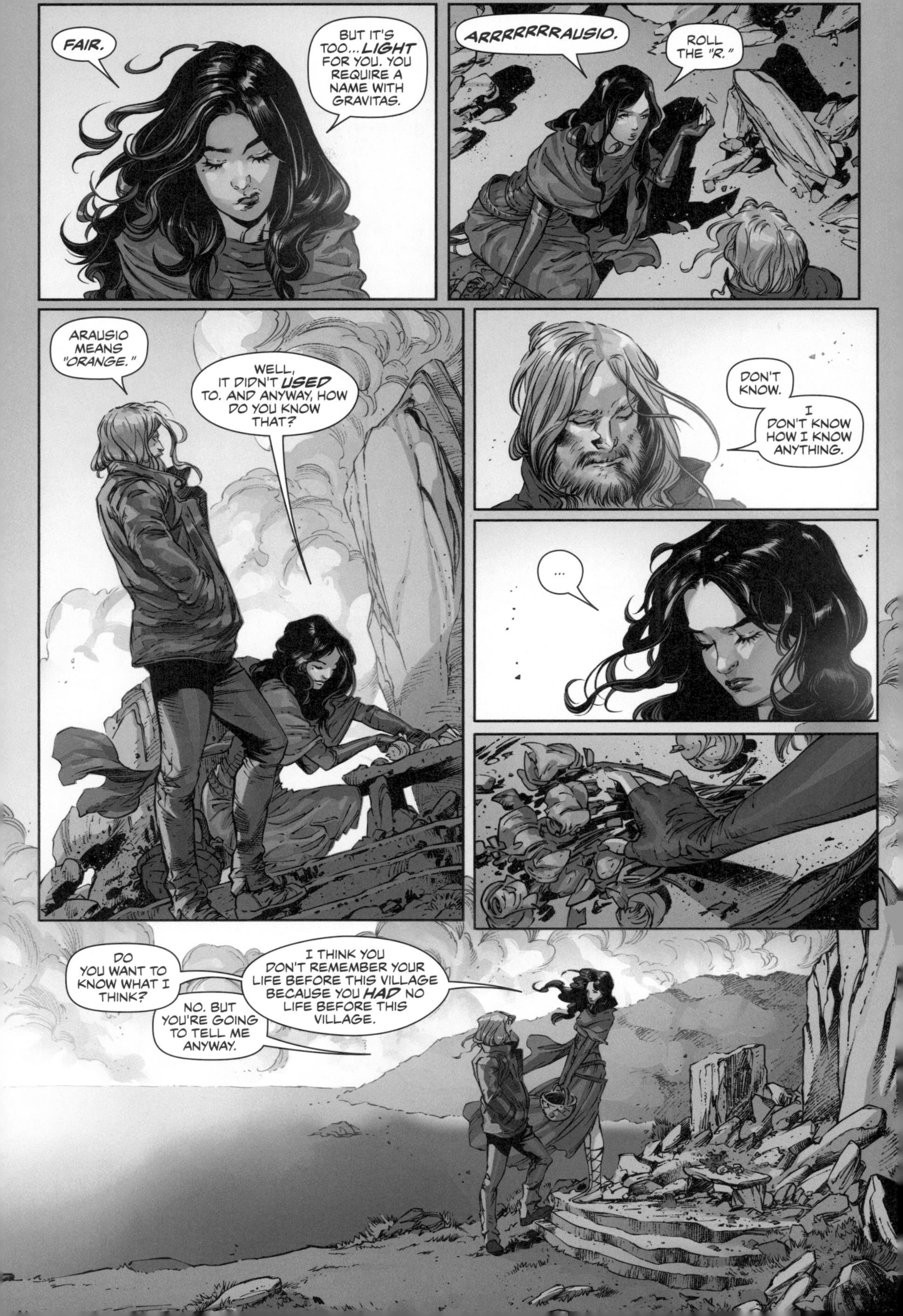
FAIR.
BUT IT'S TOO...LIGHT FOR YOU. YOU REQUIRE A NAME WITH GRAVITAS.
ARRRRRRRAUSIO.
ROLL THE "R."
ARAUSIO MEANS "ORANGE."
WELL, IT DIDN'T USED TO. AND ANYWAY, HOW DO YOU KNOW THAT?
DON'T KNOW.
I DON'T KNOW HOW I KNOW ANYTHING.
...
DO YOU WANT TO KNOW WHAT I THINK?
NO. BUT YOU'RE GOING TO TELL ME ANYWAY.
I THINK YOU DON'T REMEMBER YOUR LIFE BEFORE THIS VILLAGE BECAUSE YOU HAD NO LIFE BEFORE THIS VILLAGE.

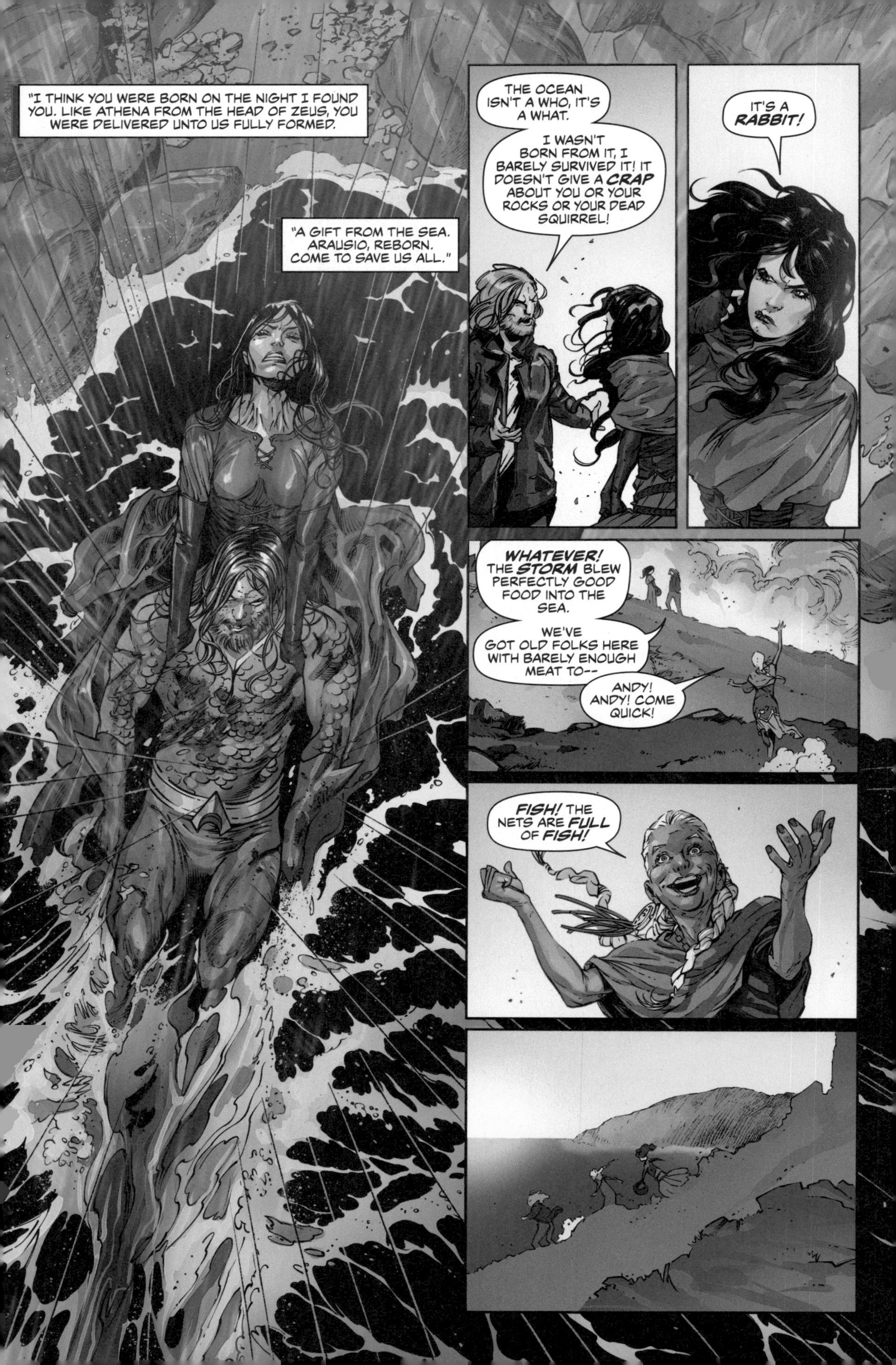

"I THINK YOU WERE BORN ON THE NIGHT I FOUND YOU. LIKE ATHENA FROM THE HEAD OF ZEUS, YOU WERE DELIVERED UNTO US FULLY FORMED.
"A GIFT FROM THE SEA. ARAUSIO, REBORN. COME TO SAVE US ALL."
THE OCEAN ISN'T A WHO, IT'S A WHAT.
I WASN'T BORN FROM IT, I BARELY SURVIVED IT! IT DOESN'T GIVE A CRAP ABOUT YOU OR YOUR ROCKS OR YOUR DEAD SQUIRREL!
IT'S A RABBIT!
WHATEVER! THE STORM BLEW PERFECTLY GOOD FOOD INTO THE SEA.
WE'VE GOT OLD FOLKS HERE WITH BARELY ENOUGH MEAT TO--
ANDY! ANDY! COME QUICK!
FISH! THE NETS ARE FULL OF FISH!

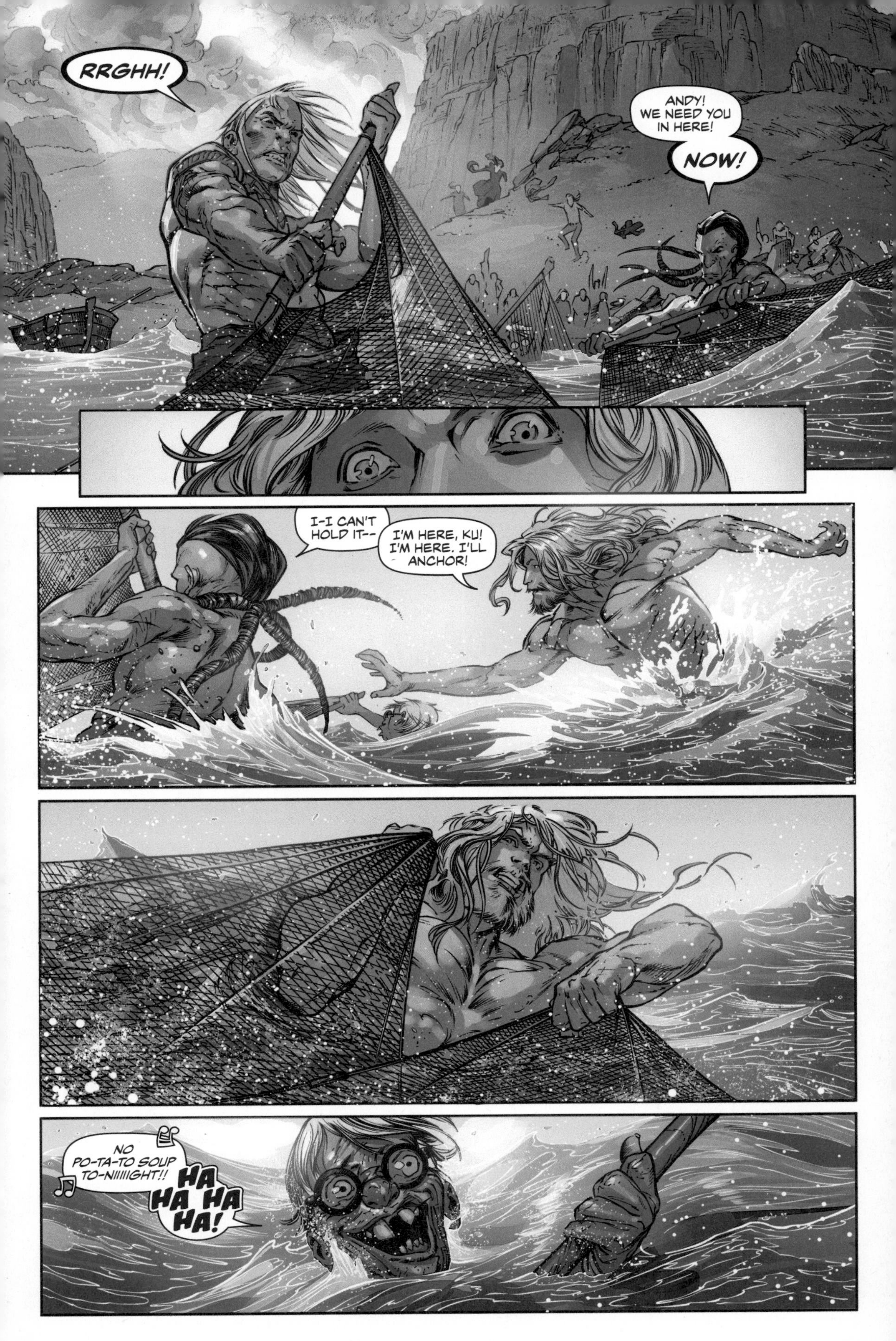
RRGHH!
ANDY! WE NEED YOU IN HERE!
NOW!
I-I CAN'T HOLD IT--
I'M HERE, KU! I'M HERE. I'LL ANCHOR!
NO PO-TA-TO SOUP TO-NIIIIIGHT!!
HA HA HA HA HA!

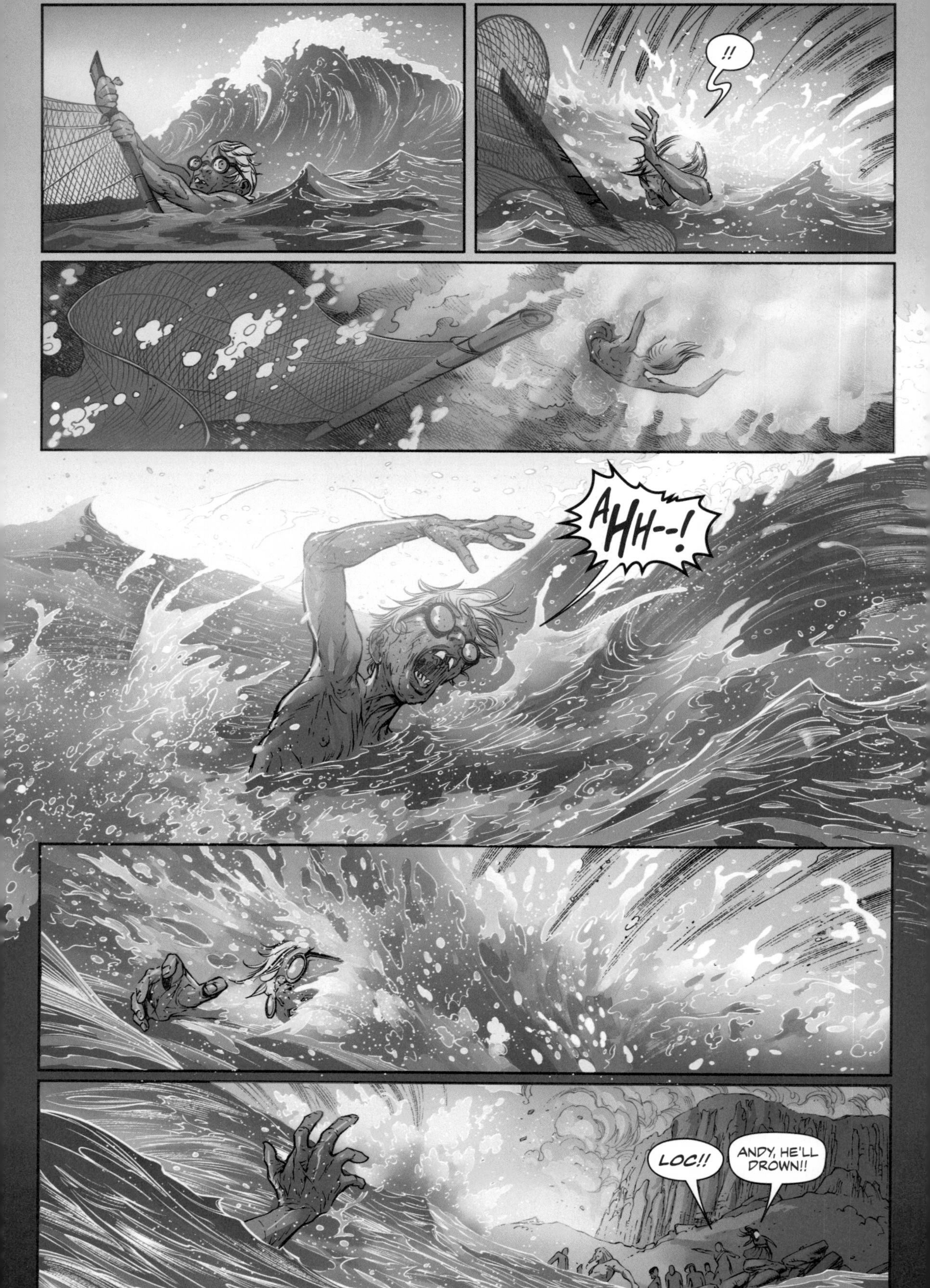
!!
AHH--!
LOC!!
ANDY, HE'LL DROWN!!

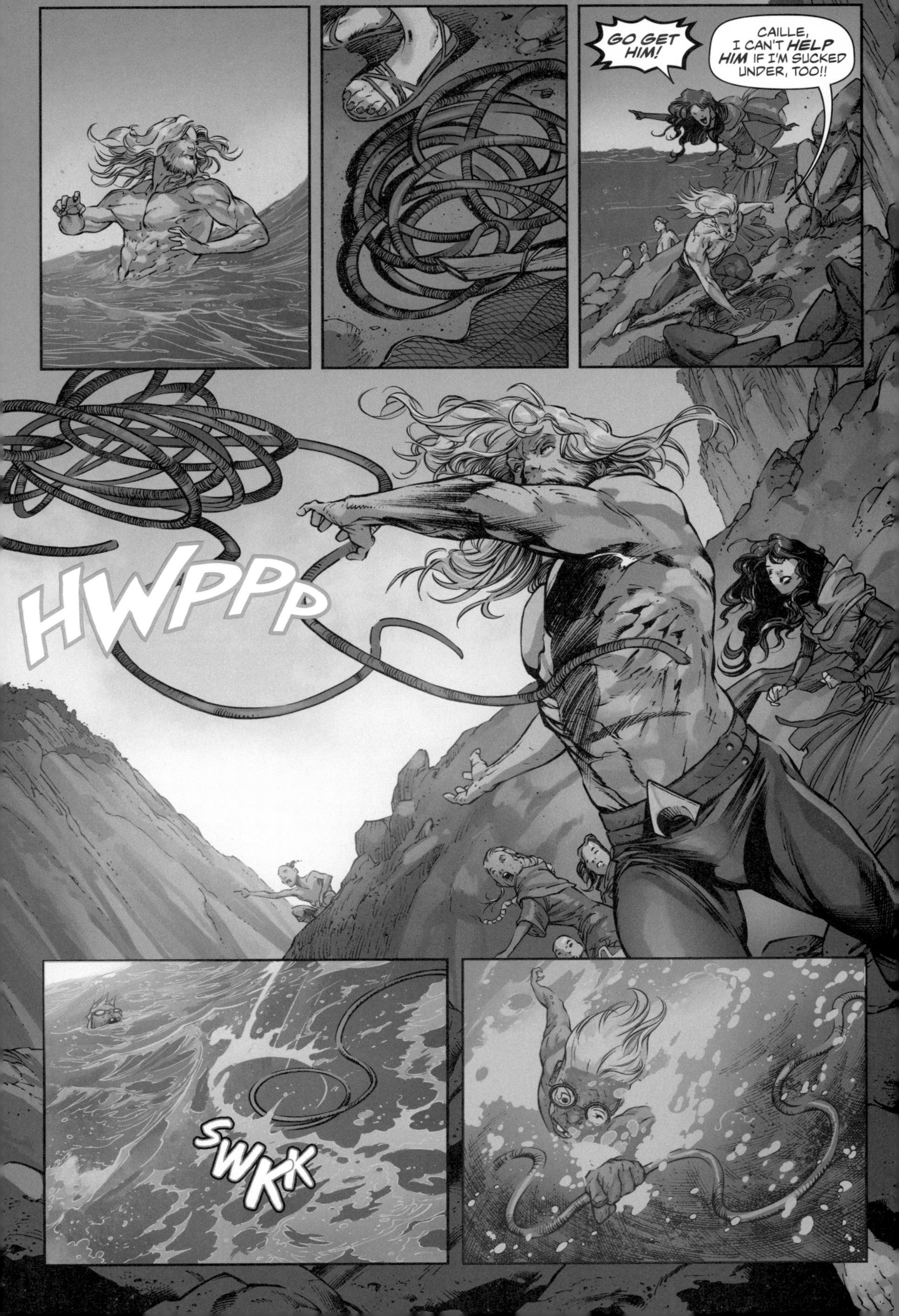
GO GET HIM!
CAILLE, I CAN'T HELP HIM IF I'M SUCKED UNDER, TOO!!
HWPPP
SWKK

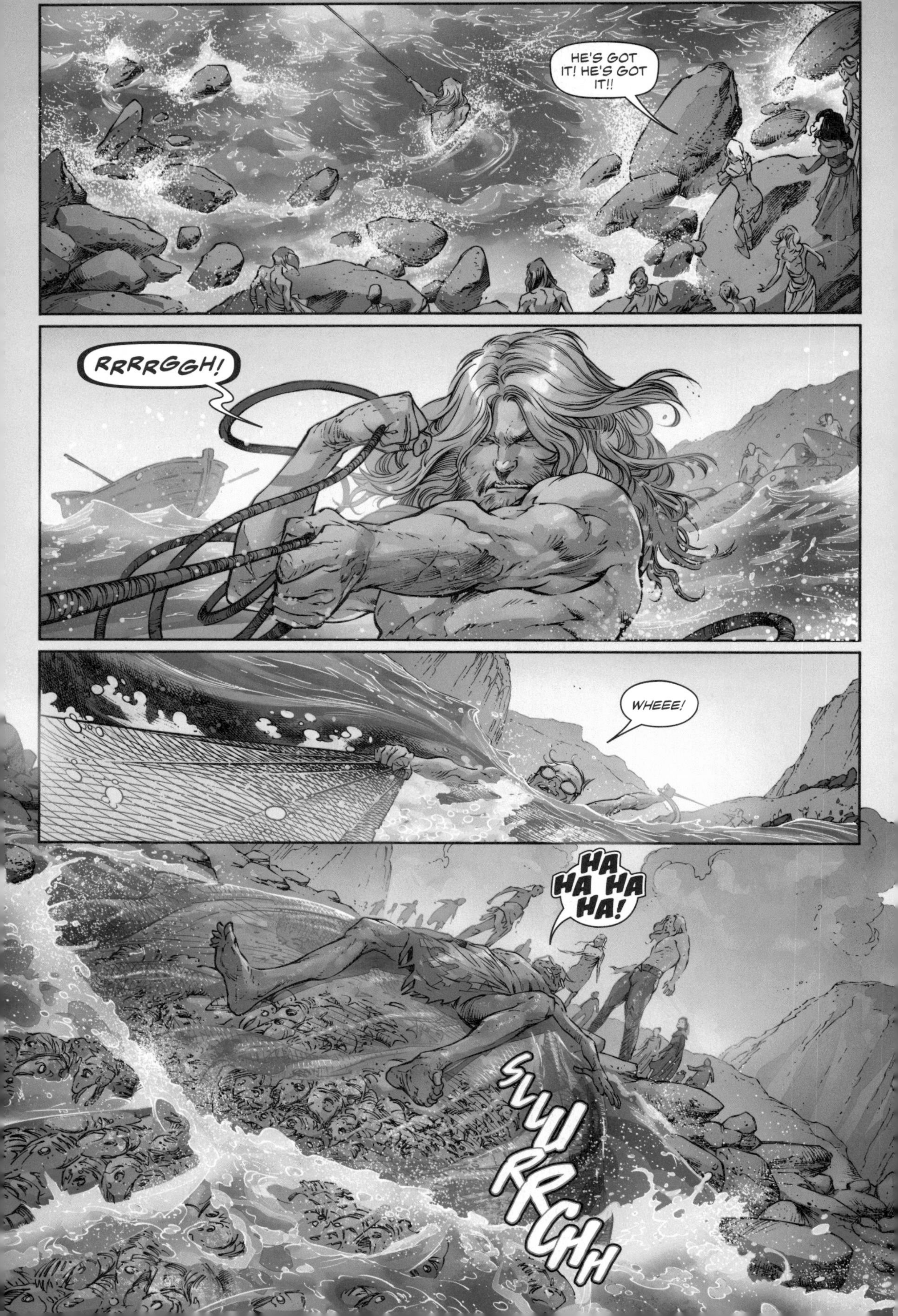
HE'S GOT IT! HE'S GOT IT!!
RRRRGGH!
WHEEE!
HA HA HA HA!
SLUURRCHH

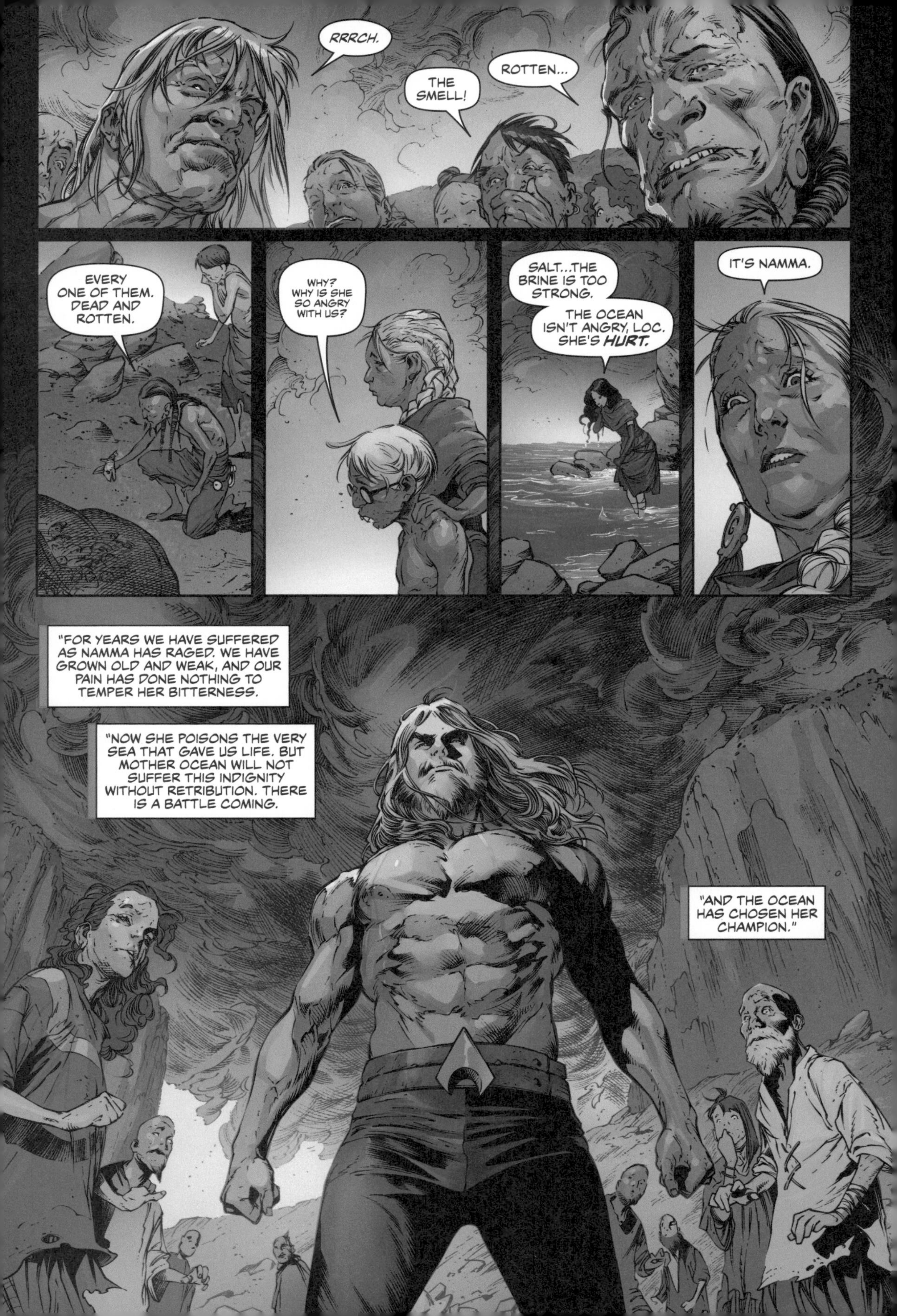
RRRCH.
THE SMELL!
ROTTEN...
EVERY ONE OF THEM. DEAD AND ROTTEN.
WHY? WHY IS SHE SO ANGRY WITH US?
SALT...THE BRINE IS TOO STRONG.
THE OCEAN ISN'T ANGRY, LOC. SHE'S HURT.
IT'S NAMMA.
"FOR YEARS WE HAVE SUFFERED AS NAMMA HAS RAGED. WE HAVE GROWN OLD AND WEAK, AND OUR PAIN HAS DONE NOTHING TO TEMPER HER BITTERNESS.
"NOW SHE POISONS THE VERY SEA THAT GAVE US LIFE. BUT MOTHER OCEAN WILL NOT SUFFER THIS INDIGNITY WITHOUT RETRIBUTION. THERE IS A BATTLE COMING.
"AND THE OCEAN HAS CHOSEN HER CHAMPION."

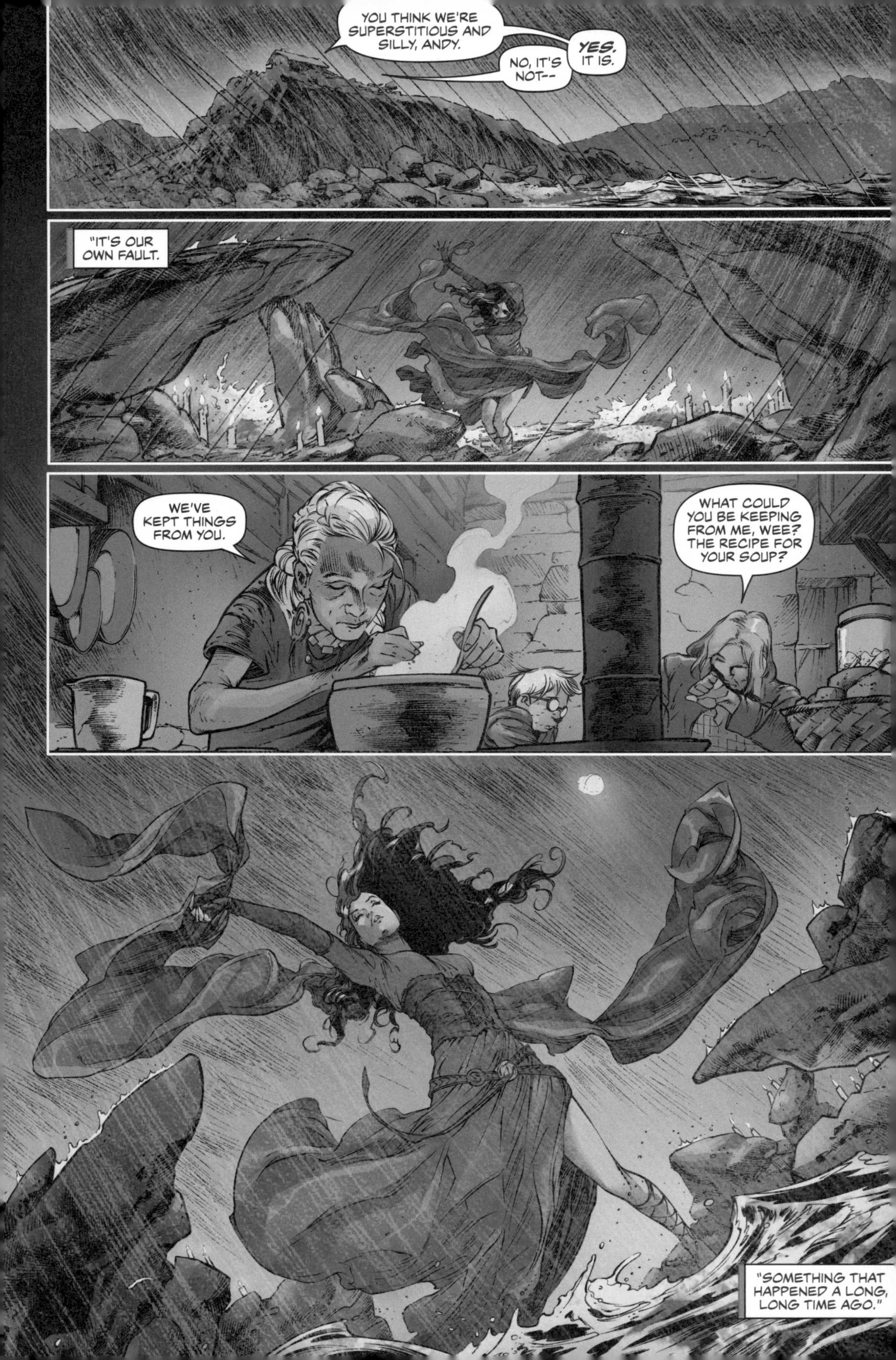
YOU THINK WE'RE SUPERSTITIOUS AND SILLY, ANDY.
YES. IT IS.
NO, IT'S NOT--
"IT'S OUR OWN FAULT.
WE'VE KEPT THINGS FROM YOU.
WHAT COULD YOU BE KEEPING FROM ME, WEE? THE RECIPE FOR YOUR SOUP?
"SOMETHING THAT HAPPENED A LONG, LONG TIME AGO."

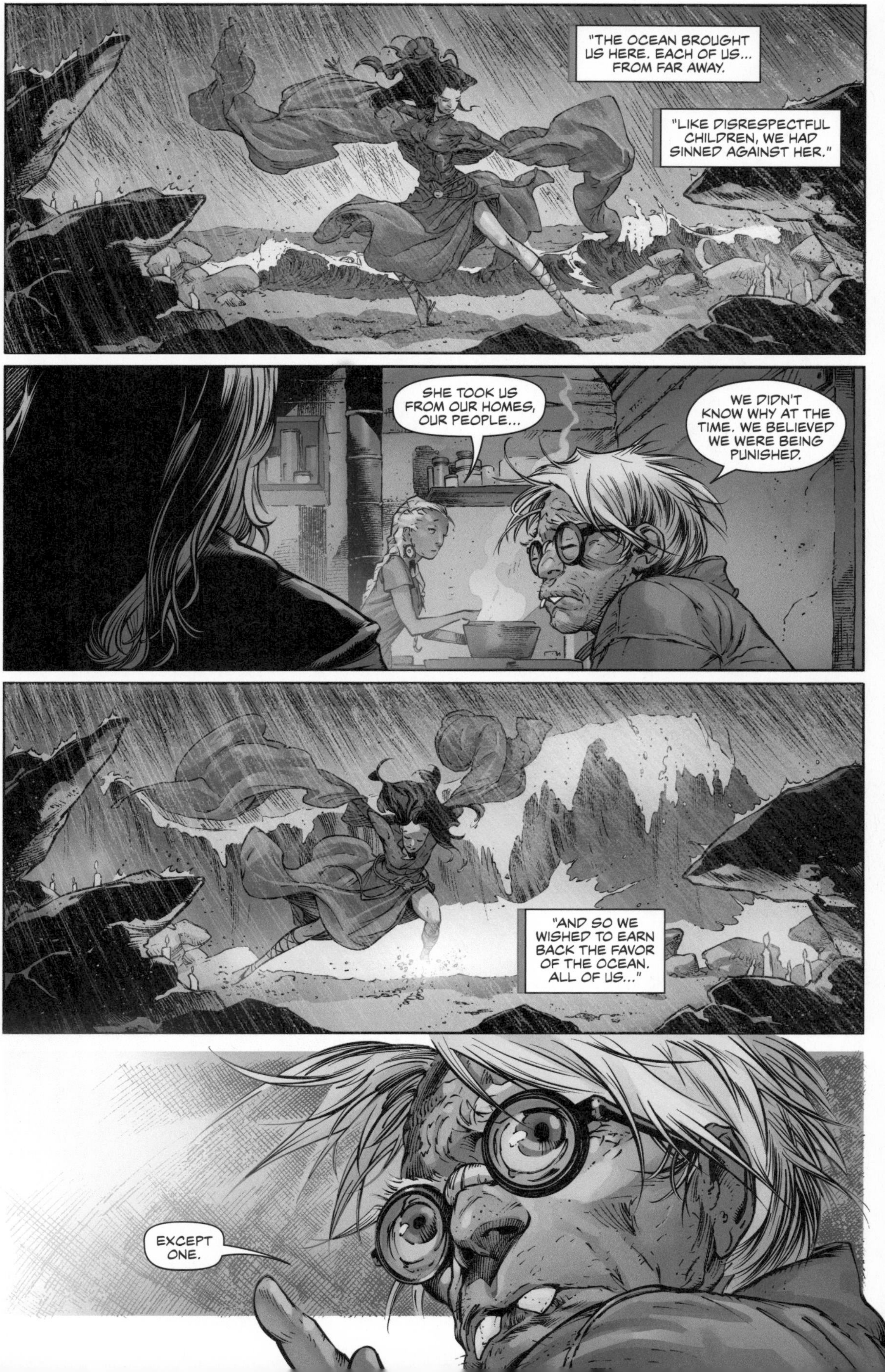
"THE OCEAN BROUGHT US HERE. EACH OF US... FROM FAR AWAY.
"LIKE DISRESPECTFUL CHILDREN, WE HAD SINNED AGAINST HER."
SHE TOOK US FROM OUR HOMES, OUR PEOPLE...
WE DIDN'T KNOW WHY AT THE TIME. WE BELIEVED WE WERE BEING PUNISHED.
"AND SO WE WISHED TO EARN BACK THE FAVOR OF THE OCEAN. ALL OF US..."
EXCEPT ONE.

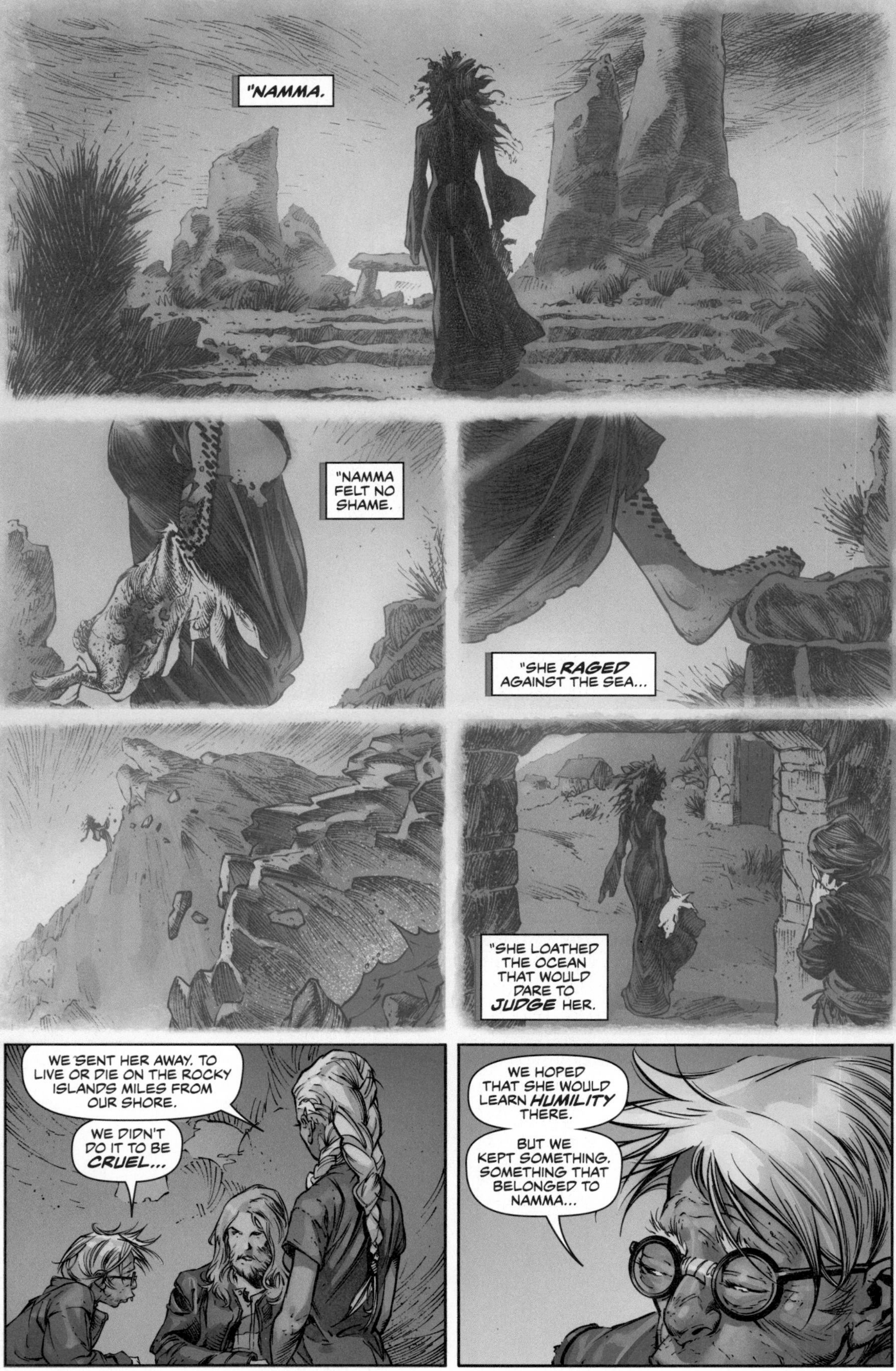
"NAMMA.
"NAMMA FELT NO SHAME.
"SHE RAGED AGAINST THE SEA...
"SHE LOATHED THE OCEAN THAT WOULD DARE TO JUDGE HER.
WE SENT HER AWAY. TO LIVE OR DIE ON THE ROCKY ISLANDS MILES FROM OUR SHORE.
WE DIDN'T DO IT TO BE CRUEL...
WE HOPED THAT SHE WOULD LEARN HUMILITY THERE.
BUT WE KEPT SOMETHING. SOMETHING THAT BELONGED TO NAMMA...

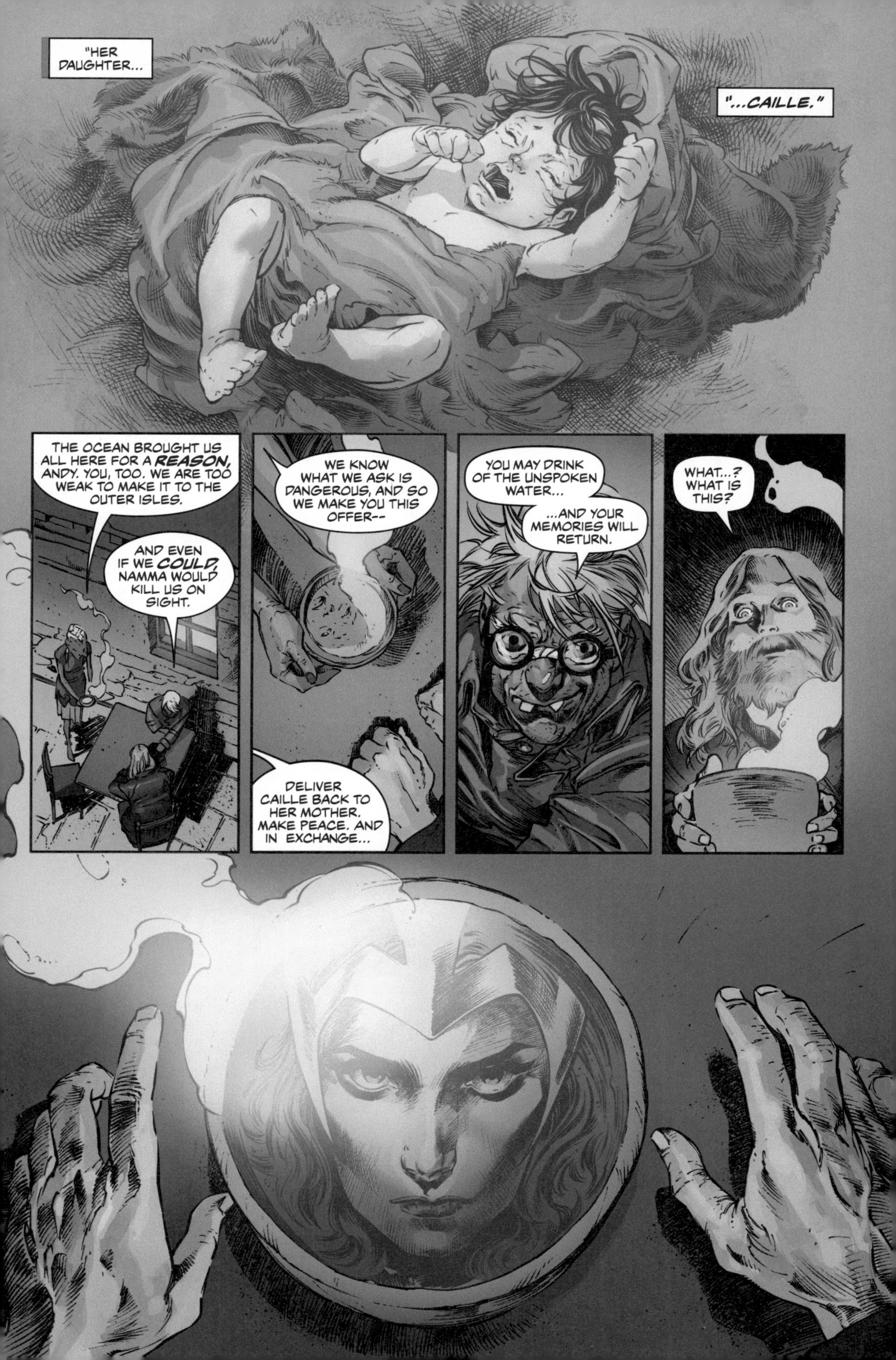
"HER DAUGHTER...
"...CAILLE."
THE OCEAN BROUGHT US ALL HERE FOR A REASON, ANDY. YOU, TOO. WE ARE TOO WEAK TO MAKE IT TO THE OUTER ISLES.
AND EVEN IF WE COULD, NAMMA WOULD KILL US ON SIGHT.
WE KNOW WHAT WE ASK IS DANGEROUS, AND SO WE MAKE YOU THIS OFFER--
DELIVER CAILLE BACK TO HER MOTHER. MAKE PEACE. AND IN EXCHANGE...
YOU MAY DRINK OF THE UNSPOKEN WATER...
...AND YOUR MEMORIES WILL RETURN.
WHAT...? WHAT IS THIS?

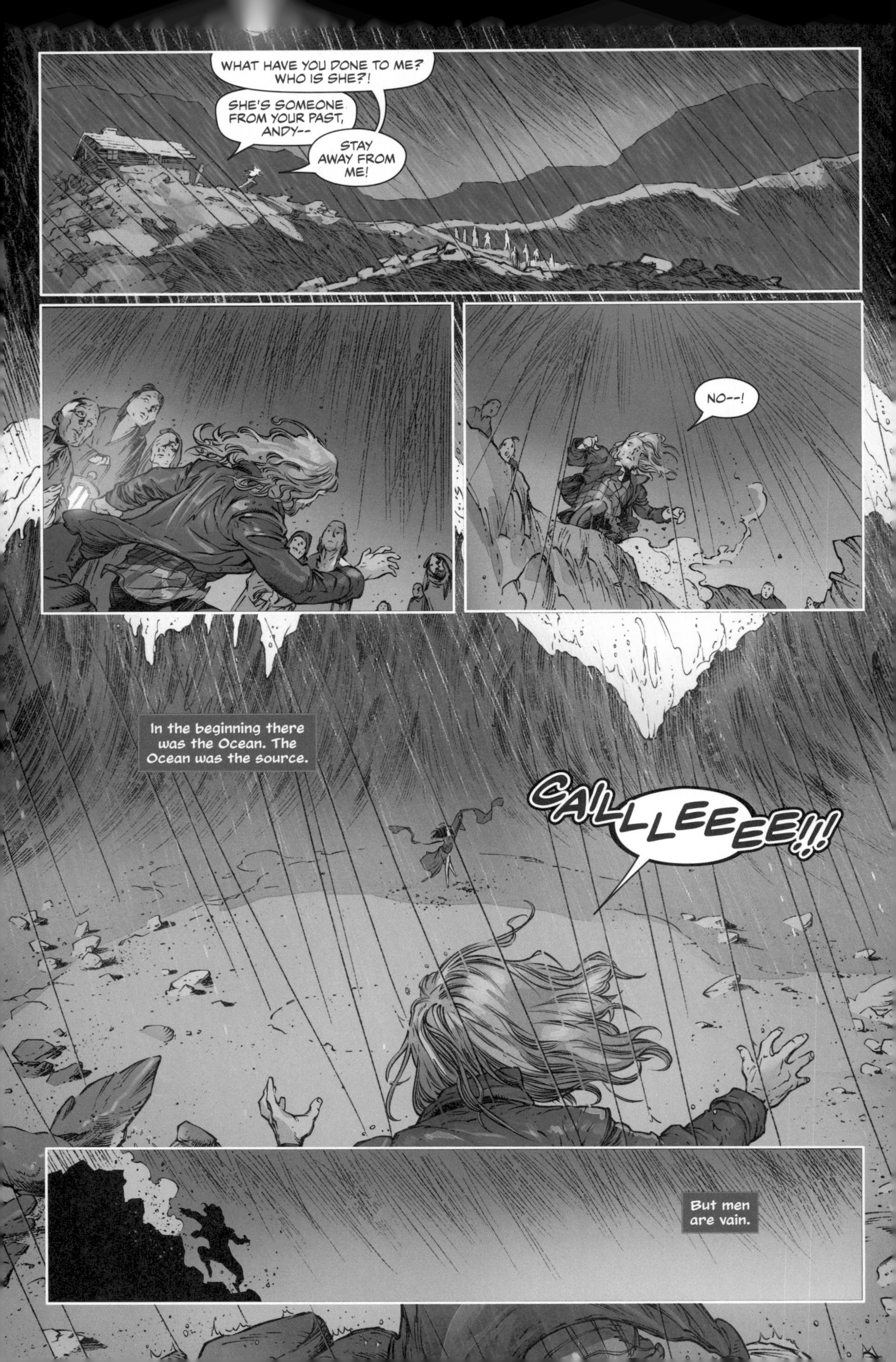
WHAT HAVE YOU DONE TO ME? WHO IS SHE?!
SHE'S SOMEONE FROM YOUR PAST, ANDY--
STAY AWAY FROM ME!
NO--!
In the beginning there was the Ocean. The Ocean was the source.
CALLLEEEEE!!!
But men are vain.

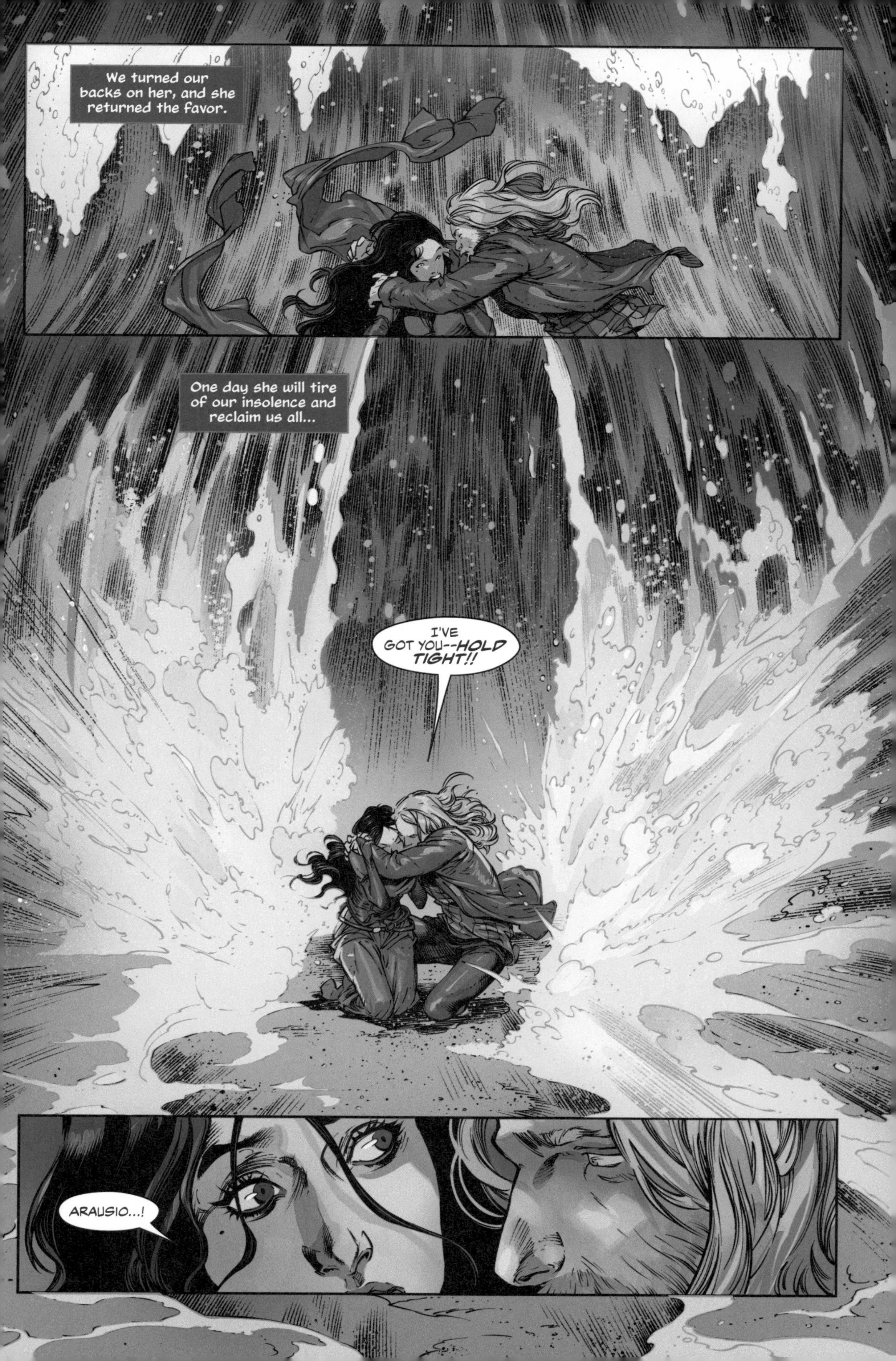
We turned our backs on her, and she returned the favor.
One day she will tire of our insolence and reclaim us all...
I'VE GOT YOU--HOLD TIGHT!!
ARAUSIO...!

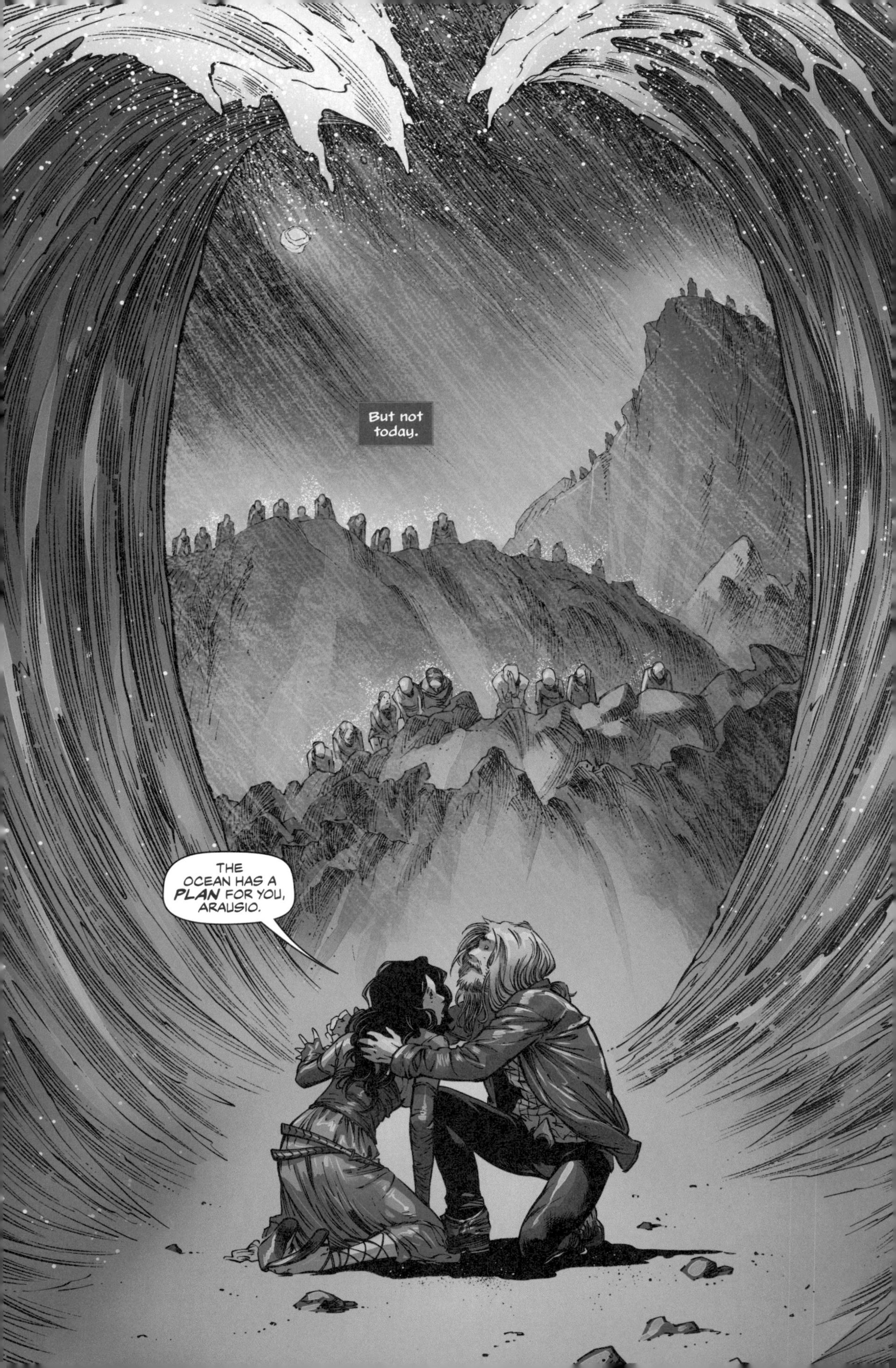
But not today.
THE OCEAN HAS A PLAN FOR YOU, ARAUSIO.

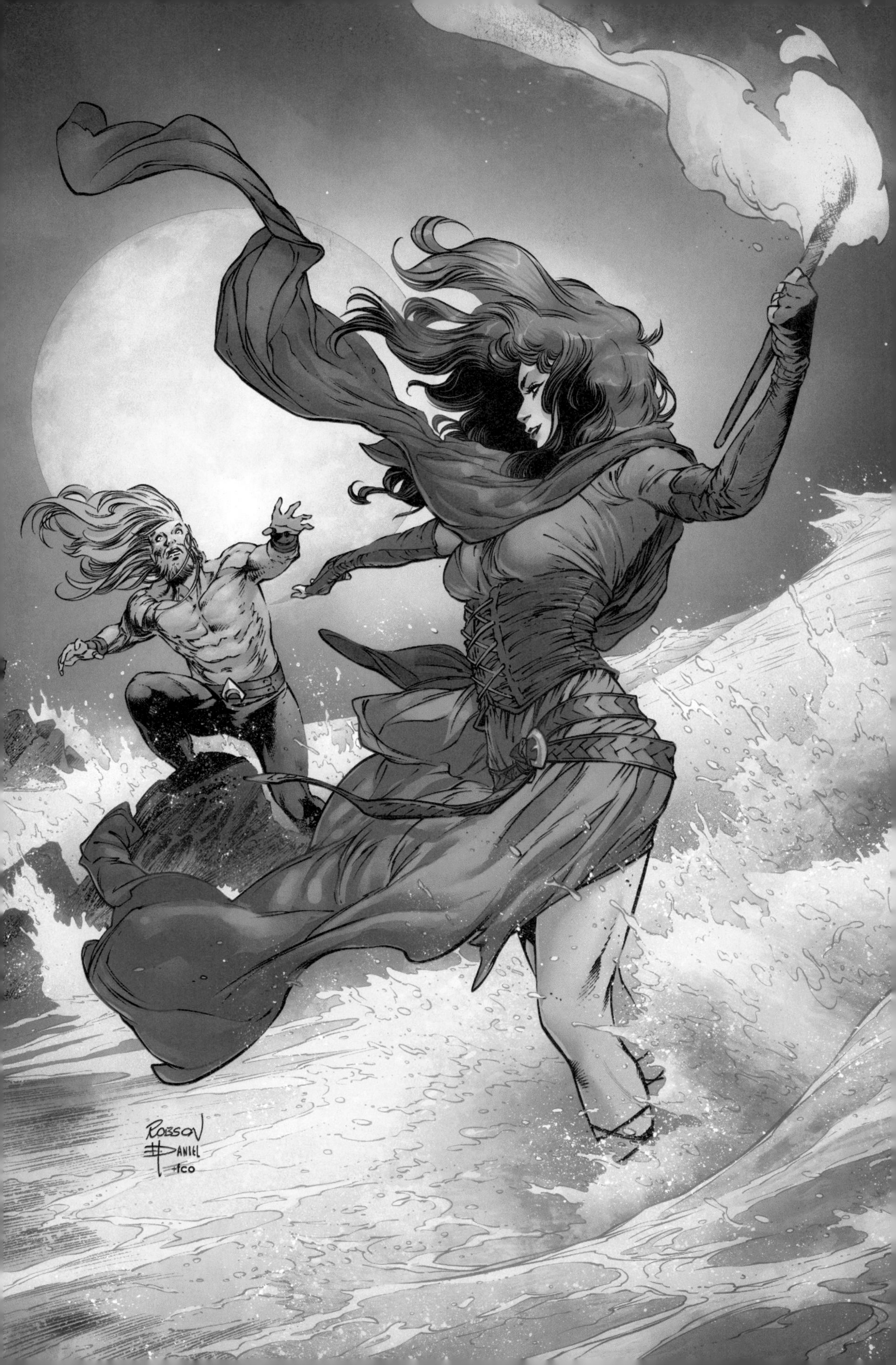
ROBSON
DANIEL
+fco

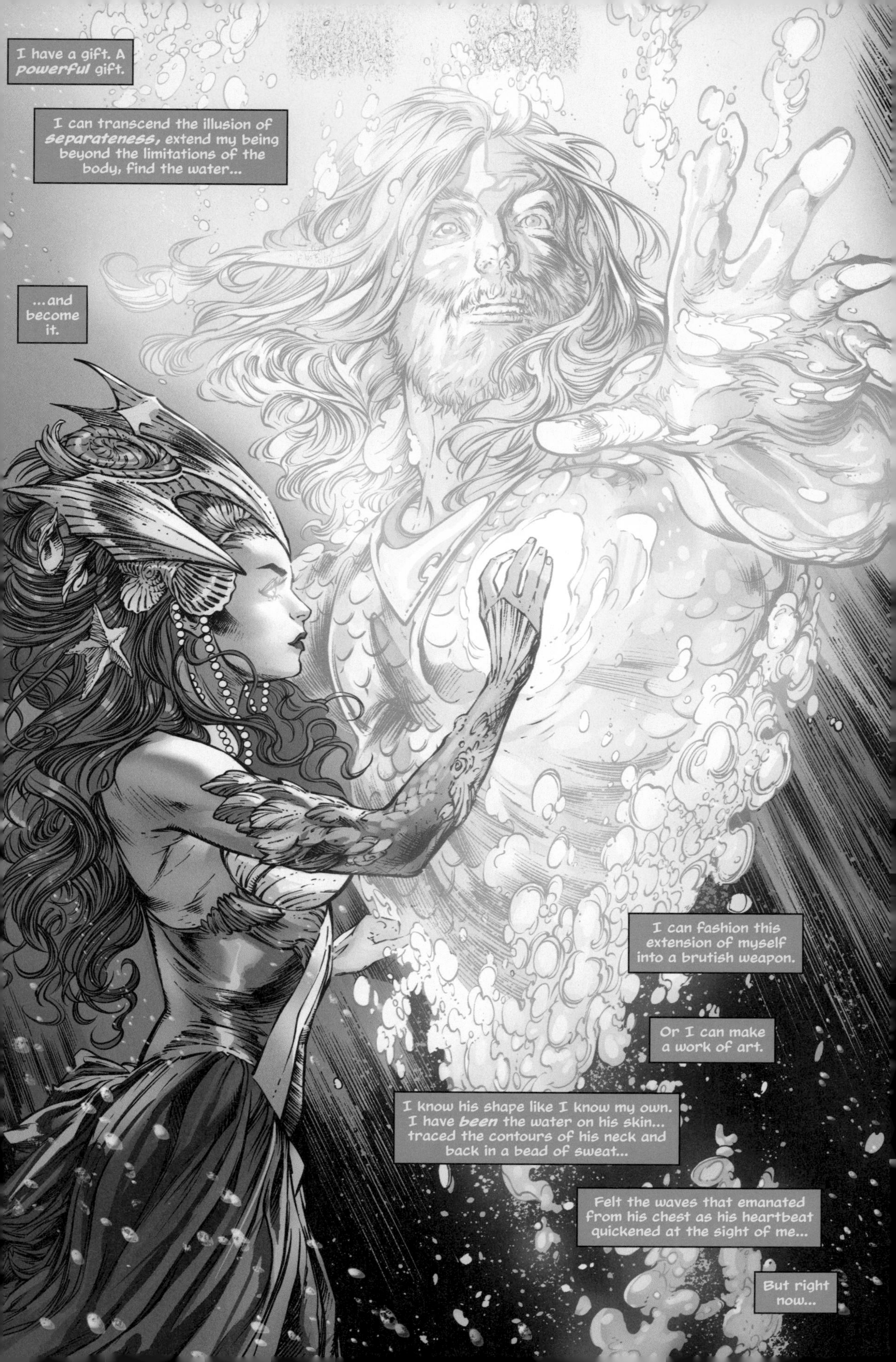
I have a gift. A *powerful* gift.
I can transcend the illusion of *separateness,* extend my being beyond the limitations of the body, find the water...
...and become it.
I can fashion this extension of myself into a brutish weapon.
Or I can make a work of art.
I know his shape like I know my own. I have *been* the water on his skin... traced the contours of his neck and back in a bead of sweat...
Felt the waves that emanated from his chest as his heartbeat quickened at the sight of me...
But right now...

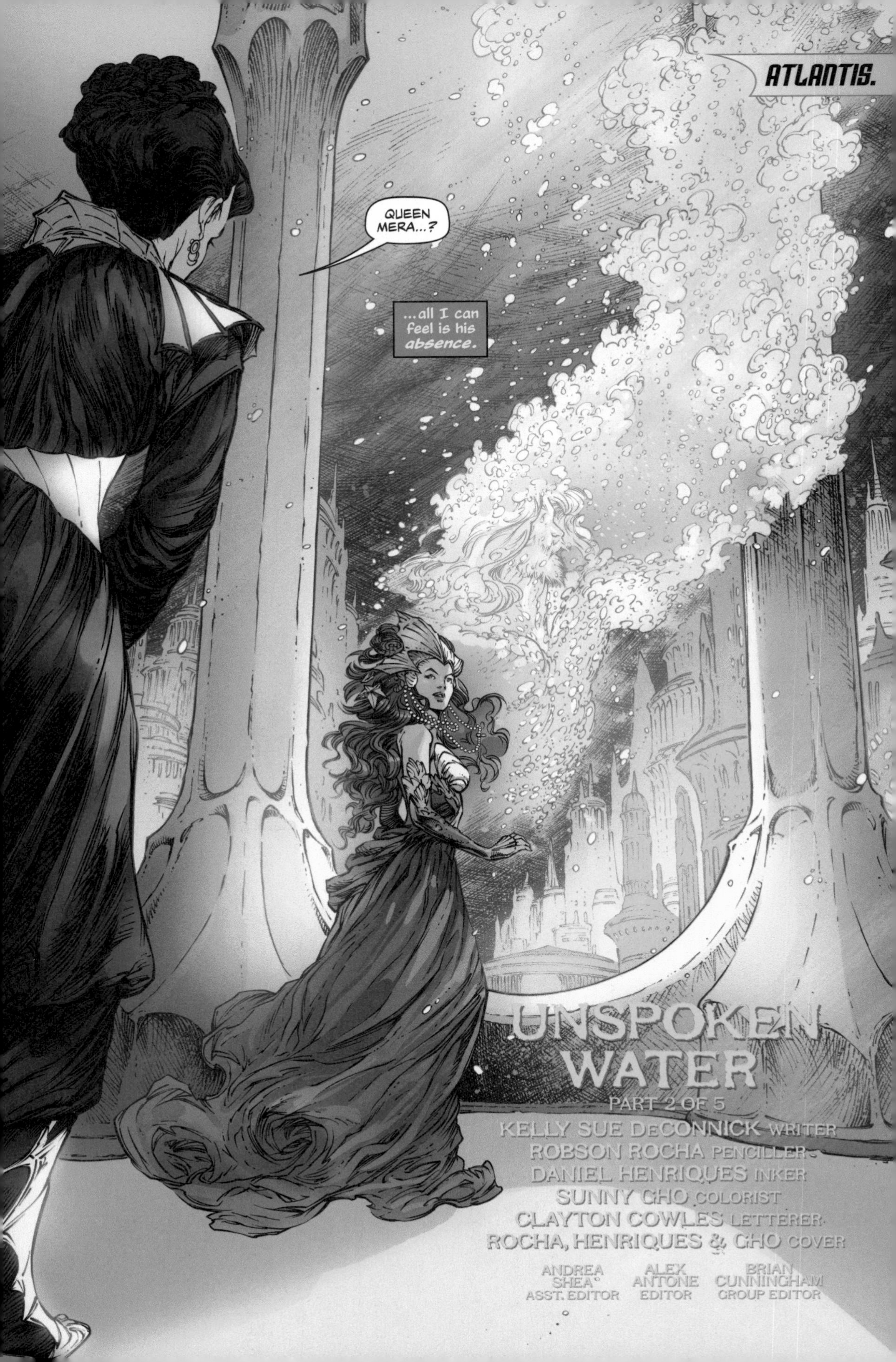
ATLANTIS.
QUEEN MERA...?
...all I can feel is his *absence*.
UNSPOKEN WATER
PART 2 OF 5
KELLY SUE DeCONNICK WRITER
ROBSON ROCHA PENCILLER
DANIEL HENRIQUES INKER
SUNNY CHO COLORIST
CLAYTON COWLES LETTERER
ROCHA, HENRIQUES & CHO COVER
ANDREA SHEA ASST. EDITOR
ALEX ANTONE EDITOR
BRIAN CUNNINGHAM GROUP EDITOR

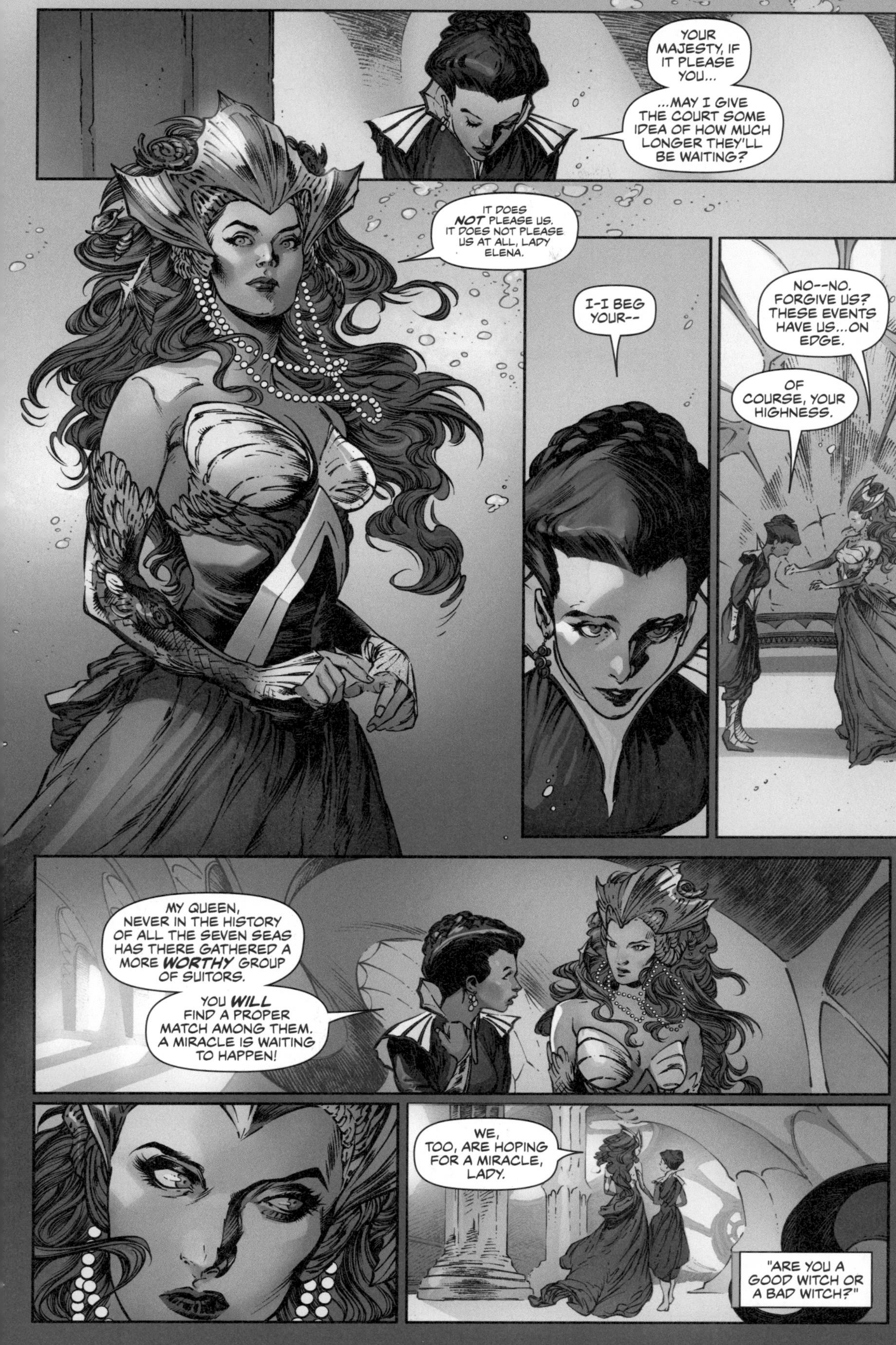
YOUR MAJESTY, IF IT PLEASE YOU...
...MAY I GIVE THE COURT SOME IDEA OF HOW MUCH LONGER THEY'LL BE WAITING?
IT DOES *NOT* PLEASE US. IT DOES NOT PLEASE US AT ALL, LADY ELENA.
I-I BEG YOUR--
NO--NO. FORGIVE US? THESE EVENTS HAVE US...ON EDGE.
OF COURSE, YOUR HIGHNESS.
MY QUEEN, NEVER IN THE HISTORY OF ALL THE SEVEN SEAS HAS THERE GATHERED A MORE *WORTHY* GROUP OF SUITORS.
YOU *WILL* FIND A PROPER MATCH AMONG THEM. A MIRACLE IS WAITING TO HAPPEN!
WE, TOO, ARE HOPING FOR A MIRACLE, LADY.
"ARE YOU A GOOD WITCH OR A BAD WITCH?"

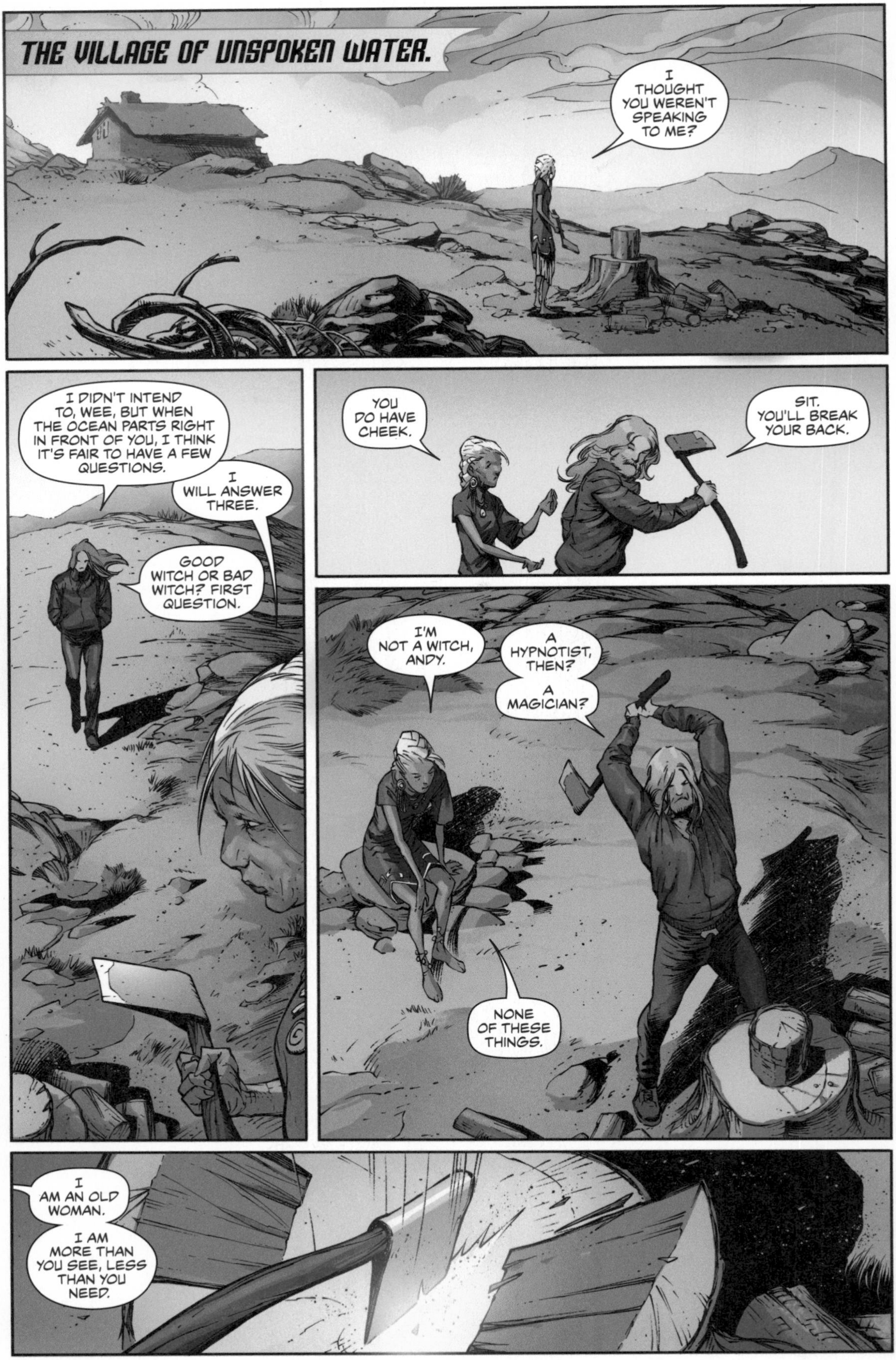
THE VILLAGE OF UNSPOKEN WATER.
I THOUGHT YOU WEREN'T SPEAKING TO ME?
I DIDN'T INTEND TO, WEE, BUT WHEN THE OCEAN PARTS RIGHT IN FRONT OF YOU, I THINK IT'S FAIR TO HAVE A FEW QUESTIONS.
I WILL ANSWER THREE.
GOOD WITCH OR BAD WITCH? FIRST QUESTION.
YOU DO HAVE CHEEK.
SIT. YOU'LL BREAK YOUR BACK.
I'M NOT A WITCH, ANDY.
A HYPNOTIST, THEN?
A MAGICIAN?
NONE OF THESE THINGS.
I AM AN OLD WOMAN.
I AM MORE THAN YOU SEE, LESS THAN YOU NEED.

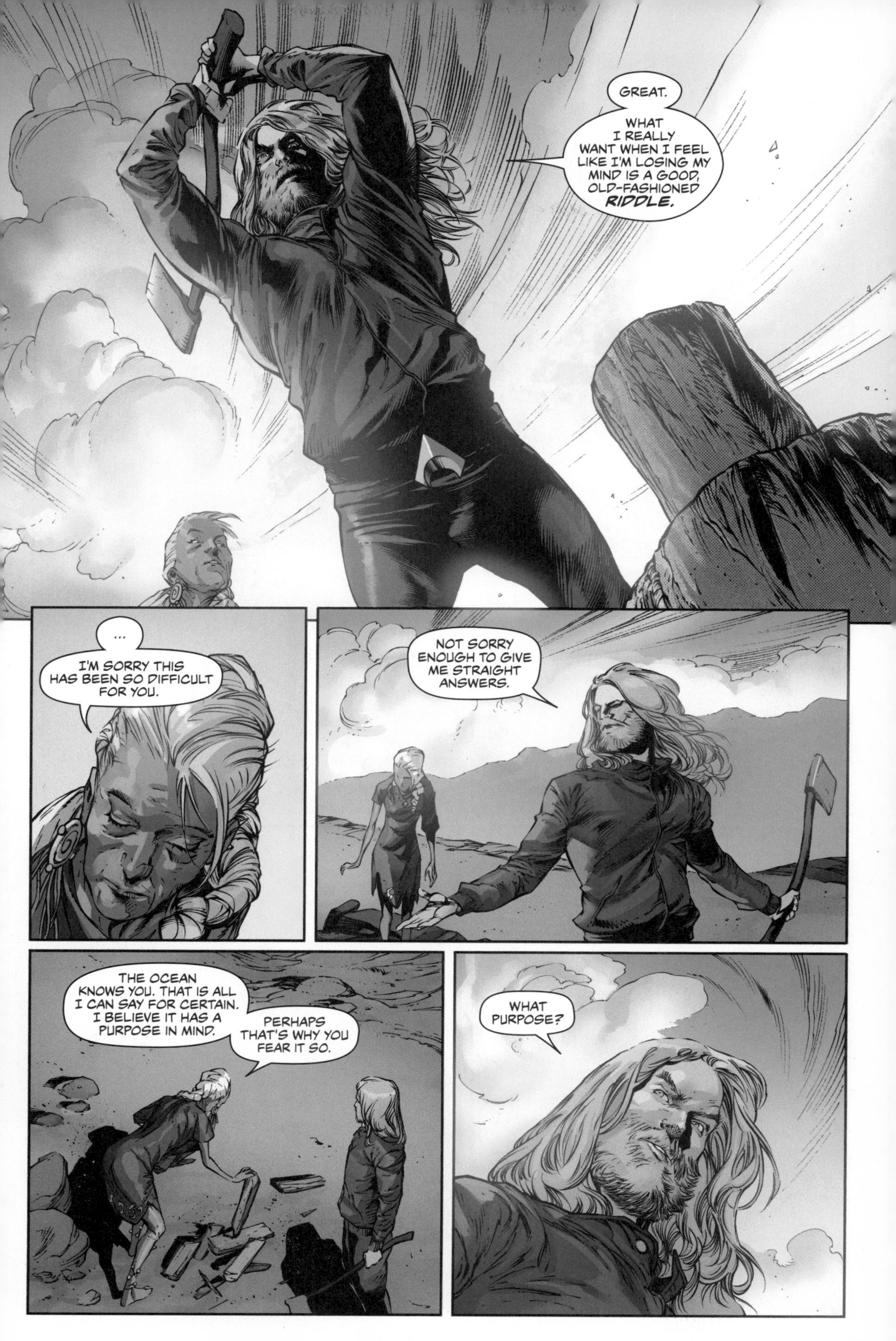
GREAT.
WHAT I REALLY WANT WHEN I FEEL LIKE I'M LOSING MY MIND IS A GOOD, OLD-FASHIONED ***RIDDLE.***
...
I'M SORRY THIS HAS BEEN SO DIFFICULT FOR YOU.
NOT SORRY ENOUGH TO GIVE ME STRAIGHT ANSWERS.
THE OCEAN KNOWS YOU. THAT IS ALL I CAN SAY FOR CERTAIN. I BELIEVE IT HAS A PURPOSE IN MIND.
PERHAPS THAT'S WHY YOU FEAR IT SO.
WHAT PURPOSE?

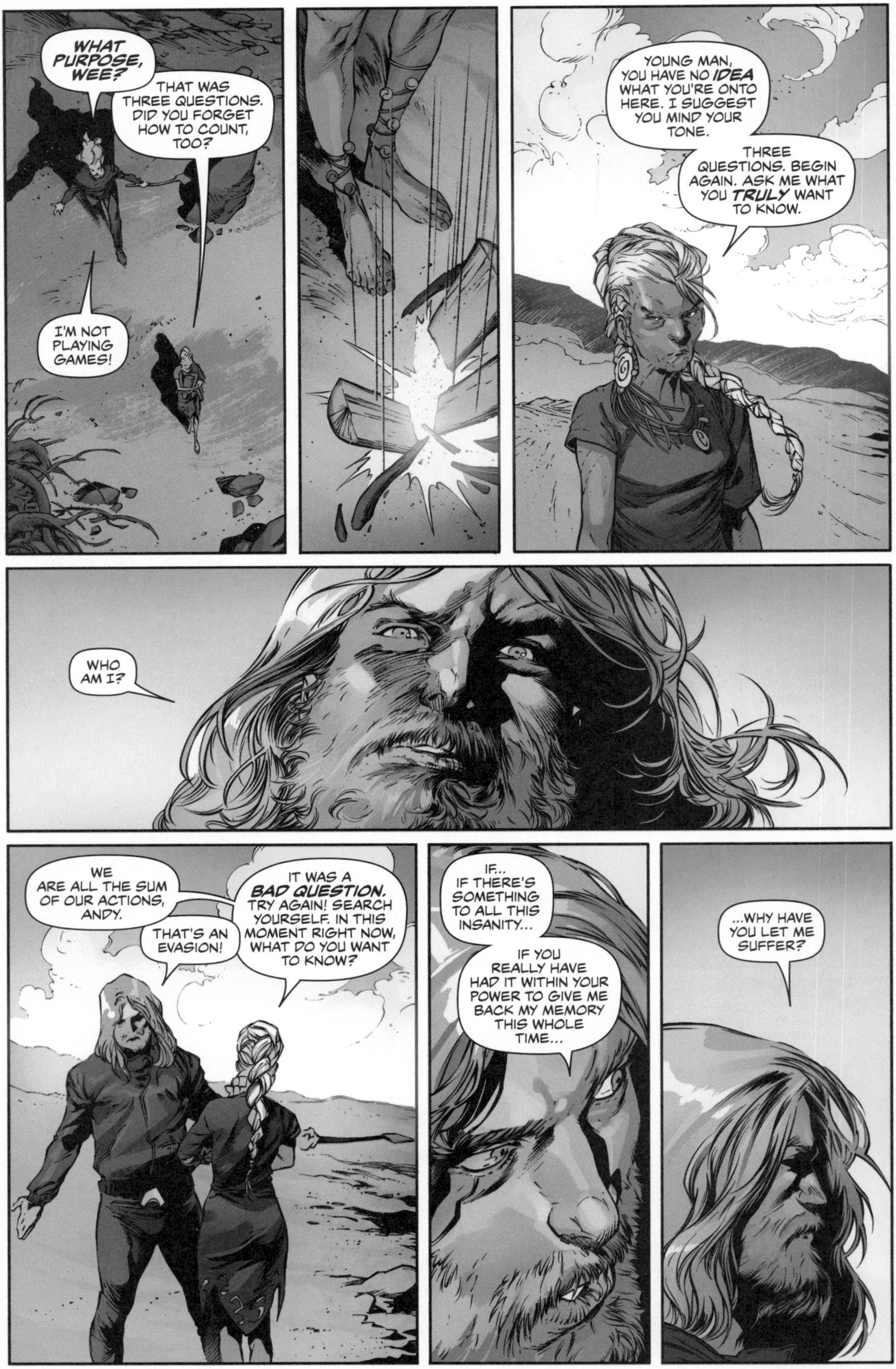
WHAT PURPOSE, WEE?
THAT WAS THREE QUESTIONS. DID YOU FORGET HOW TO COUNT, TOO?
I'M NOT PLAYING GAMES!
YOUNG MAN, YOU HAVE NO IDEA WHAT YOU'RE ONTO HERE. I SUGGEST YOU MIND YOUR TONE.
THREE QUESTIONS. BEGIN AGAIN. ASK ME WHAT YOU TRULY WANT TO KNOW.
WHO AM I?
WE ARE ALL THE SUM OF OUR ACTIONS, ANDY.
THAT'S AN EVASION!
IT WAS A BAD QUESTION. TRY AGAIN! SEARCH YOURSELF. IN THIS MOMENT RIGHT NOW, WHAT DO YOU WANT TO KNOW?
IF... IF THERE'S SOMETHING TO ALL THIS INSANITY...
IF YOU REALLY HAVE HAD IT WITHIN YOUR POWER TO GIVE ME BACK MY MEMORY THIS WHOLE TIME...
...WHY HAVE YOU LET ME SUFFER?

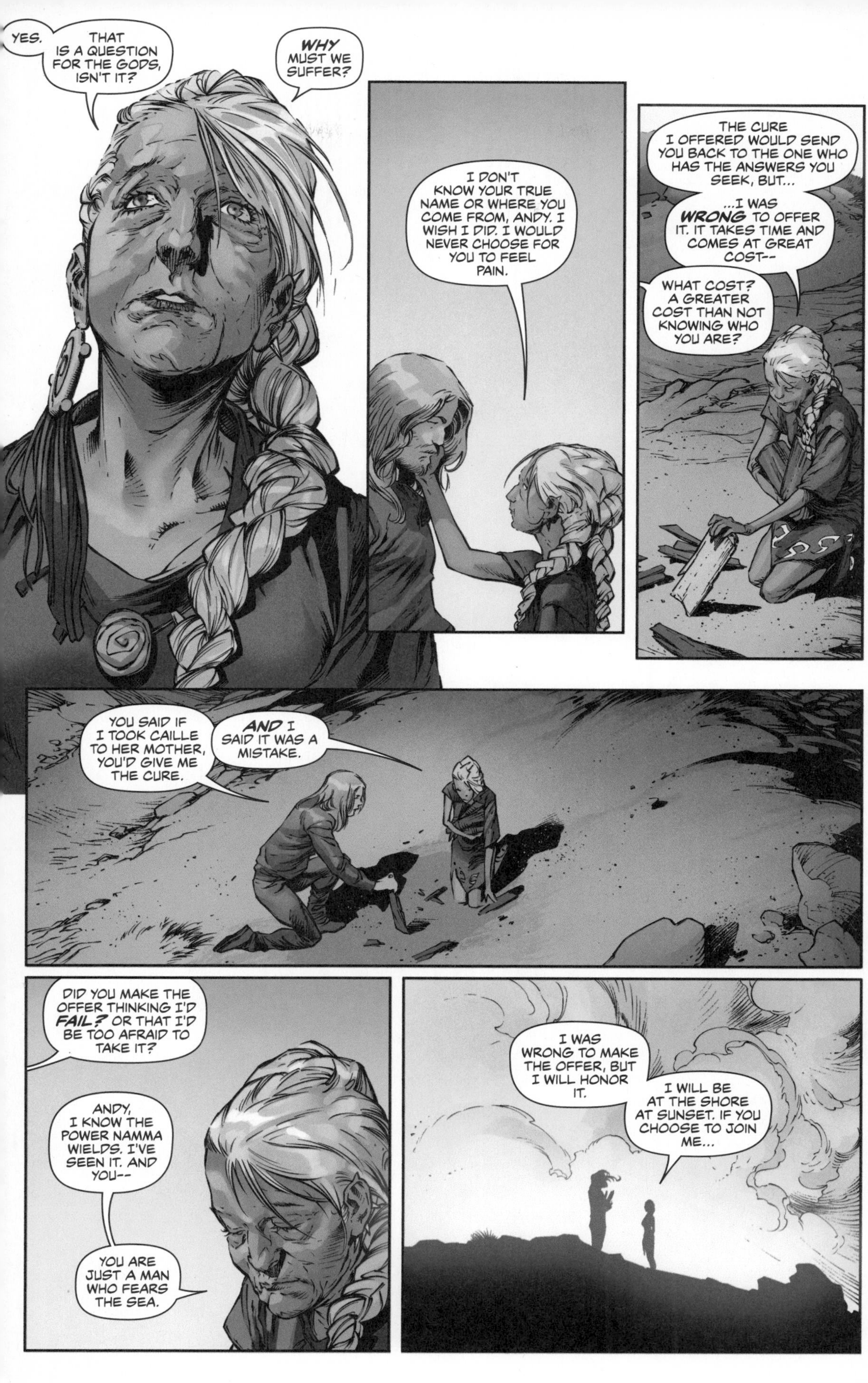
YES.
THAT IS A QUESTION FOR THE GODS, ISN'T IT?
WHY MUST WE SUFFER?
I DON'T KNOW YOUR TRUE NAME OR WHERE YOU COME FROM, ANDY. I WISH I DID. I WOULD NEVER CHOOSE FOR YOU TO FEEL PAIN.
THE CURE I OFFERED WOULD SEND YOU BACK TO THE ONE WHO HAS THE ANSWERS YOU SEEK, BUT...
...I WAS WRONG TO OFFER IT. IT TAKES TIME AND COMES AT GREAT COST--
WHAT COST? A GREATER COST THAN NOT KNOWING WHO YOU ARE?
YOU SAID IF I TOOK CAILLE TO HER MOTHER, YOU'D GIVE ME THE CURE.
AND I SAID IT WAS A MISTAKE.
DID YOU MAKE THE OFFER THINKING I'D FAIL? OR THAT I'D BE TOO AFRAID TO TAKE IT?
ANDY, I KNOW THE POWER NAMMA WIELDS. I'VE SEEN IT. AND YOU--
YOU ARE JUST A MAN WHO FEARS THE SEA.
I WAS WRONG TO MAKE THE OFFER, BUT I WILL HONOR IT.
I WILL BE AT THE SHORE AT SUNSET. IF YOU CHOOSE TO JOIN ME...

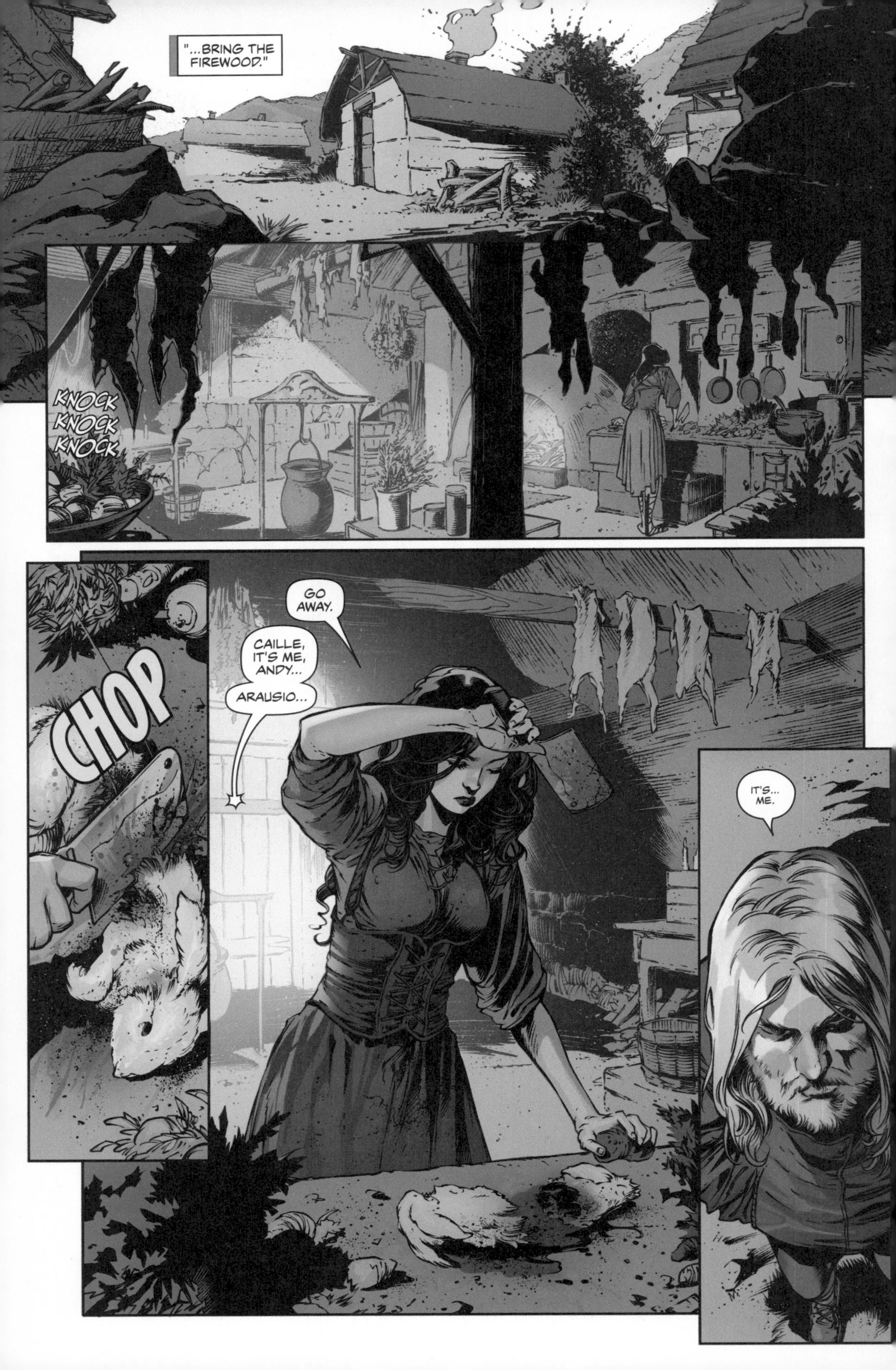
"...BRING THE FIREWOOD."
KNOCK KNOCK KNOCK
CHOP
GO AWAY.
CAILLE, IT'S ME, ANDY...
ARAUSIO...
IT'S... ME.

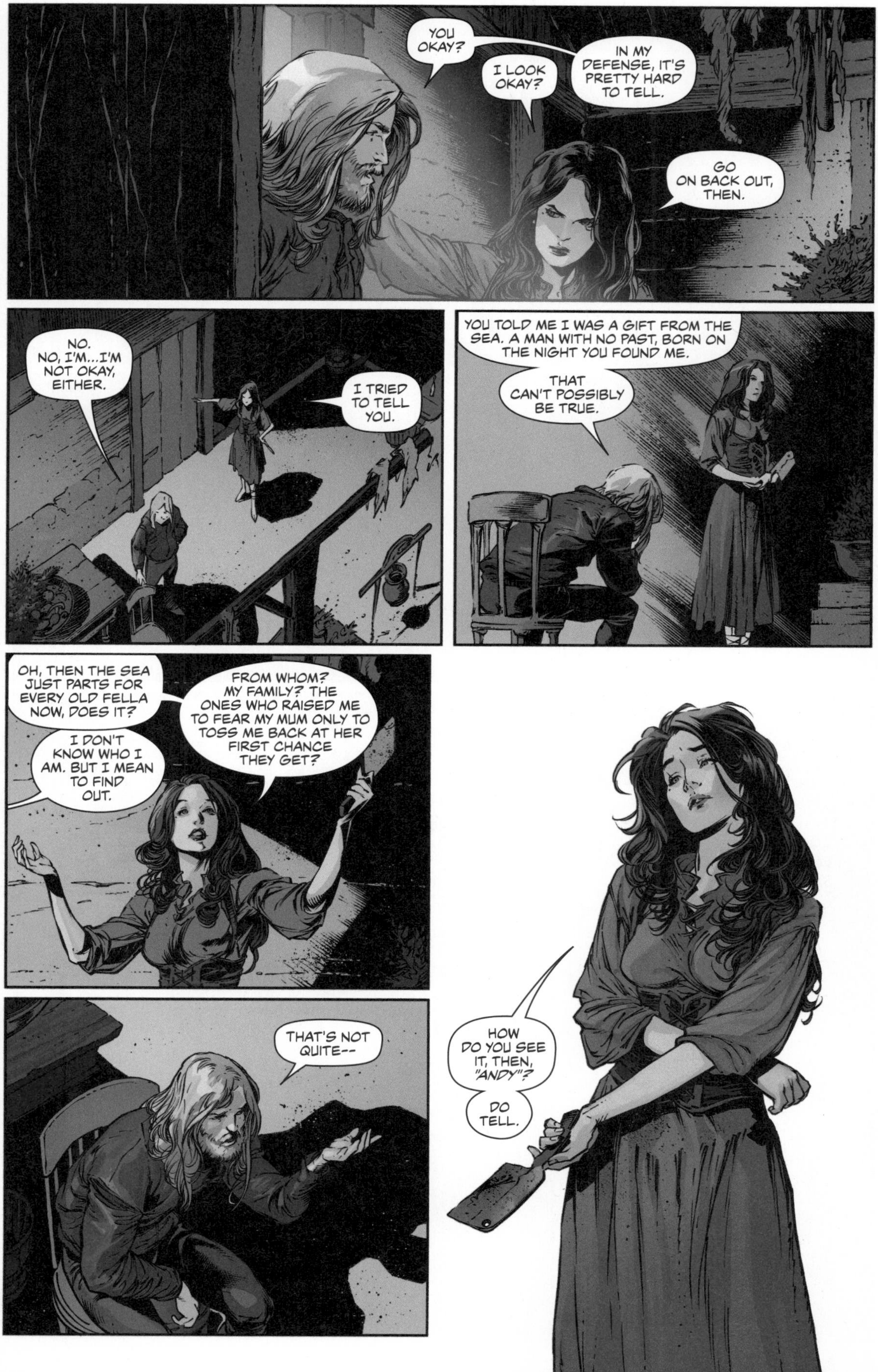
YOU OKAY?
I LOOK OKAY?
IN MY DEFENSE, IT'S PRETTY HARD TO TELL.
GO ON BACK OUT, THEN.
NO. NO, I'M...I'M NOT OKAY, EITHER.
I TRIED TO TELL YOU.
YOU TOLD ME I WAS A GIFT FROM THE SEA. A MAN WITH NO PAST, BORN ON THE NIGHT YOU FOUND ME.
THAT CAN'T POSSIBLY BE TRUE.
OH, THEN THE SEA JUST PARTS FOR EVERY OLD FELLA NOW, DOES IT?
I DON'T KNOW WHO I AM. BUT I MEAN TO FIND OUT.
FROM WHOM? MY FAMILY? THE ONES WHO RAISED ME TO FEAR MY MUM ONLY TO TOSS ME BACK AT HER FIRST CHANCE THEY GET?
THAT'S NOT QUITE--
HOW DO YOU SEE IT, THEN, "ANDY"?
DO TELL.

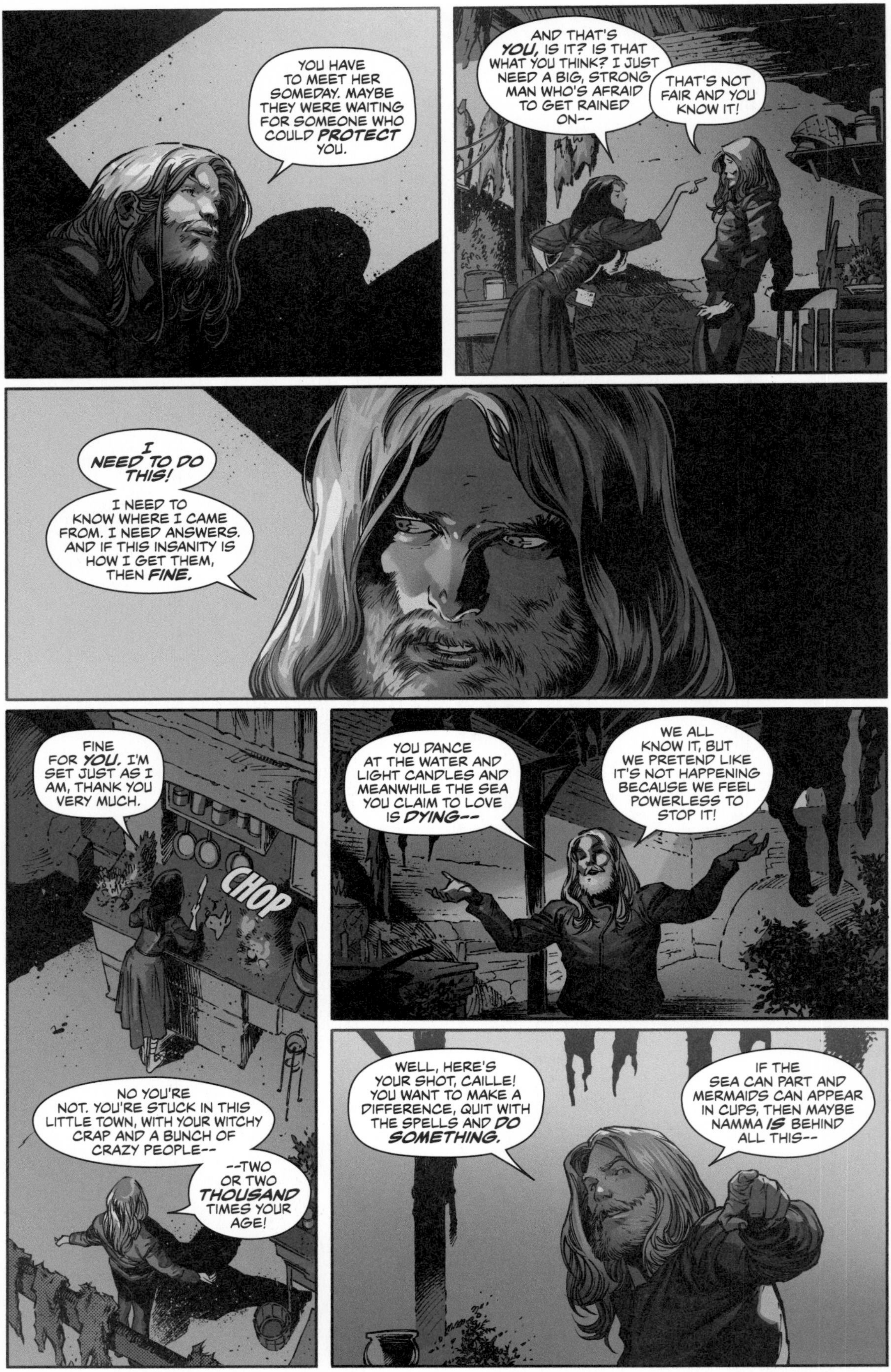
YOU HAVE TO MEET HER SOMEDAY. MAYBE THEY WERE WAITING FOR SOMEONE WHO COULD PROTECT YOU.
AND THAT'S YOU, IS IT? IS THAT WHAT YOU THINK? I JUST NEED A BIG, STRONG MAN WHO'S AFRAID TO GET RAINED ON--
THAT'S NOT FAIR AND YOU KNOW IT!
I NEED TO DO THIS!
I NEED TO KNOW WHERE I CAME FROM. I NEED ANSWERS. AND IF THIS INSANITY IS HOW I GET THEM, THEN FINE.
FINE FOR YOU. I'M SET JUST AS I AM, THANK YOU VERY MUCH.
CHOP
YOU DANCE AT THE WATER AND LIGHT CANDLES AND MEANWHILE THE SEA YOU CLAIM TO LOVE IS DYING--
WE ALL KNOW IT, BUT WE PRETEND LIKE IT'S NOT HAPPENING BECAUSE WE FEEL POWERLESS TO STOP IT!
NO YOU'RE NOT. YOU'RE STUCK IN THIS LITTLE TOWN, WITH YOUR WITCHY CRAP AND A BUNCH OF CRAZY PEOPLE--
--TWO OR TWO THOUSAND TIMES YOUR AGE!
WELL, HERE'S YOUR SHOT, CAILLE! YOU WANT TO MAKE A DIFFERENCE, QUIT WITH THE SPELLS AND DO SOMETHING.
IF THE SEA CAN PART AND MERMAIDS CAN APPEAR IN CUPS, THEN MAYBE NAMMA IS BEHIND ALL THIS--

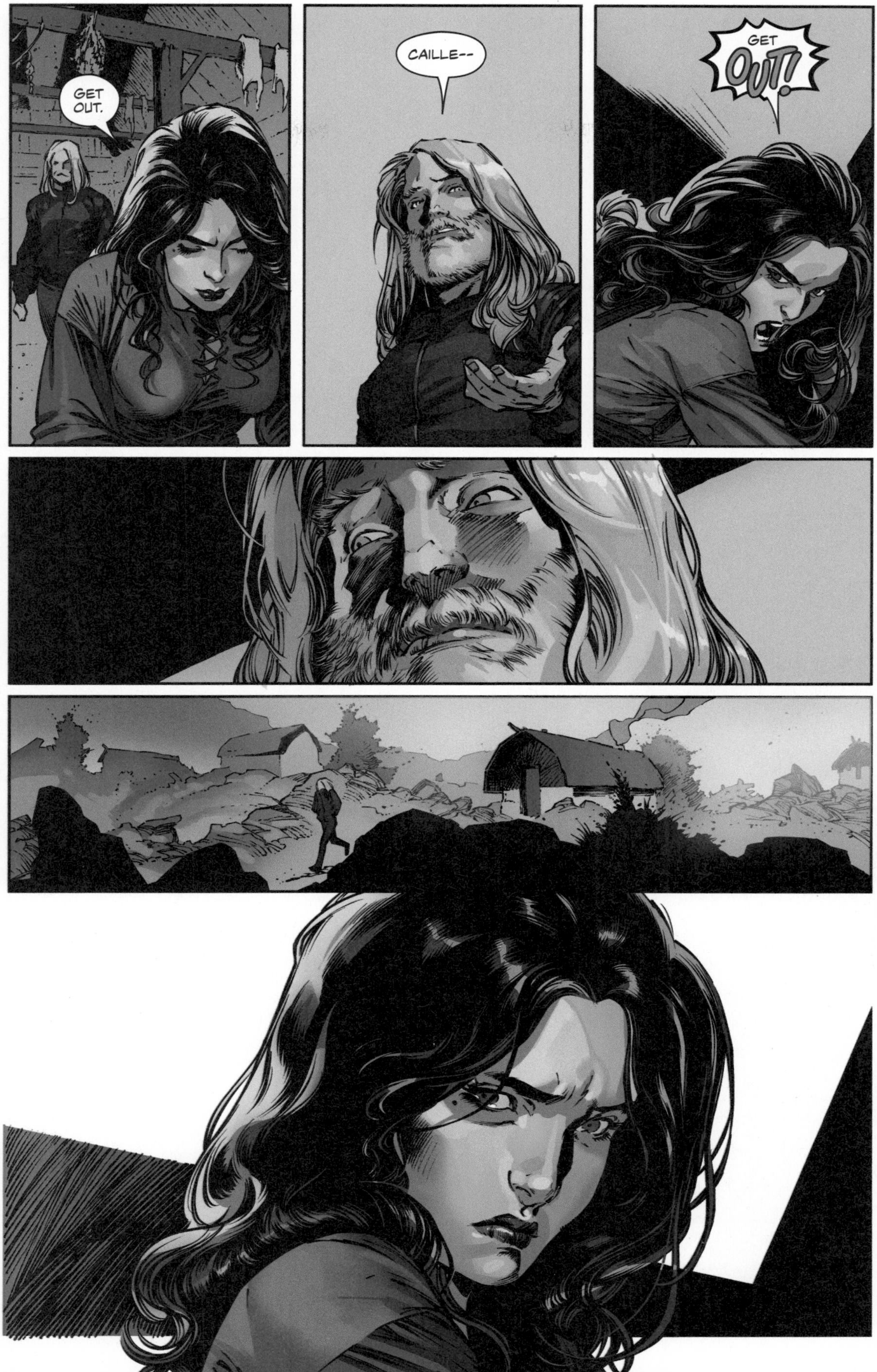
GET OUT.
CAILLE--
GET OUT!

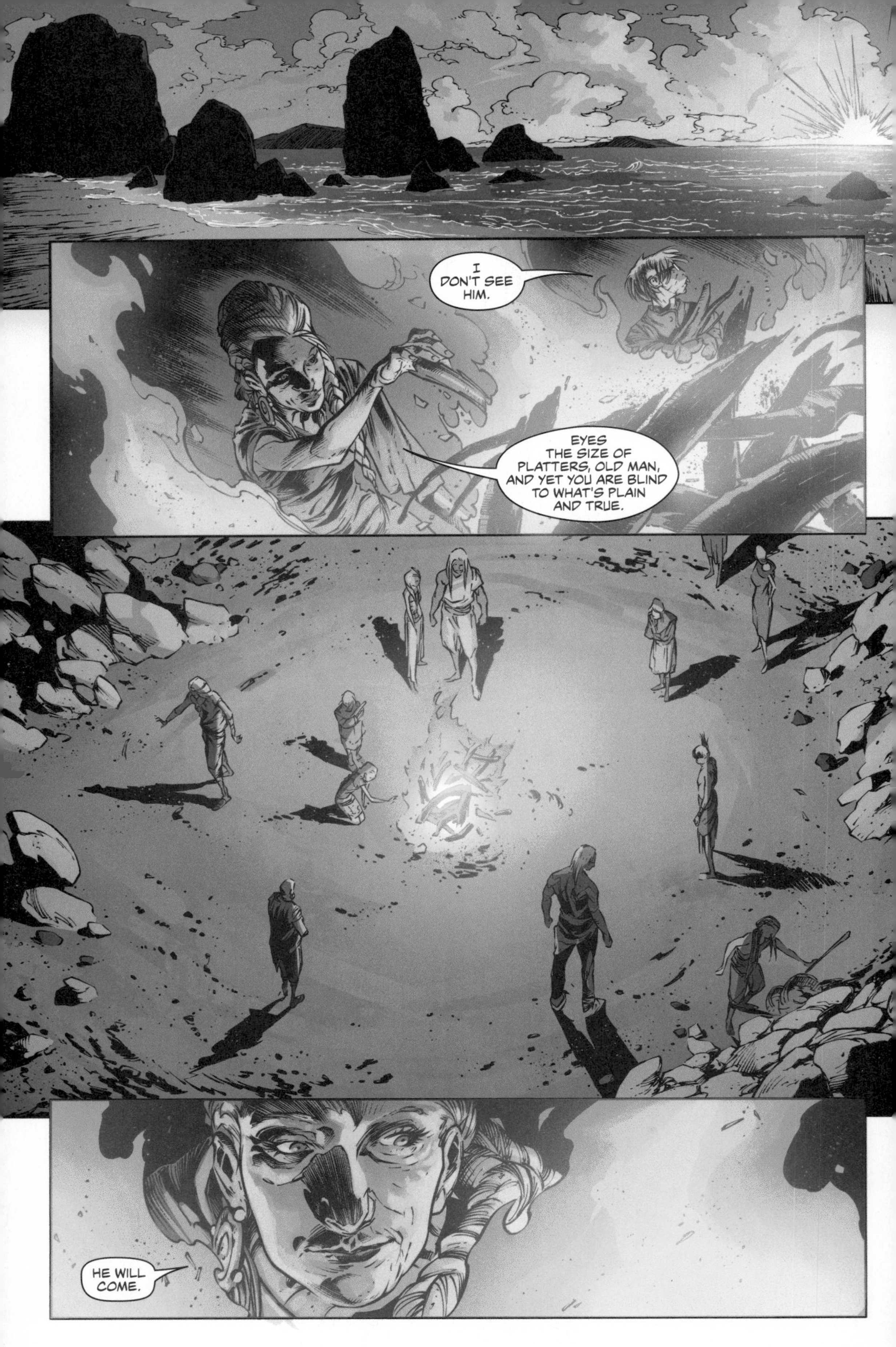
I DON'T SEE HIM.
EYES THE SIZE OF PLATTERS, OLD MAN, AND YET YOU ARE BLIND TO WHAT'S PLAIN AND TRUE.
HE WILL COME.

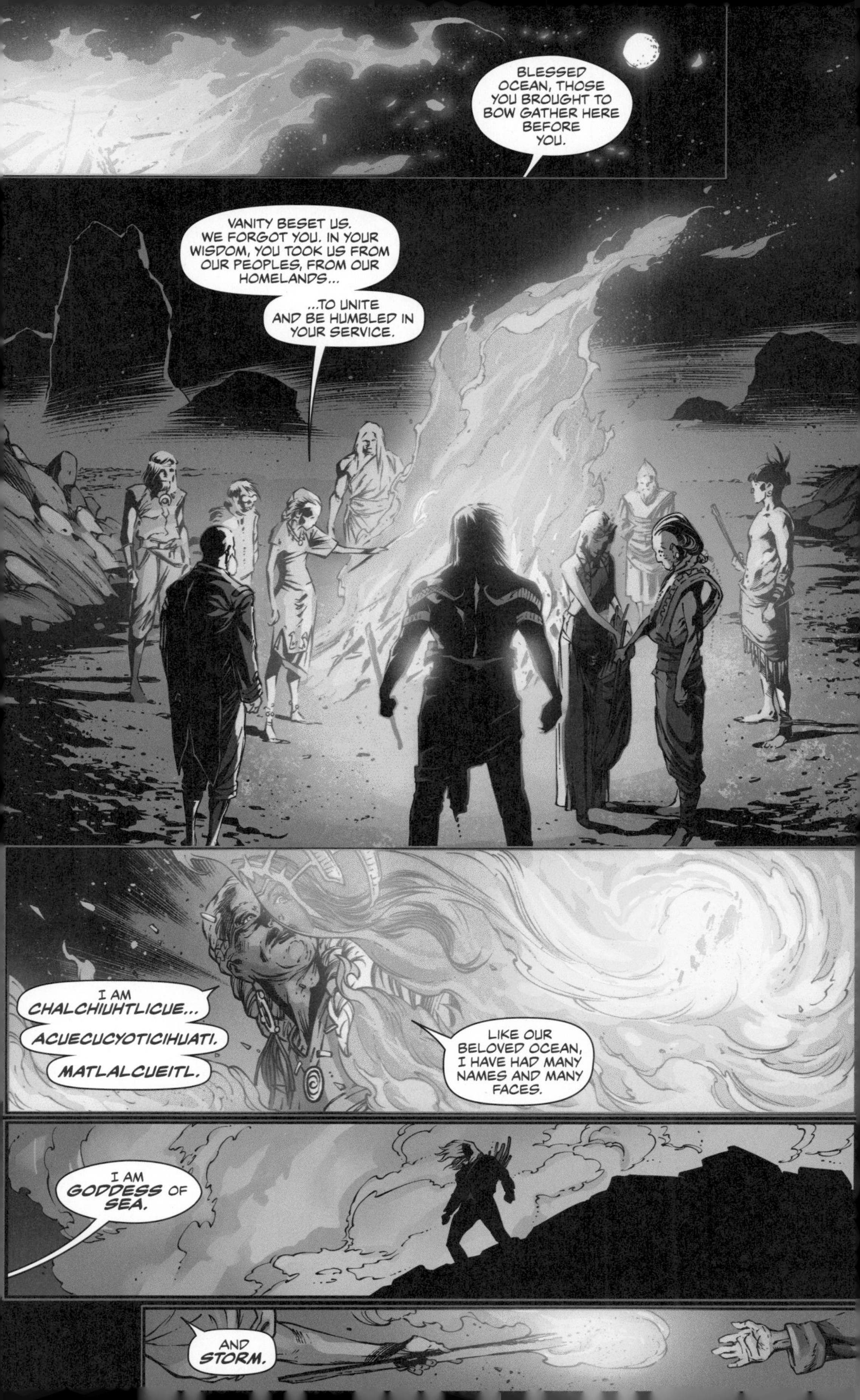
BLESSED OCEAN, THOSE YOU BROUGHT TO BOW GATHER HERE BEFORE YOU.
VANITY BESET US. WE FORGOT YOU. IN YOUR WISDOM, YOU TOOK US FROM OUR PEOPLES, FROM OUR HOMELANDS...
...TO UNITE AND BE HUMBLED IN YOUR SERVICE.
I AM CHALCHIUHTLICUE...
ACUECUCYOTICIHUATI.
MATLALCUEITL.
LIKE OUR BELOVED OCEAN, I HAVE HAD MANY NAMES AND MANY FACES.
I AM GODDESS OF SEA.
AND STORM.

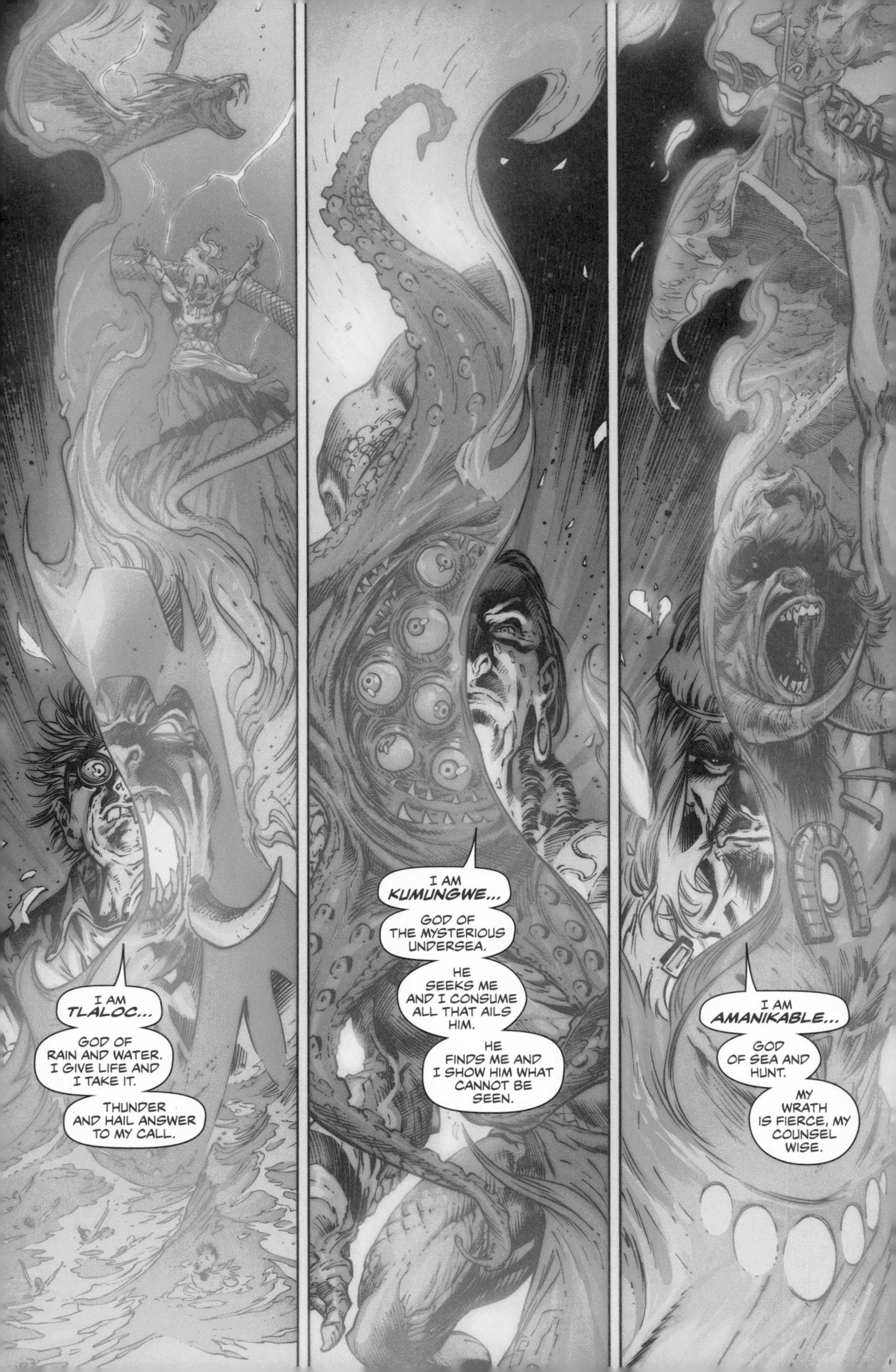
I AM TLALOC...
GOD OF RAIN AND WATER. I GIVE LIFE AND I TAKE IT.
THUNDER AND HAIL ANSWER TO MY CALL.
I AM KUMUNGWE...
GOD OF THE MYSTERIOUS UNDERSEA.
HE SEEKS ME AND I CONSUME ALL THAT AILS HIM.
HE FINDS ME AND I SHOW HIM WHAT CANNOT BE SEEN.
I AM AMANIKABLE...
GOD OF SEA AND HUNT.
MY WRATH IS FIERCE, MY COUNSEL WISE.

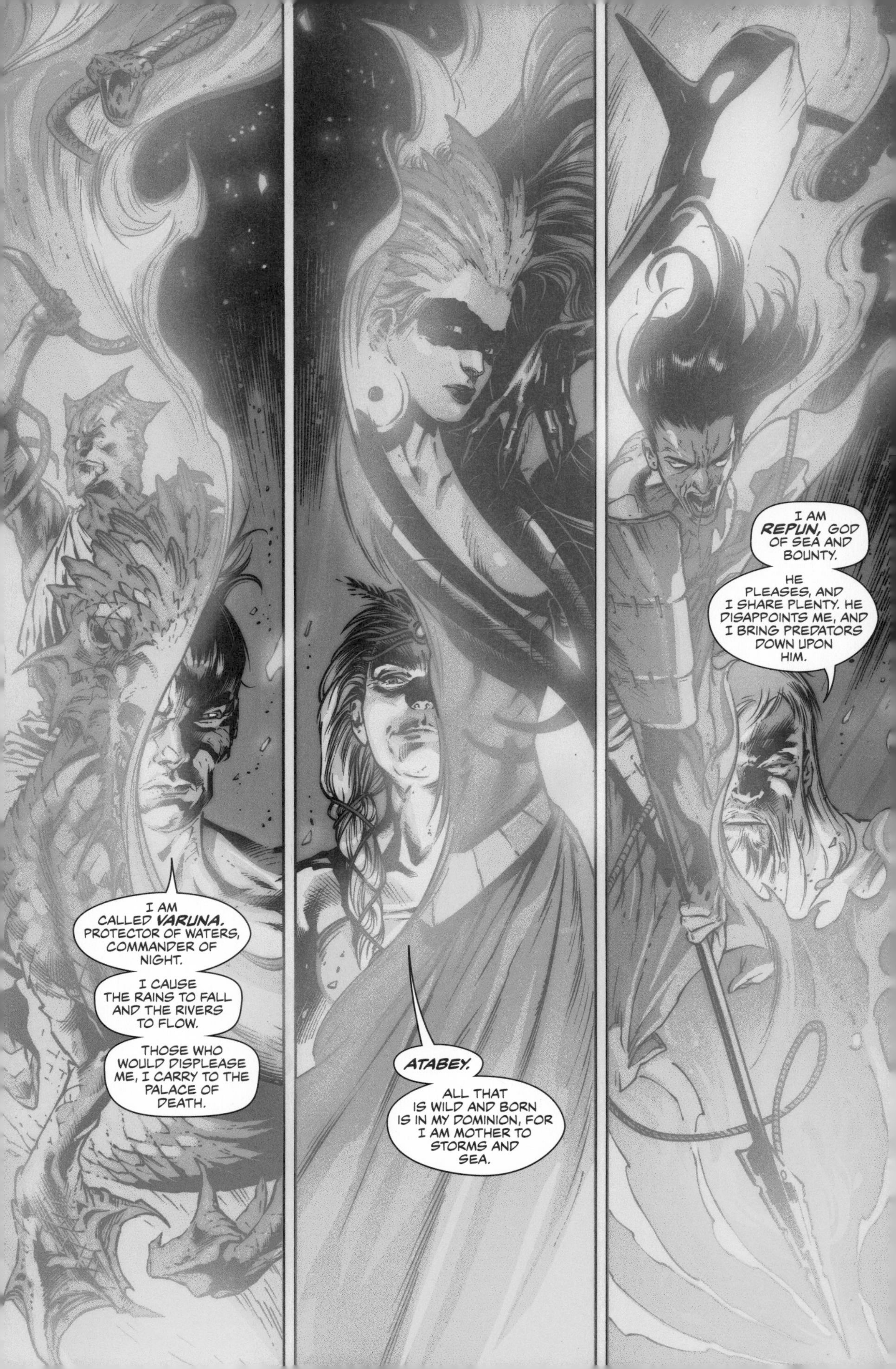
I AM CALLED VARUNA. PROTECTOR OF WATERS, COMMANDER OF NIGHT.
I CAUSE THE RAINS TO FALL AND THE RIVERS TO FLOW.
THOSE WHO WOULD DISPLEASE ME, I CARRY TO THE PALACE OF DEATH.
ATABEY.
ALL THAT IS WILD AND BORN IS IN MY DOMINION, FOR I AM MOTHER TO STORMS AND SEA.
I AM REPUN, GOD OF SEA AND BOUNTY.
HE PLEASES, AND I SHARE PLENTY. HE DISAPPOINTS ME, AND I BRING PREDATORS DOWN UPON HIM.

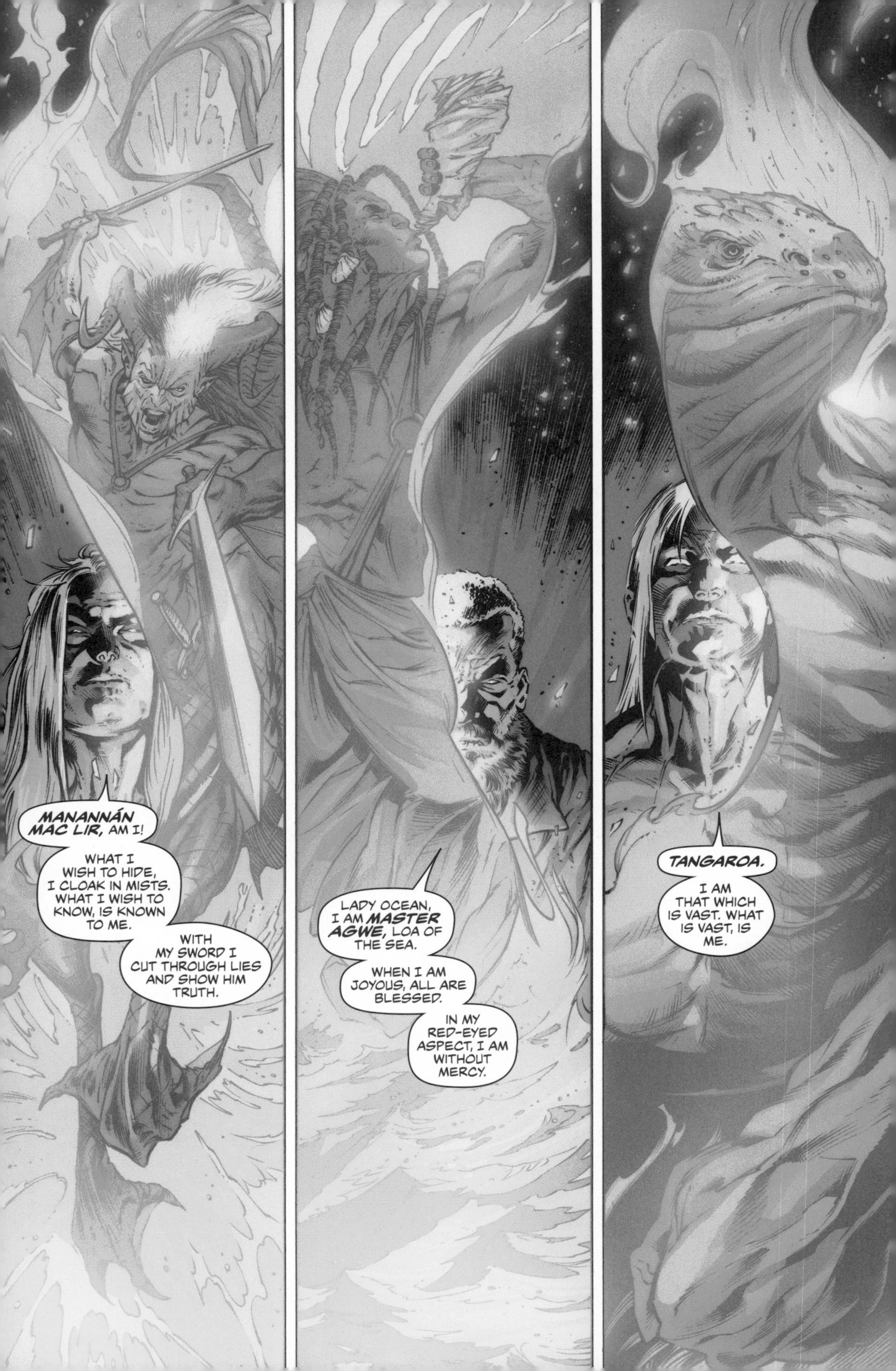

MANANNÁN MAC LIR, AM I!
WHAT I WISH TO HIDE, I CLOAK IN MISTS. WHAT I WISH TO KNOW, IS KNOWN TO ME.
WITH MY SWORD I CUT THROUGH LIES AND SHOW HIM TRUTH.
LADY OCEAN, I AM MASTER AGWE, LOA OF THE SEA.
WHEN I AM JOYOUS, ALL ARE BLESSED.
IN MY RED-EYED ASPECT, I AM WITHOUT MERCY.
TANGAROA.
I AM THAT WHICH IS VAST. WHAT IS VAST, IS ME.

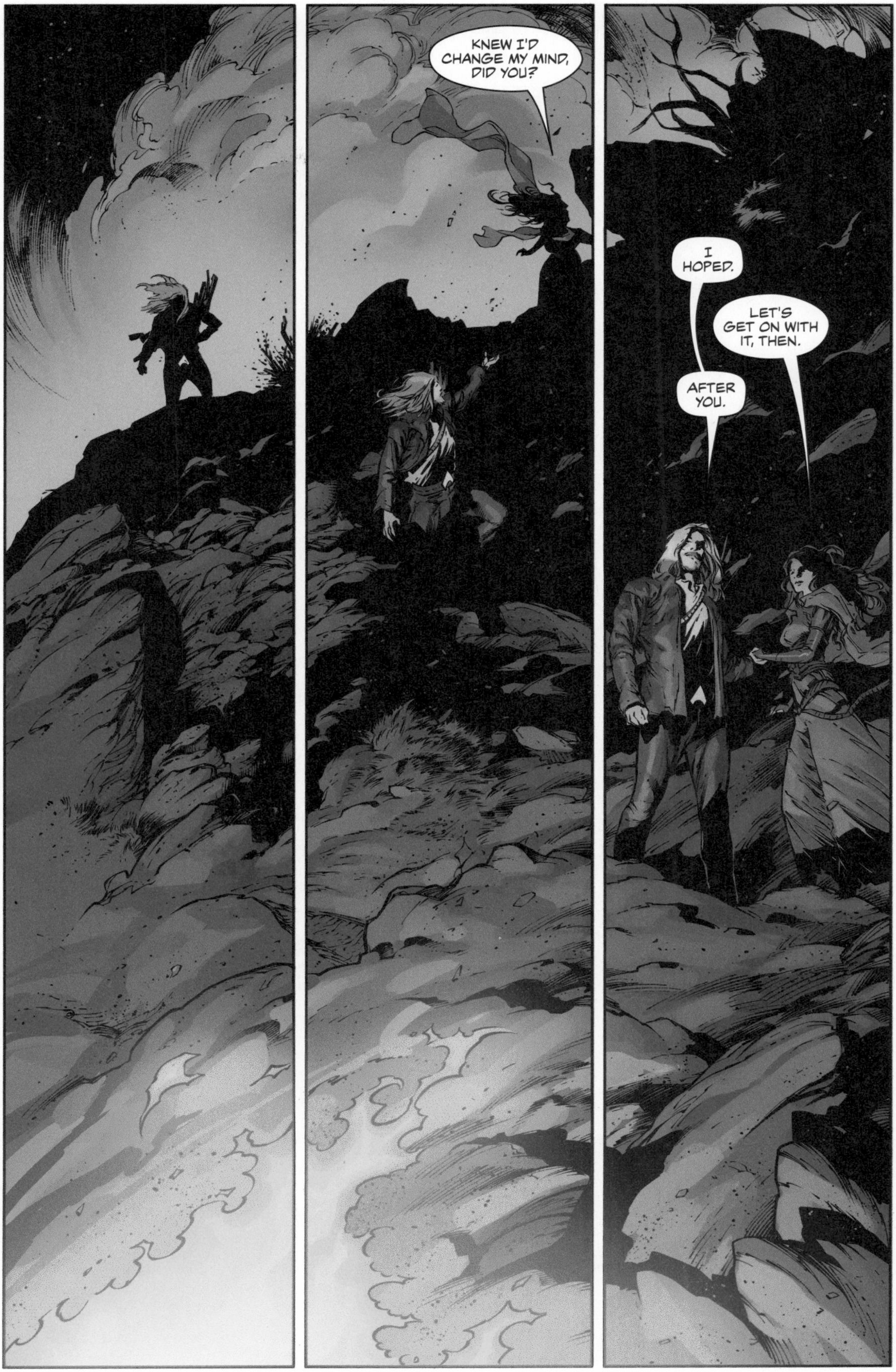
KNEW I'D CHANGE MY MIND, DID YOU?
I HOPED.
AFTER YOU.
LET'S GET ON WITH IT, THEN.

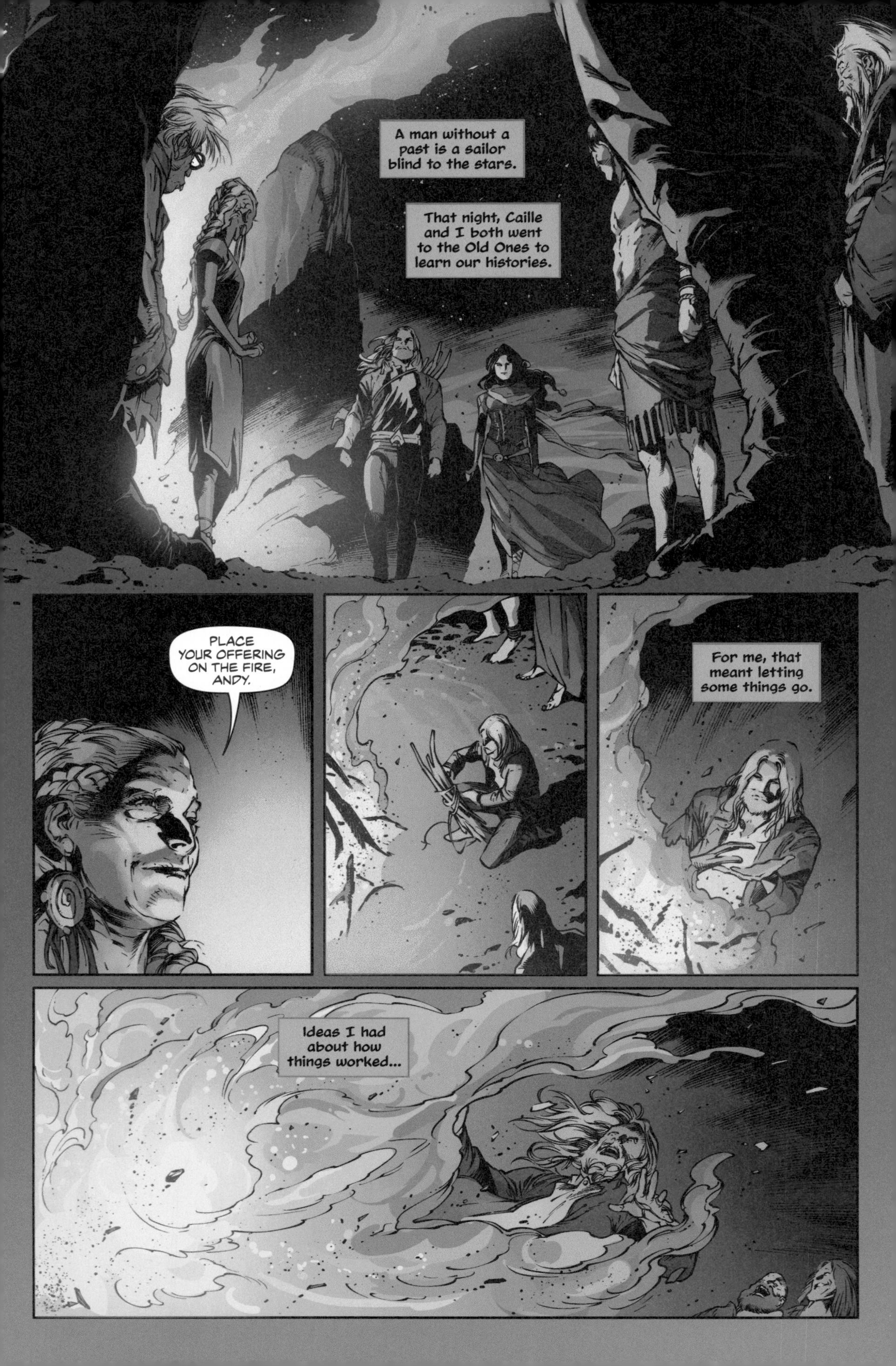
A man without a past is a sailor blind to the stars.
That night, Caille and I both went to the Old Ones to learn our histories.
PLACE YOUR OFFERING ON THE FIRE, ANDY.
For me, that meant letting some things go.
Ideas I had about how things worked...

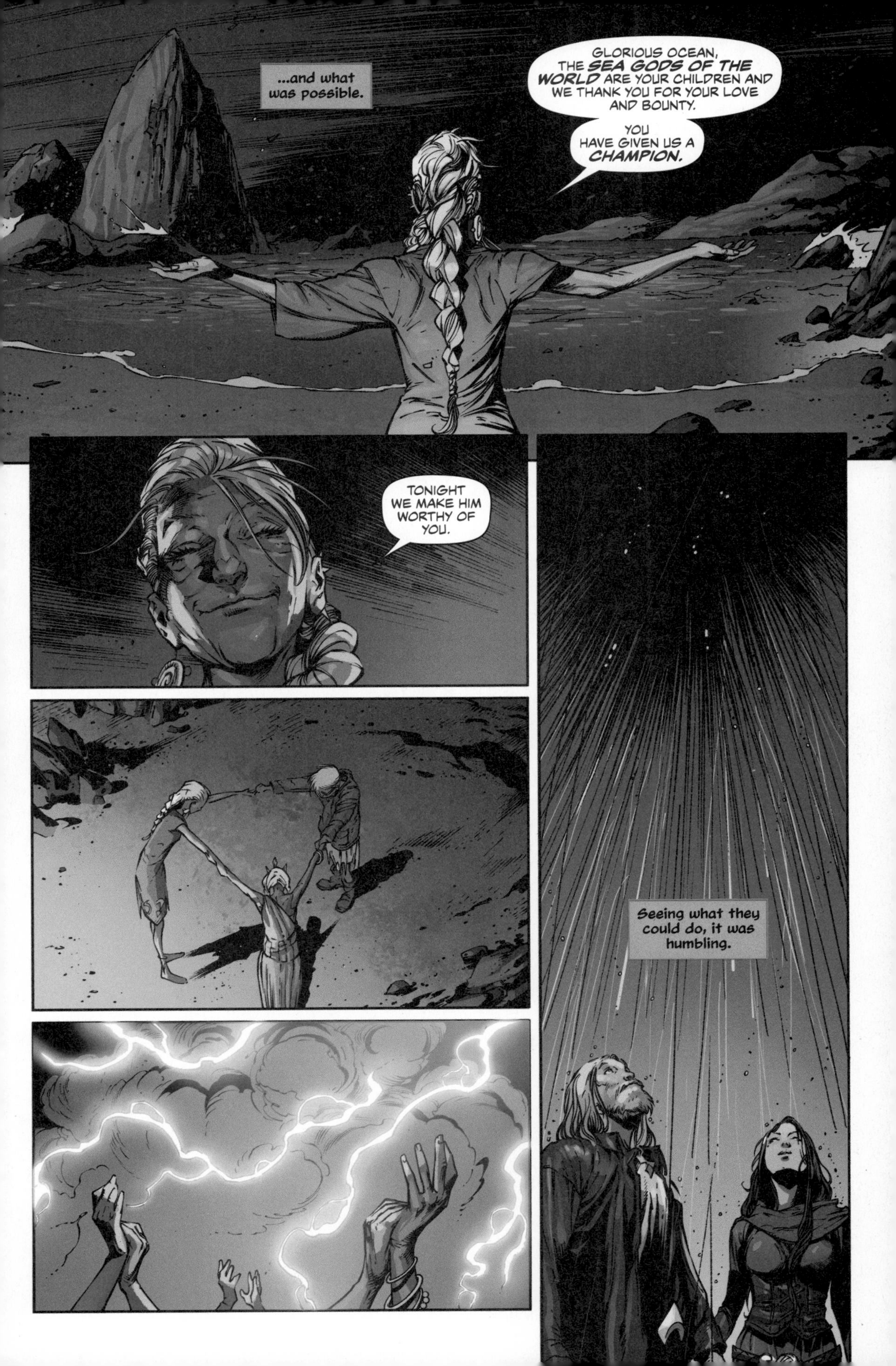
...and what was possible.
GLORIOUS OCEAN, THE SEA GODS OF THE WORLD ARE YOUR CHILDREN AND WE THANK YOU FOR YOUR LOVE AND BOUNTY.
YOU HAVE GIVEN US A CHAMPION.
TONIGHT WE MAKE HIM WORTHY OF YOU.
Seeing what they could do, it was humbling.

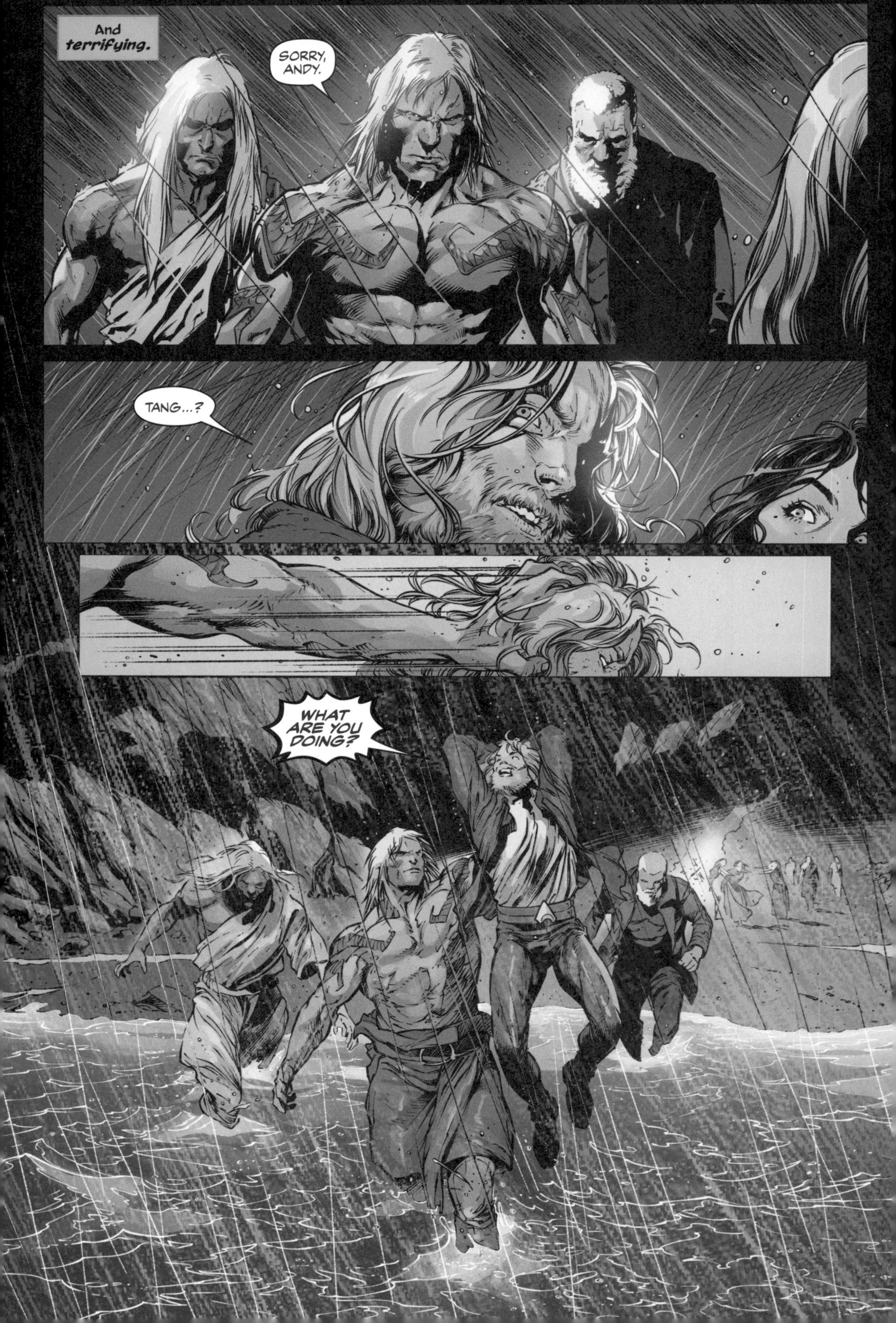
And *terrifying.*
SORRY, ANDY.
TANG...?
WHAT ARE YOU DOING?

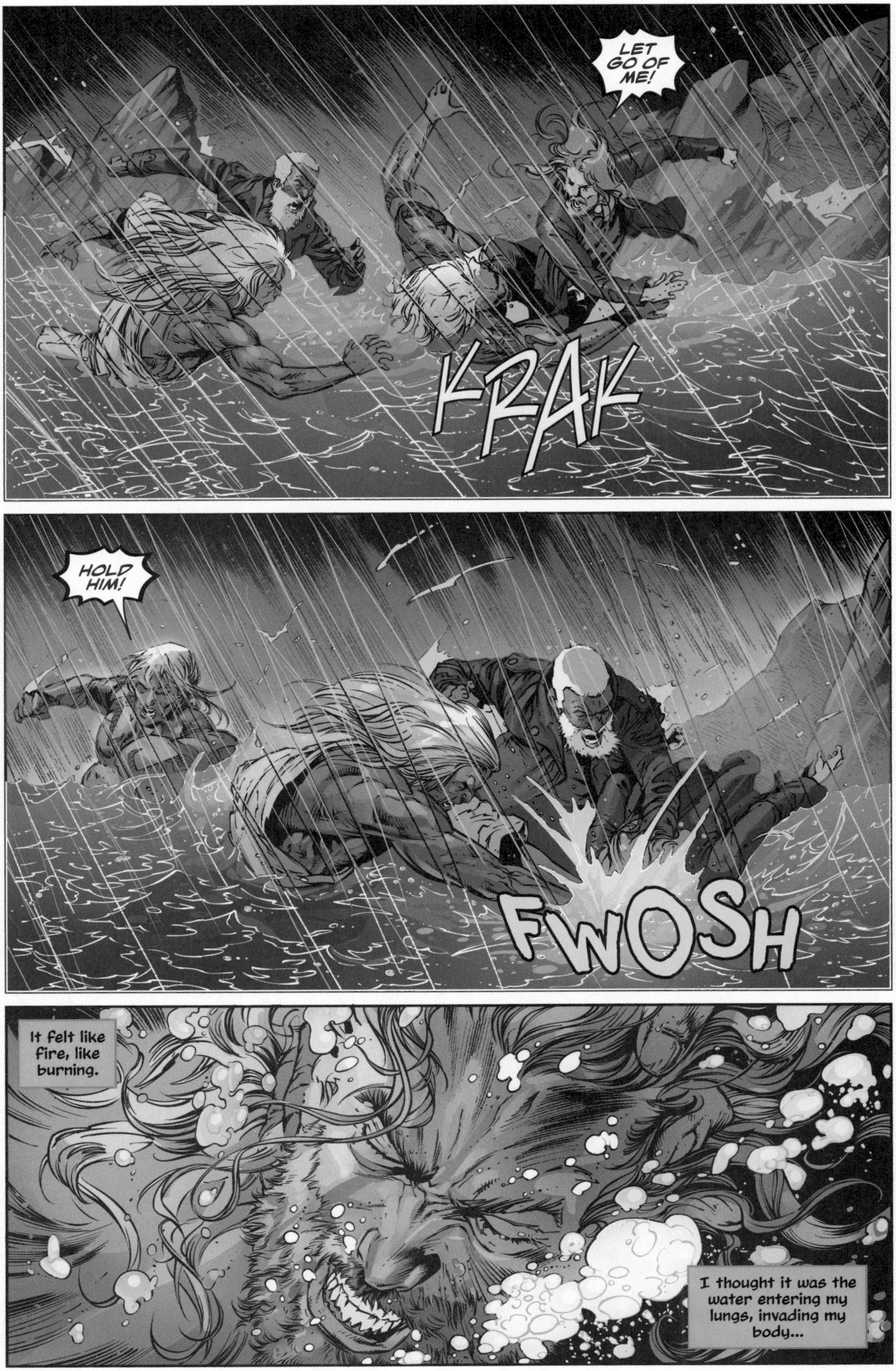
LET GO OF ME!
KRAK
HOLD HIM!
FWOSH
It felt like fire, like burning.
I thought it was the water entering my lungs, invading my body...

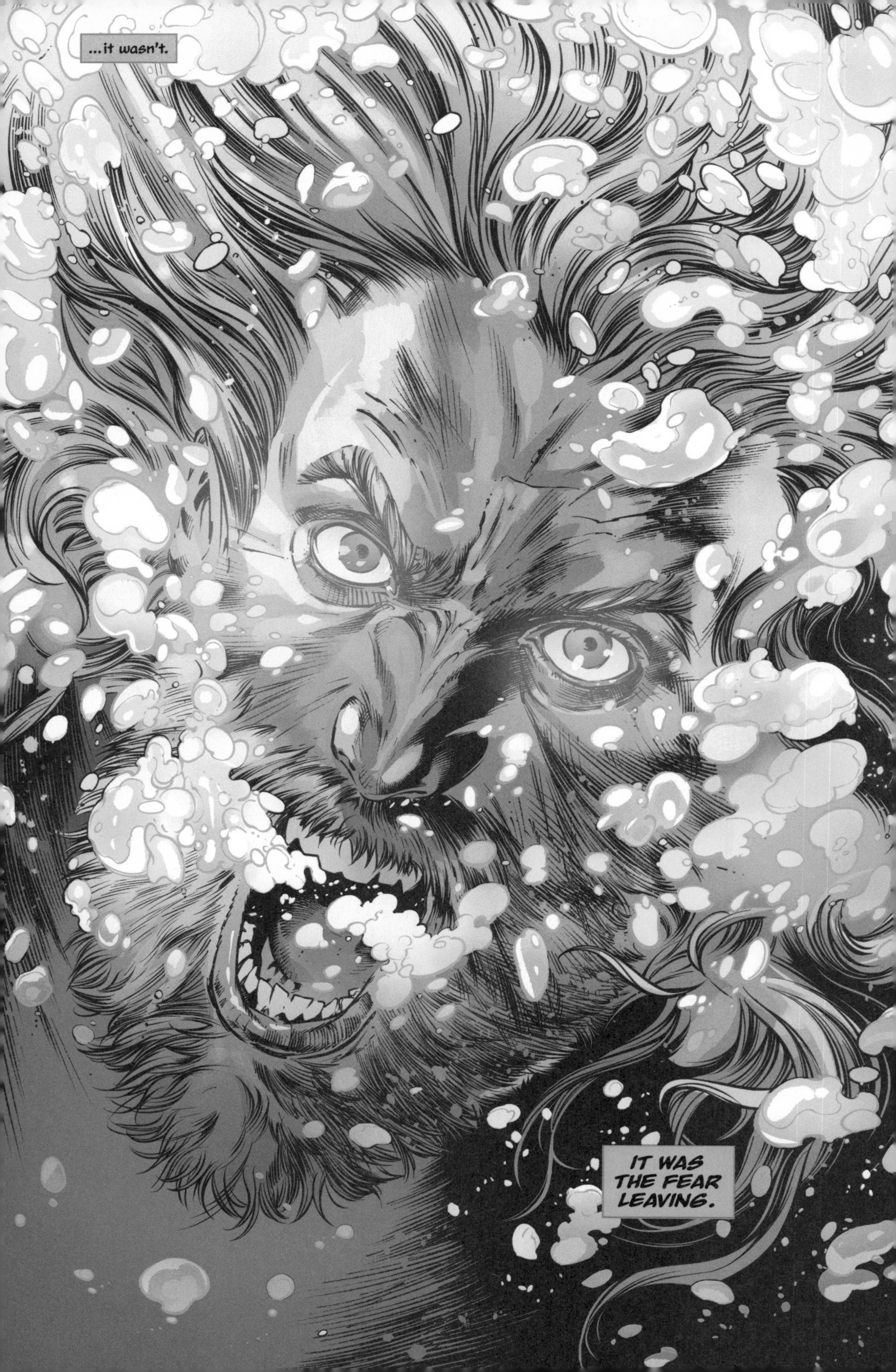
...it wasn't.
IT WAS THE FEAR LEAVING.

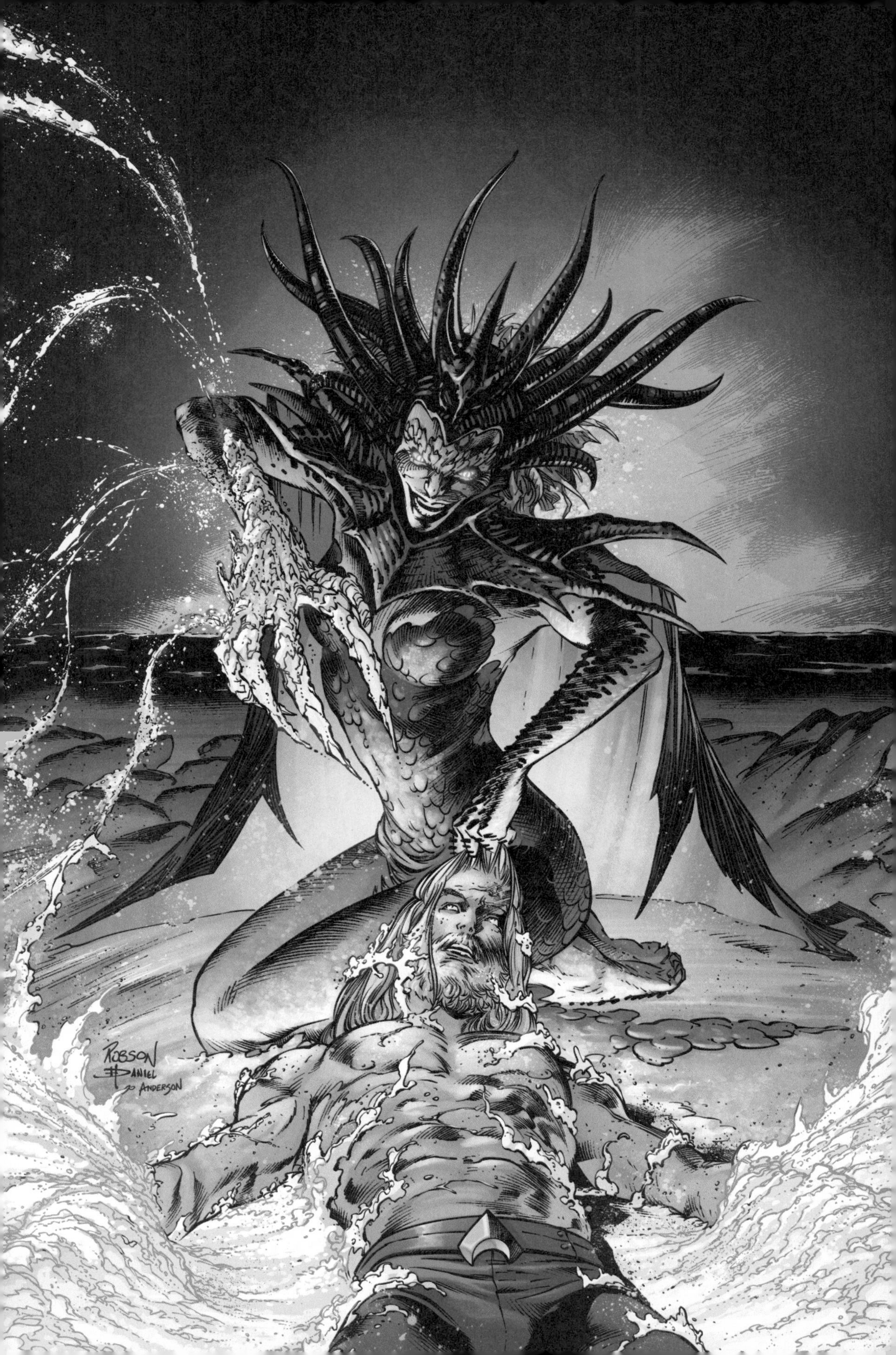
ROBSON
DANIEL
ANDERSON

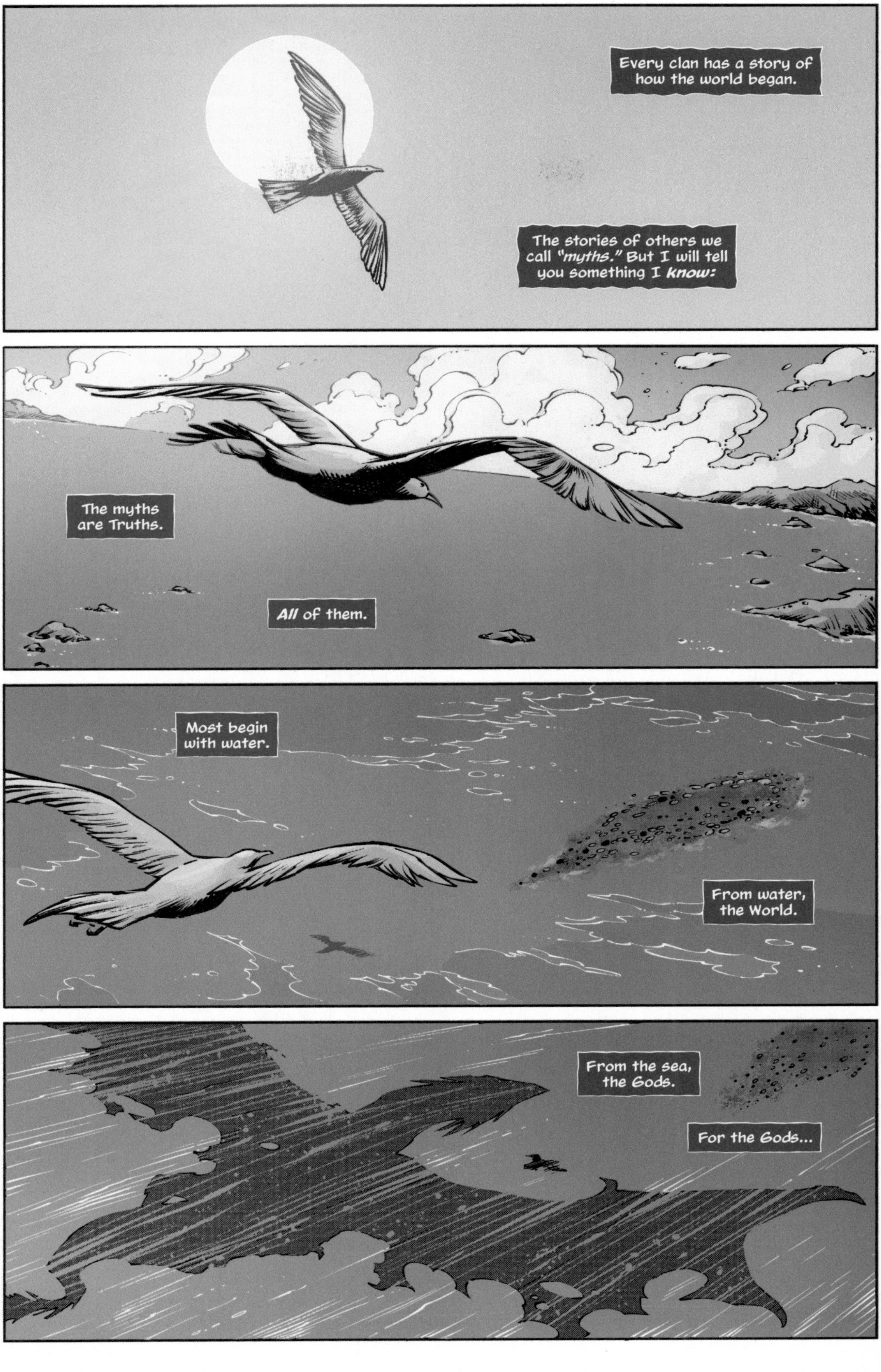
Every clan has a story of how the world began.
The stories of others we call *"myths."* But I will tell you something I ***know:***
The myths are Truths.
All of them.
Most begin with water.
From water, the World.
From the sea, the Gods.
For the Gods...

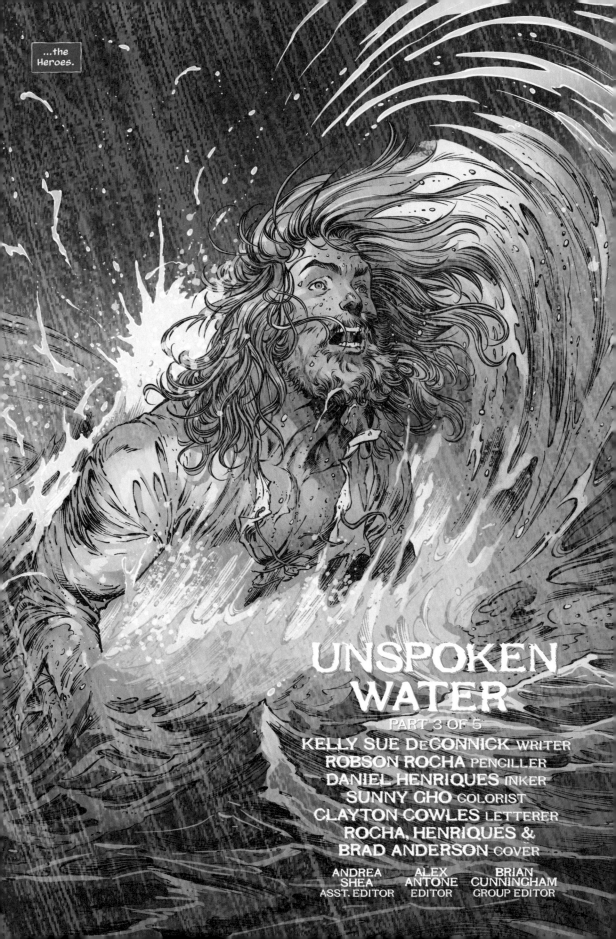

UNSPOKEN WATER

PART 3 OF 5

KELLY SUE DeCONNICK WRITER
ROBSON ROCHA PENCILLER
DANIEL HENRIQUES INKER
SUNNY GHO COLORIST
CLAYTON COWLES LETTERER
ROCHA, HENRIQUES &
BRAD ANDERSON COVER

ANDREA SHEA ASST. EDITOR
ALEX ANTONE EDITOR
BRIAN CUNNINGHAM GROUP EDITOR

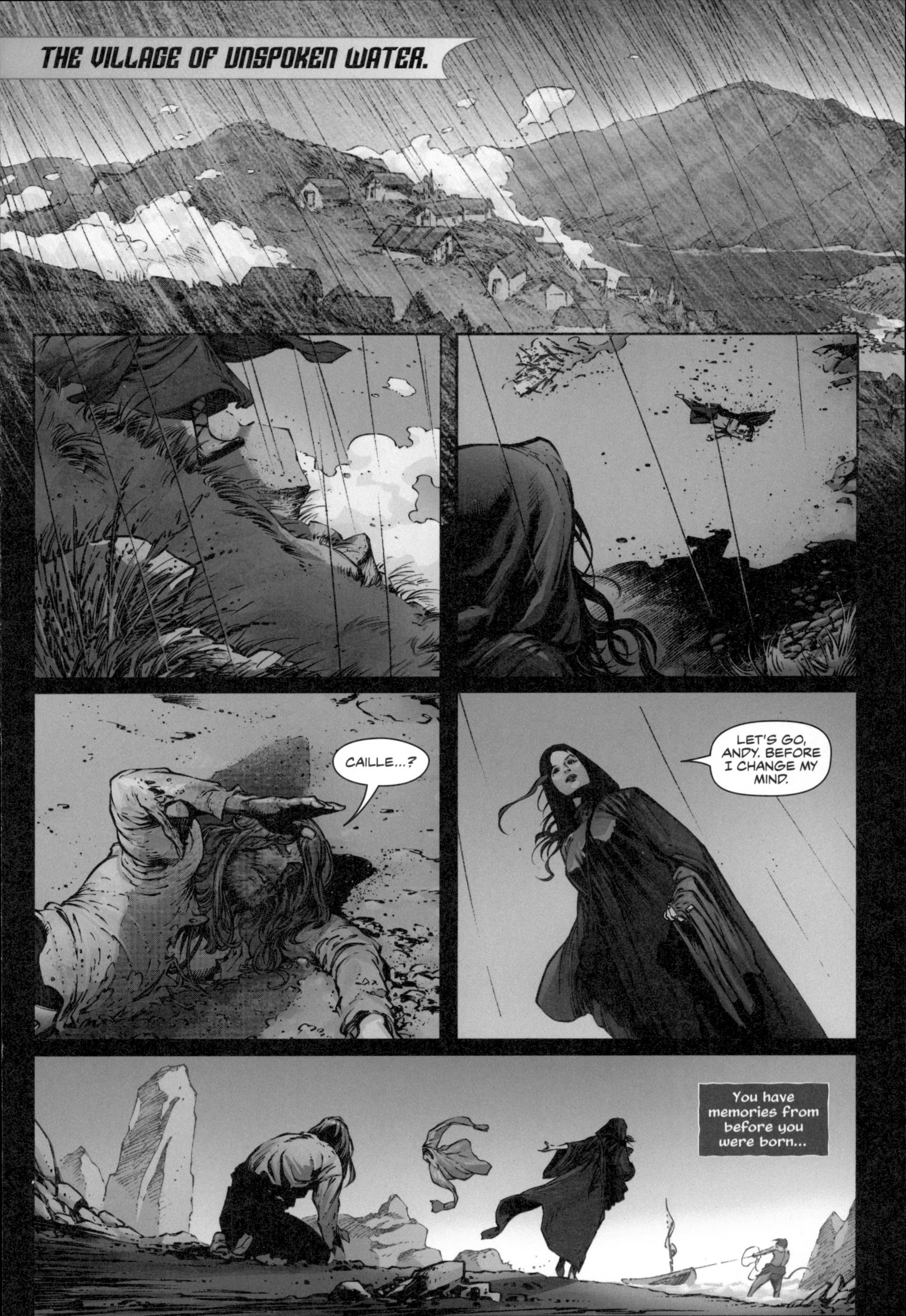
THE VILLAGE OF UNSPOKEN WATER.
CAILLE...?
LET'S GO, ANDY. BEFORE I CHANGE MY MIND.
You have memories from before you were born...

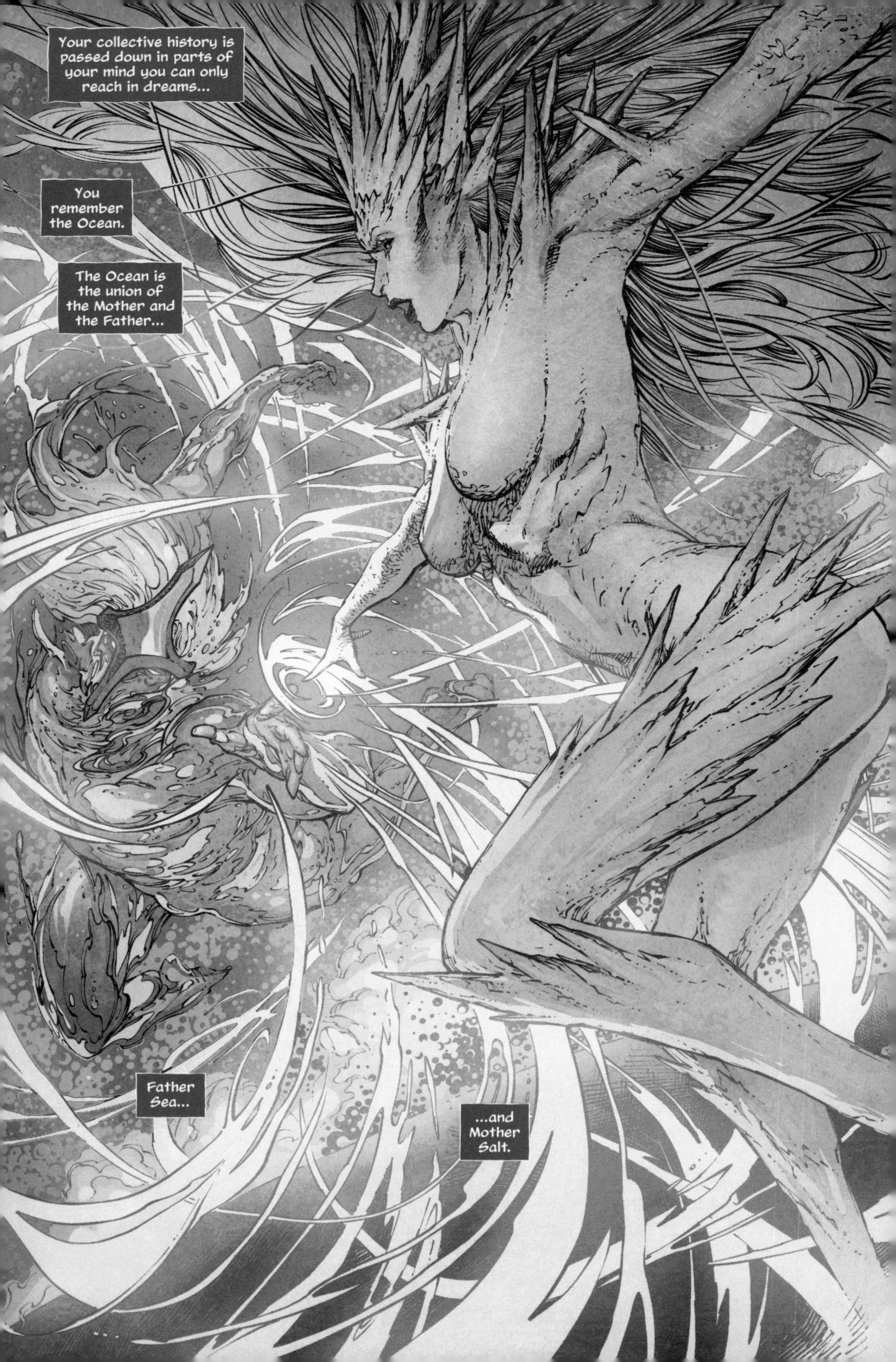
Your collective history is passed down in parts of your mind you can only reach in dreams...
You remember the Ocean.
The Ocean is the union of the Mother and the Father...
Father Sea...
...and Mother Salt.

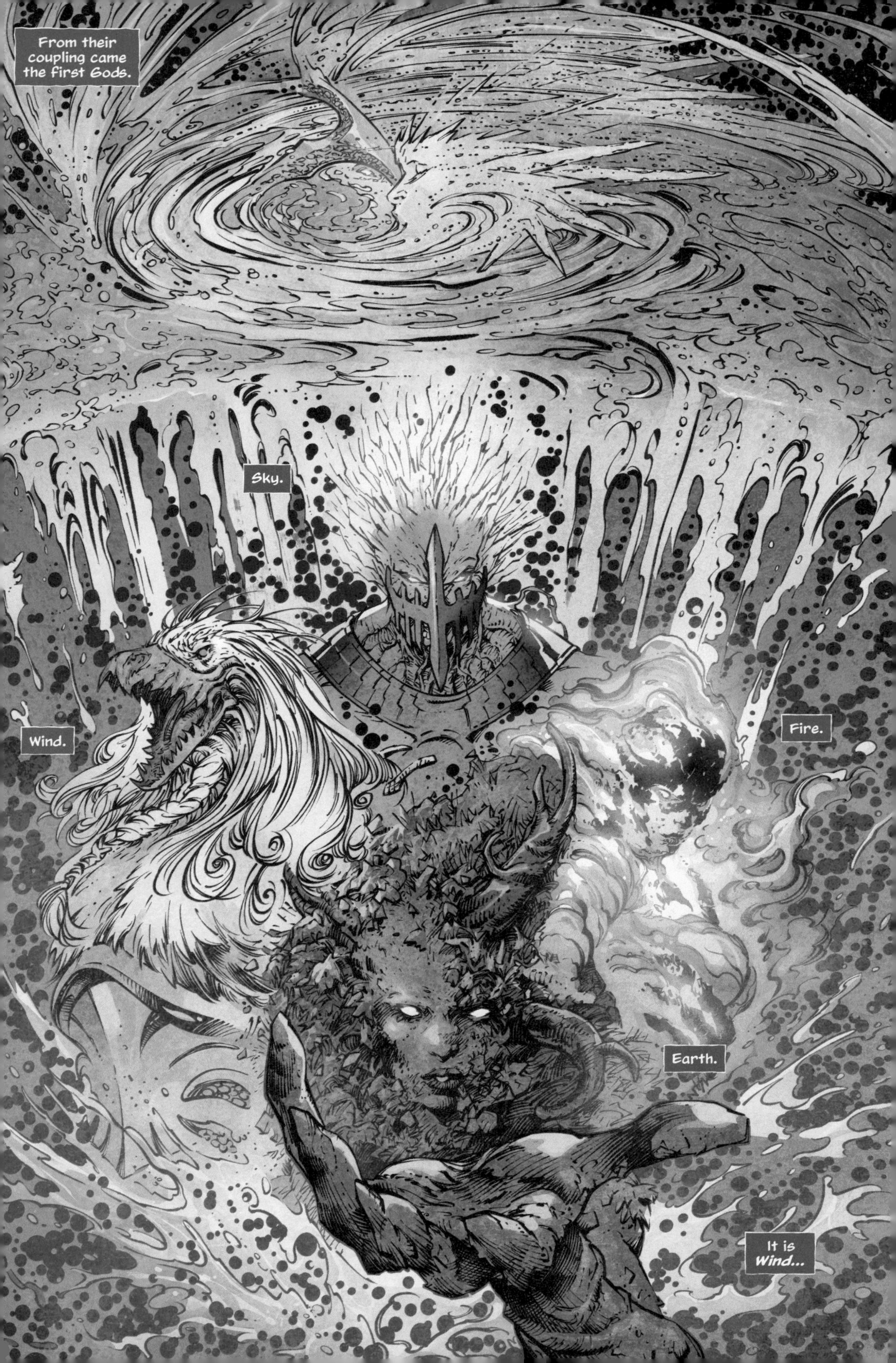
From their coupling came the first Gods.
Sky.
Wind.
Fire.
Earth.
It is *Wind...*

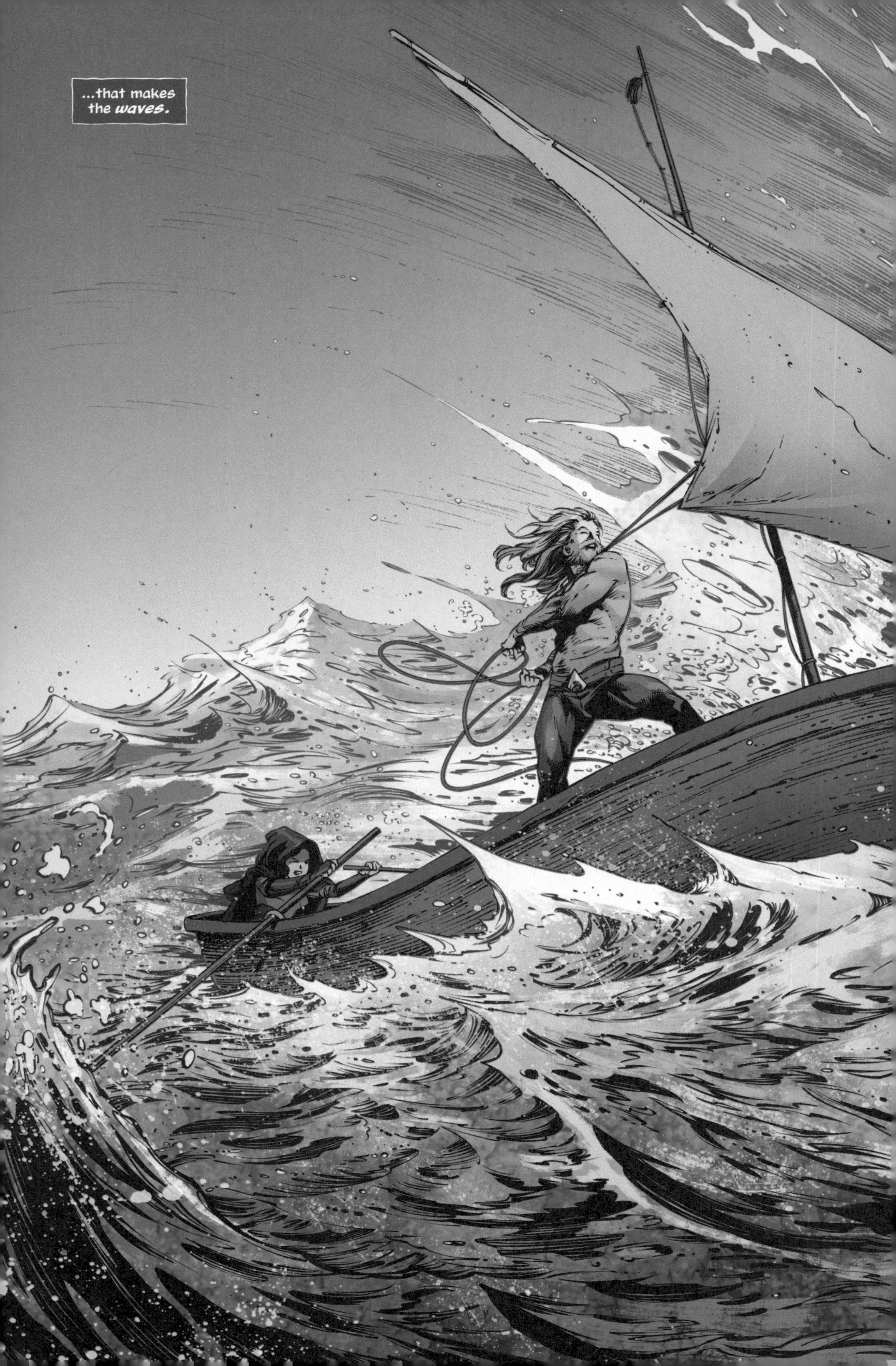
...that makes the *waves.*

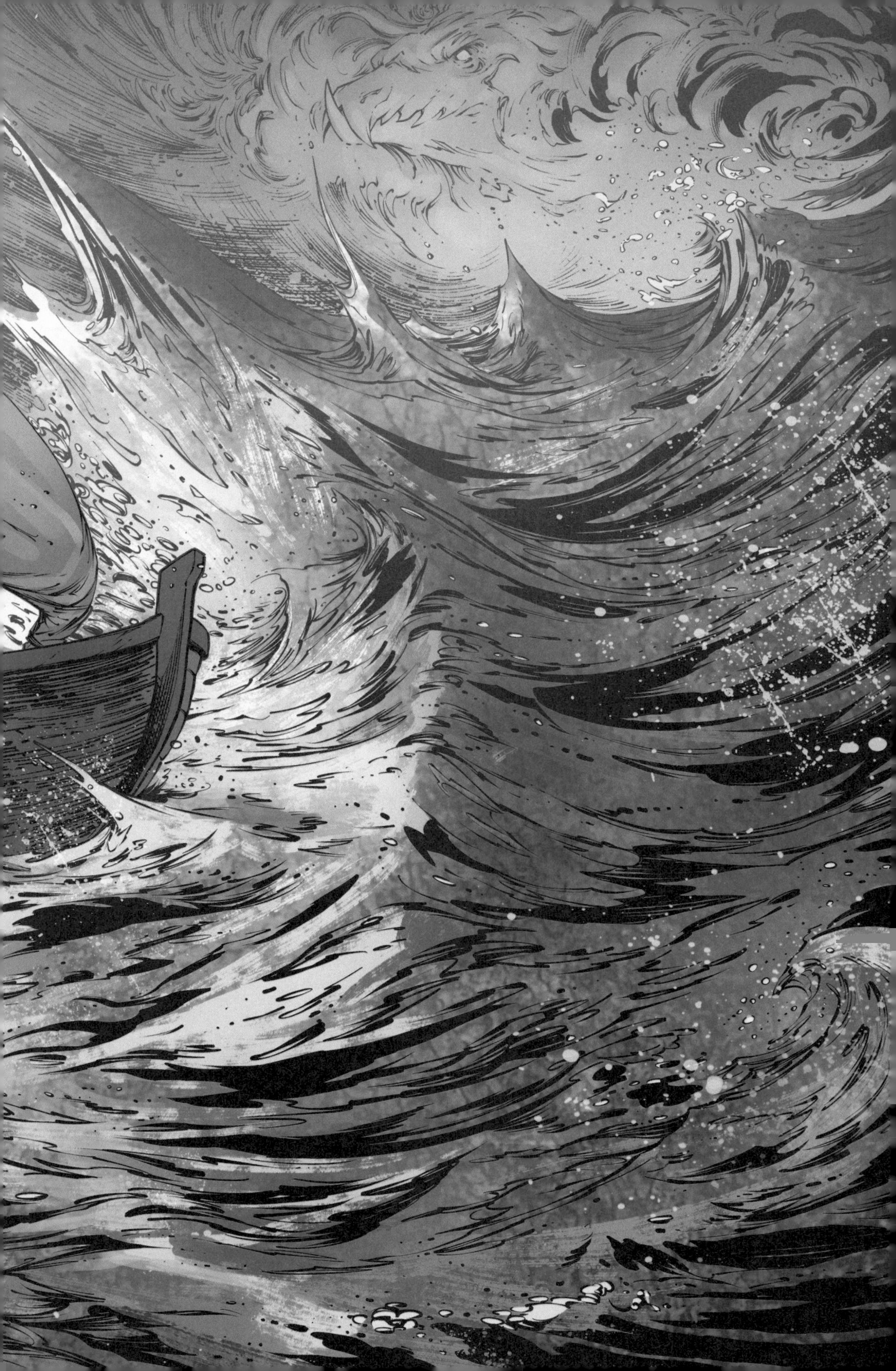

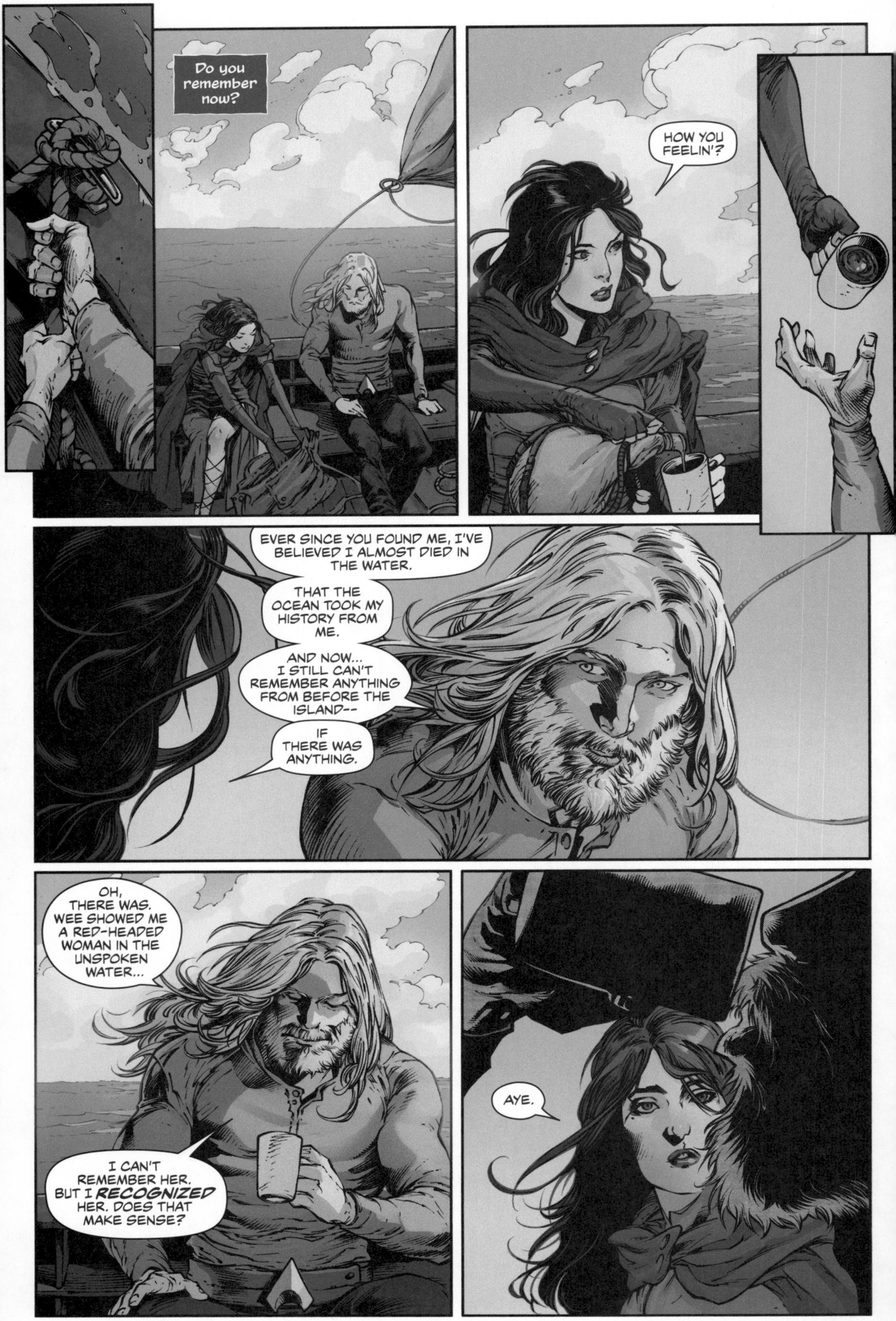

Do you remember now?
HOW YOU FEELIN'?
EVER SINCE YOU FOUND ME, I'VE BELIEVED I ALMOST DIED IN THE WATER.
THAT THE OCEAN TOOK MY HISTORY FROM ME.
AND NOW... I STILL CAN'T REMEMBER ANYTHING FROM BEFORE THE ISLAND--
IF THERE WAS ANYTHING.
OH, THERE WAS. WEE SHOWED ME A RED-HEADED WOMAN IN THE UNSPOKEN WATER...
I CAN'T REMEMBER HER. BUT I RECOGNIZED HER. DOES THAT MAKE SENSE?
AYE.

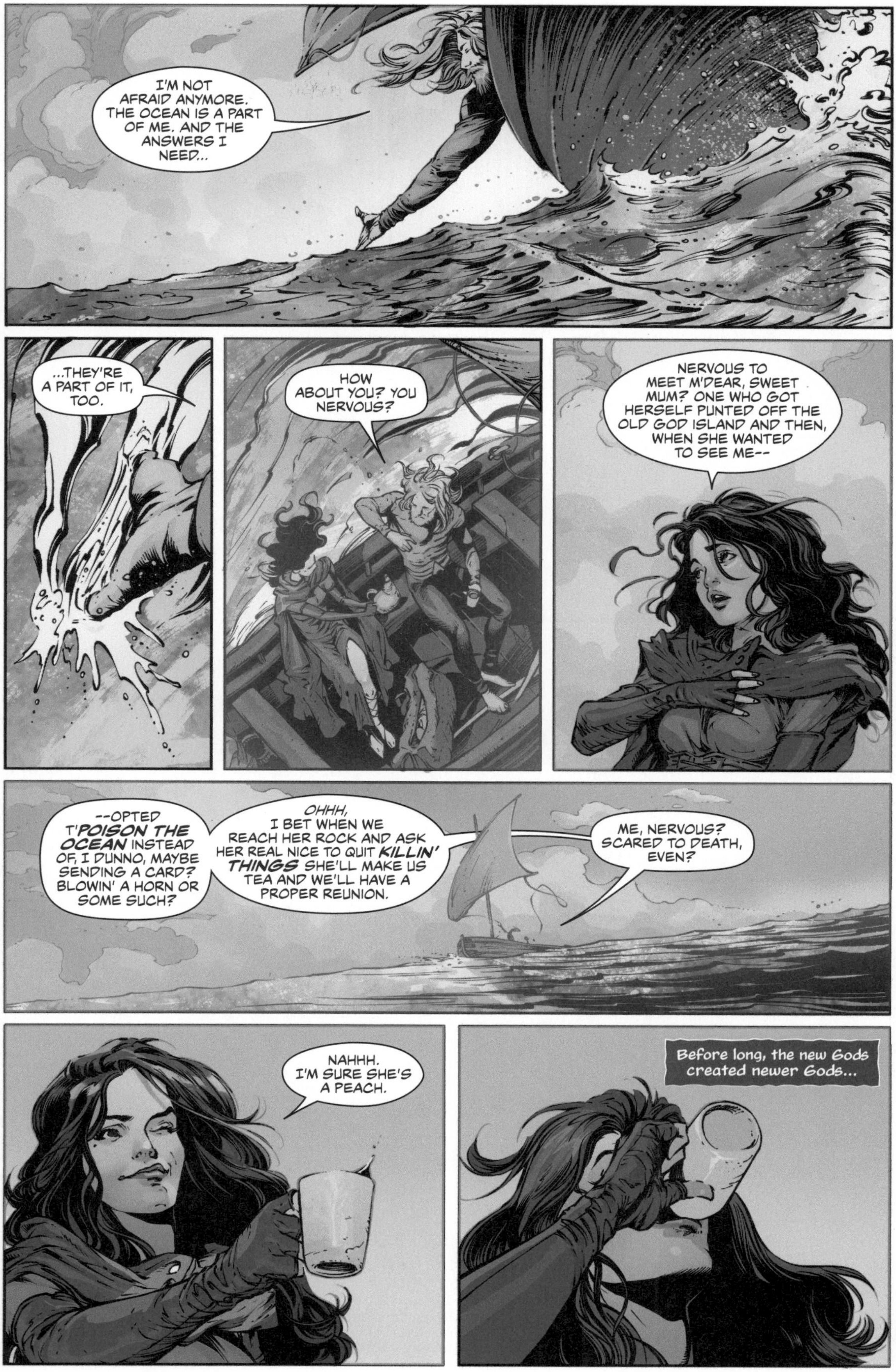
I'M NOT AFRAID ANYMORE. THE OCEAN IS A PART OF ME. AND THE ANSWERS I NEED...
...THEY'RE A PART OF IT, TOO.
HOW ABOUT YOU? YOU NERVOUS?
NERVOUS TO MEET M'DEAR, SWEET MUM? ONE WHO GOT HERSELF PUNTED OFF THE OLD GOD ISLAND AND THEN, WHEN SHE WANTED TO SEE ME--
--OPTED T'POISON THE OCEAN INSTEAD OF, I DUNNO, MAYBE SENDING A CARD? BLOWIN' A HORN OR SOME SUCH?
OHHH, I BET WHEN WE REACH HER ROCK AND ASK HER REAL NICE TO QUIT KILLIN' THINGS SHE'LL MAKE US TEA AND WE'LL HAVE A PROPER REUNION.
ME, NERVOUS? SCARED TO DEATH, EVEN?
NAHHH. I'M SURE SHE'S A PEACH.
Before long, the new Gods created newer Gods...

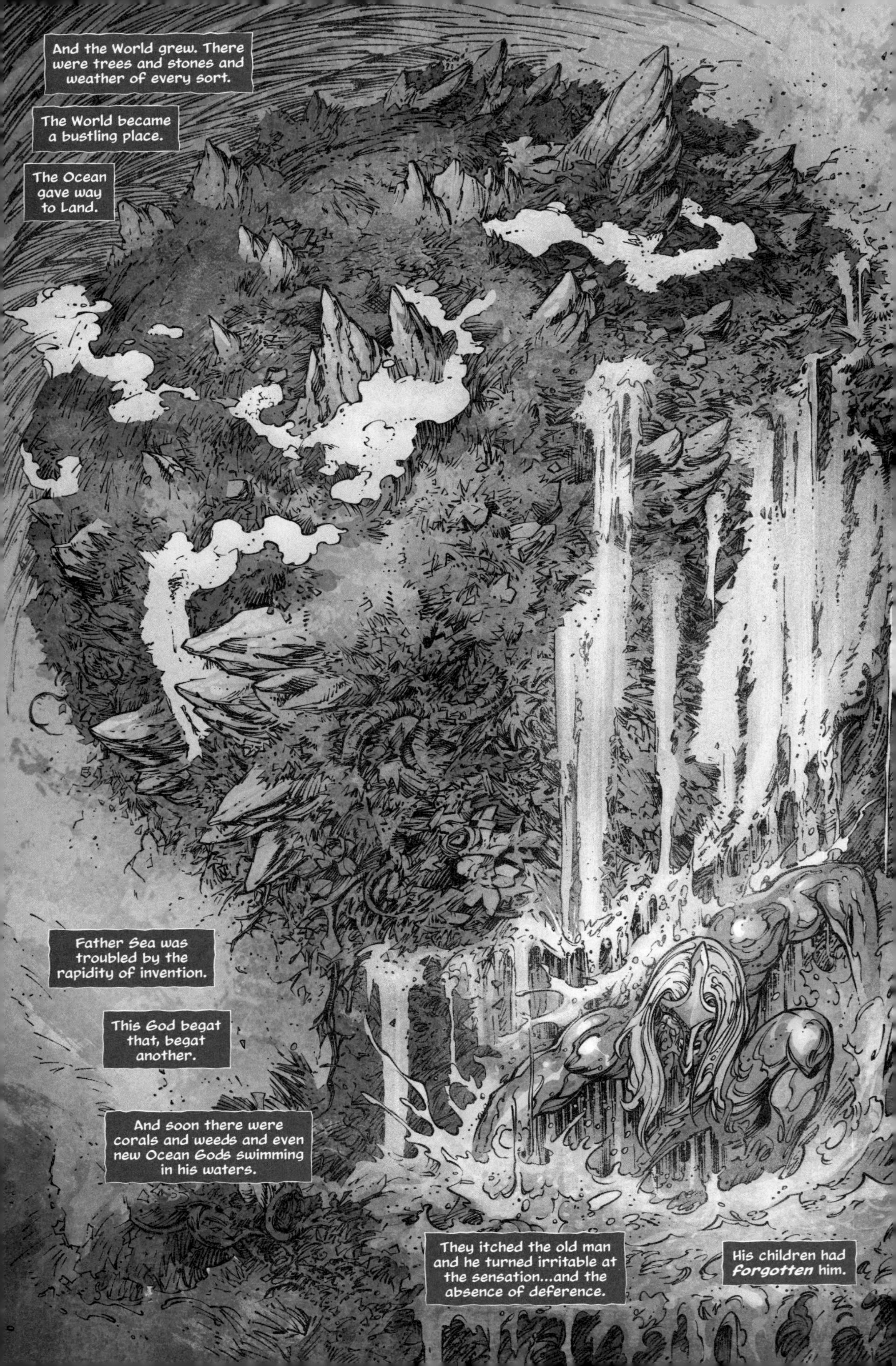
And the World grew. There were trees and stones and weather of every sort.
The World became a bustling place.
The Ocean gave way to Land.
Father Sea was troubled by the rapidity of invention.
This God begat that, begat another.
And soon there were corals and weeds and even new Ocean Gods swimming in his waters.
They itched the old man and he turned irritable at the sensation...and the absence of deference.
His children had *forgotten* him.

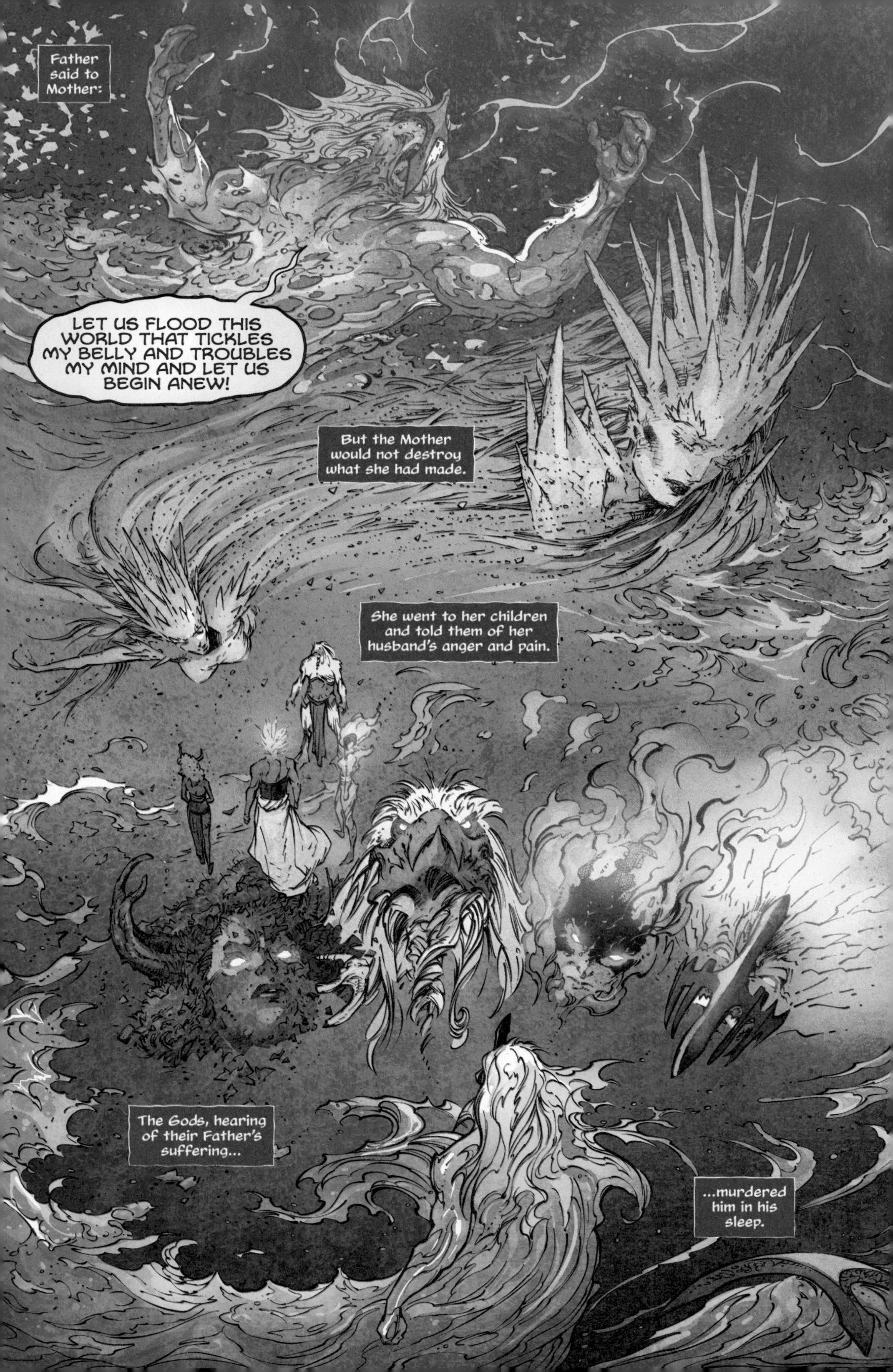
Father said to Mother:
LET US FLOOD THIS WORLD THAT TICKLES MY BELLY AND TROUBLES MY MIND AND LET US BEGIN ANEW!
But the Mother would not destroy what she had made.
She went to her children and told them of her husband's anger and pain.
The Gods, hearing of their Father's suffering...
...murdered him in his sleep.

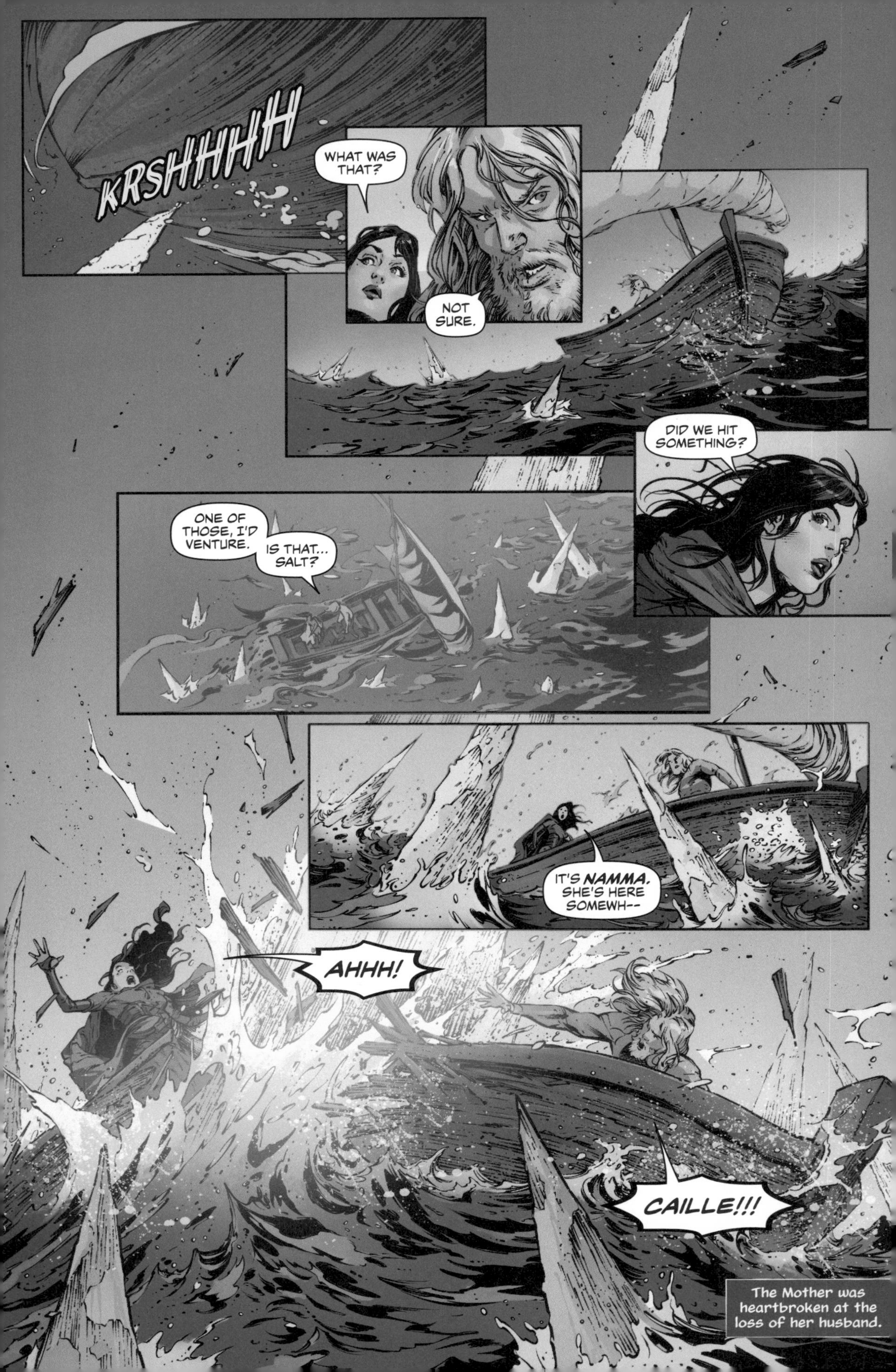
KRSHHHHH
WHAT WAS THAT?
NOT SURE.
DID WE HIT SOMETHING?
ONE OF THOSE, I'D VENTURE.
IS THAT... SALT?
IT'S NAMMA. SHE'S HERE SOMEWH--
AHHH!
CAILLE!!!
The Mother was heartbroken at the loss of her husband.

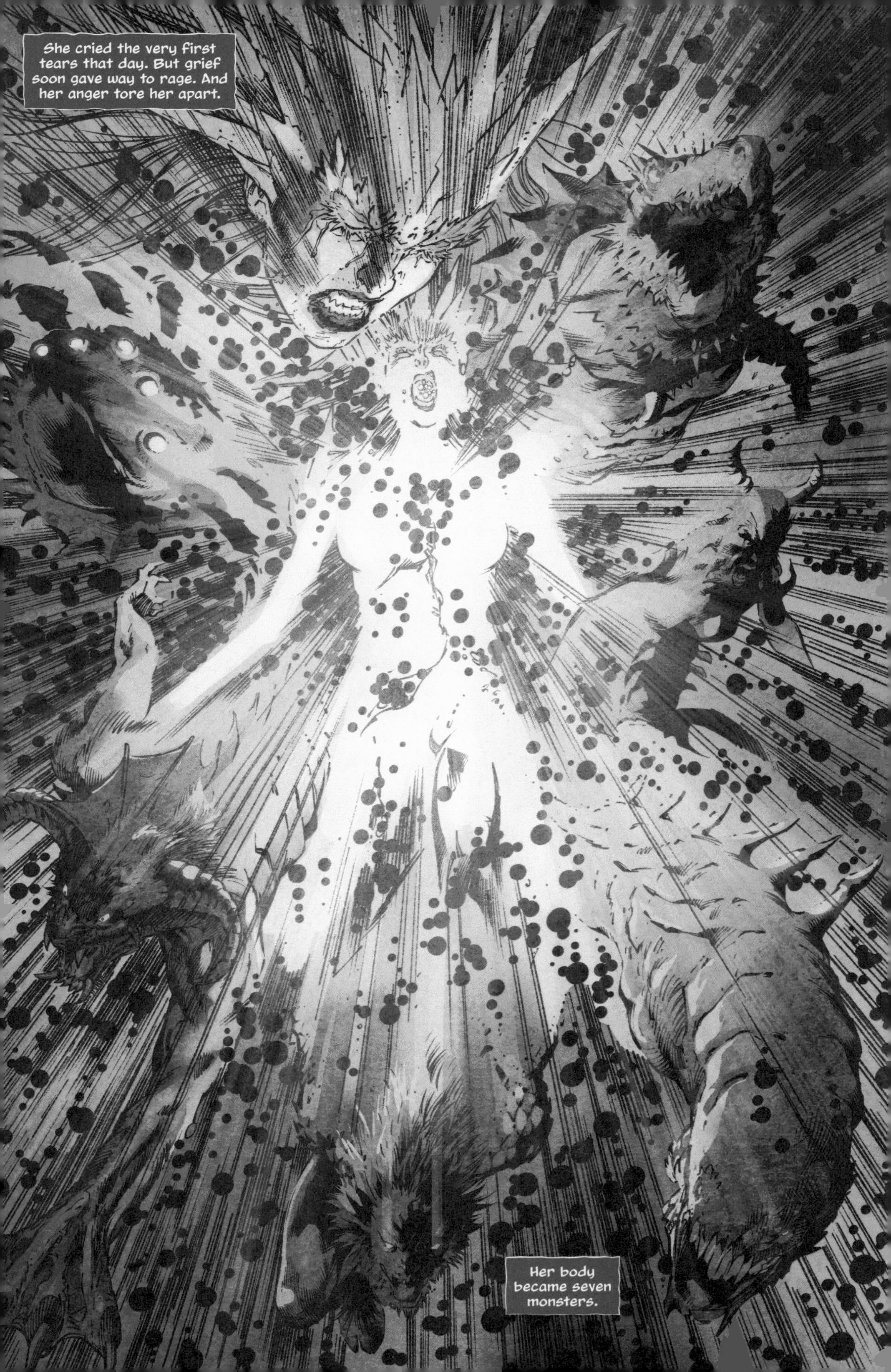
She cried the very first tears that day. But grief soon gave way to rage. And her anger tore her apart.
Her body became seven monsters.

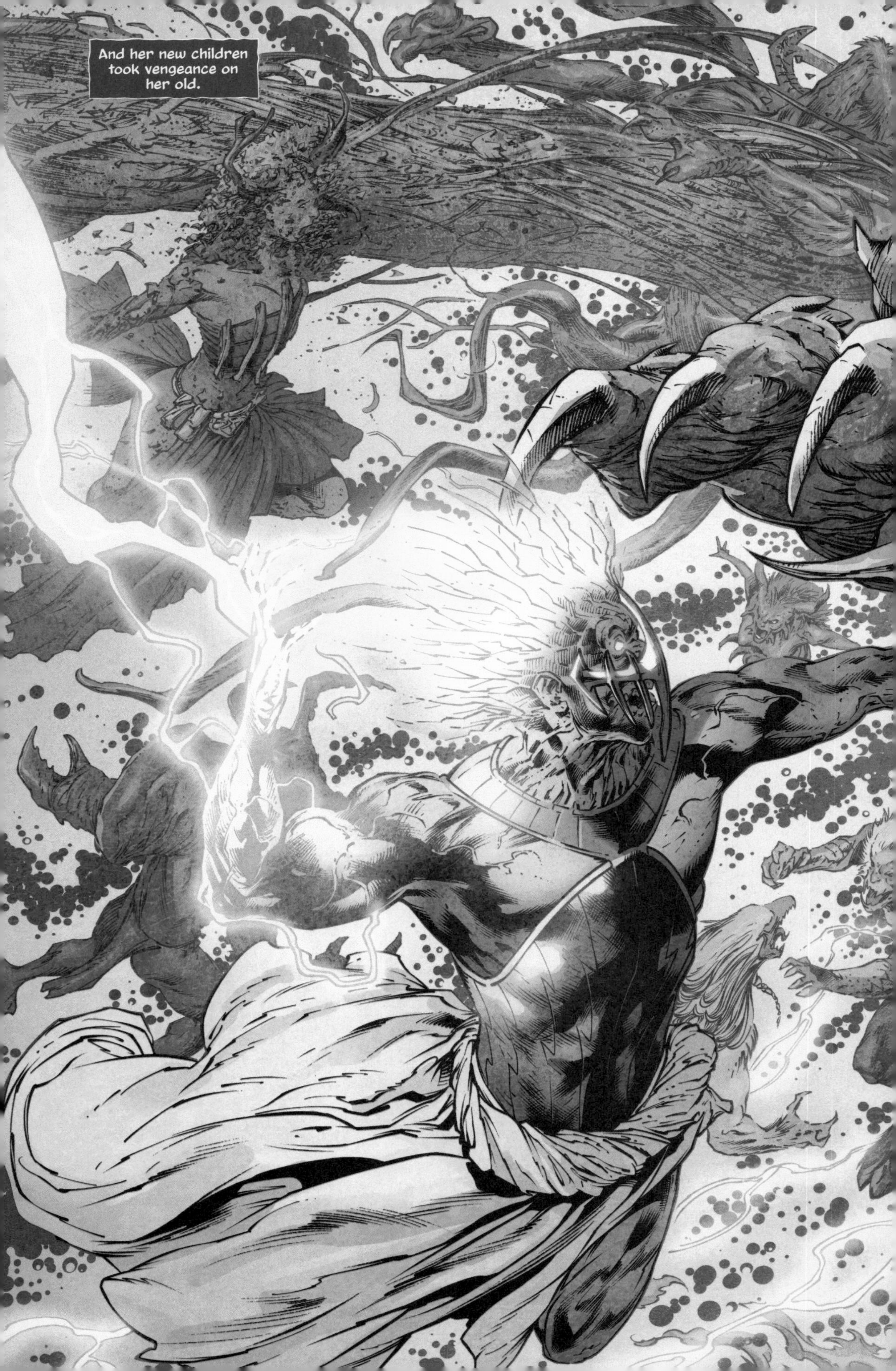
And her new children took vengeance on her old.

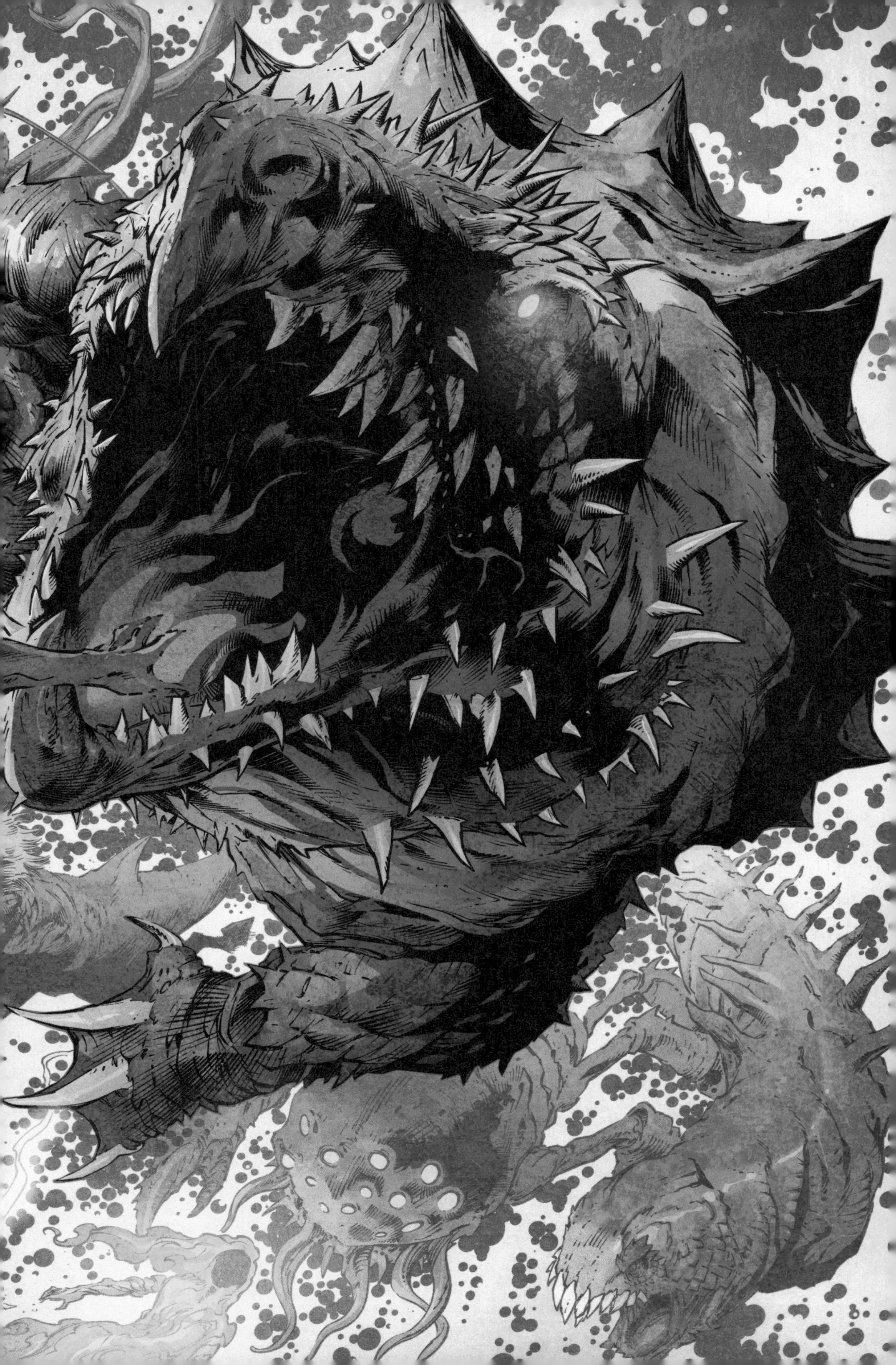

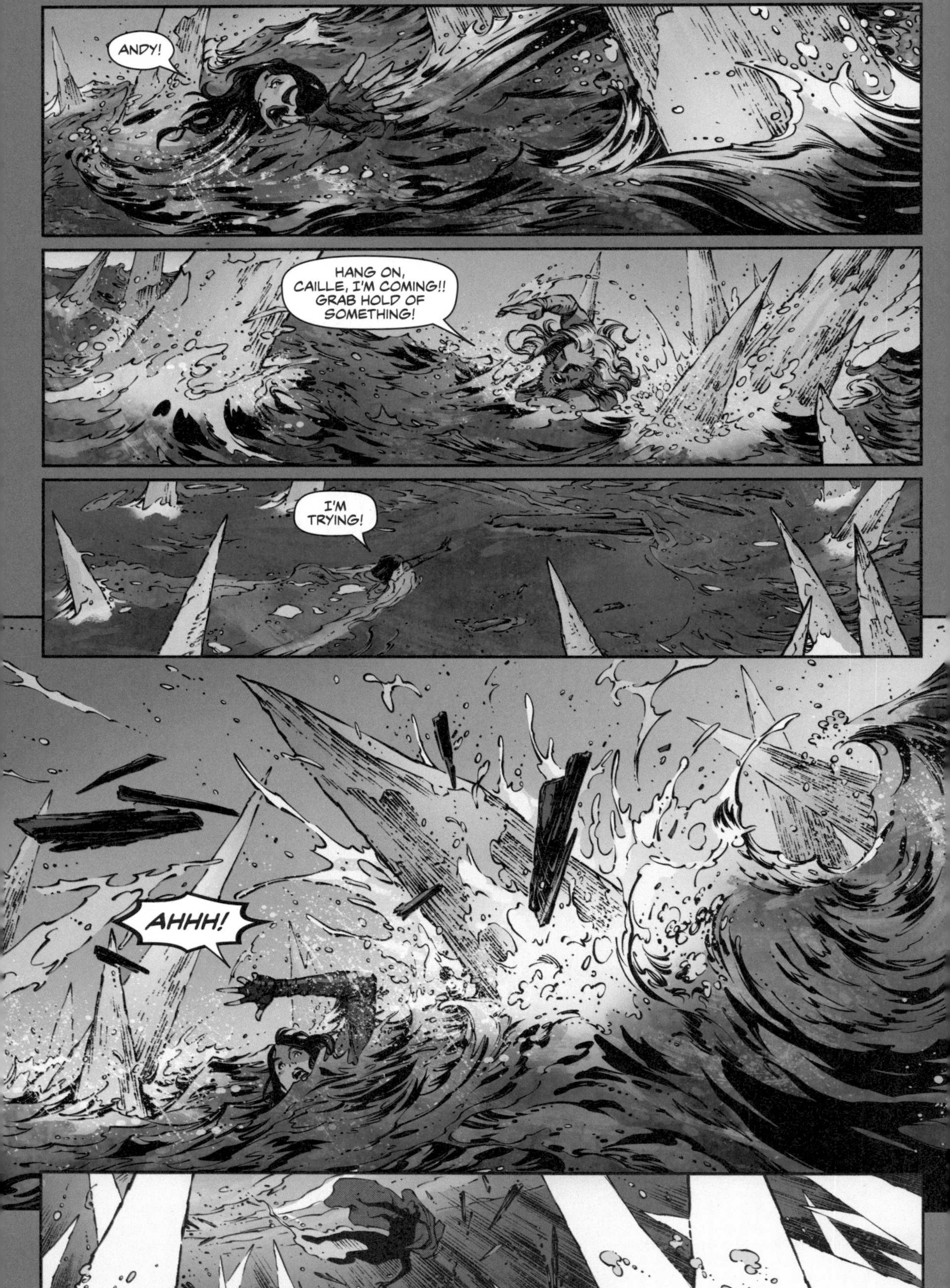
ANDY!
HANG ON, CAILLE, I'M COMING!! GRAB HOLD OF SOMETHING!
I'M TRYING!
AHHH!

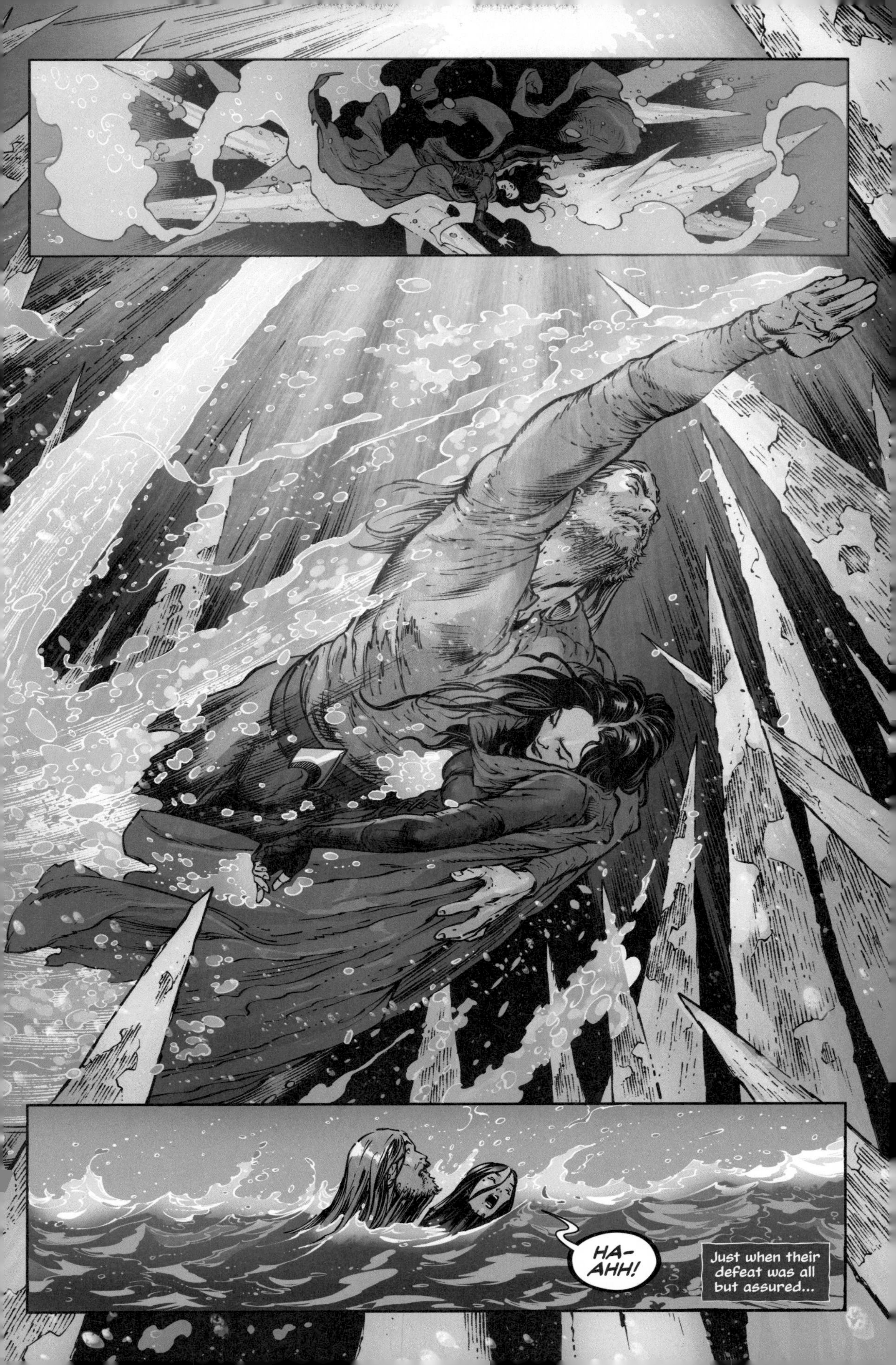
HA-AHH!
Just when their defeat was all but assured...

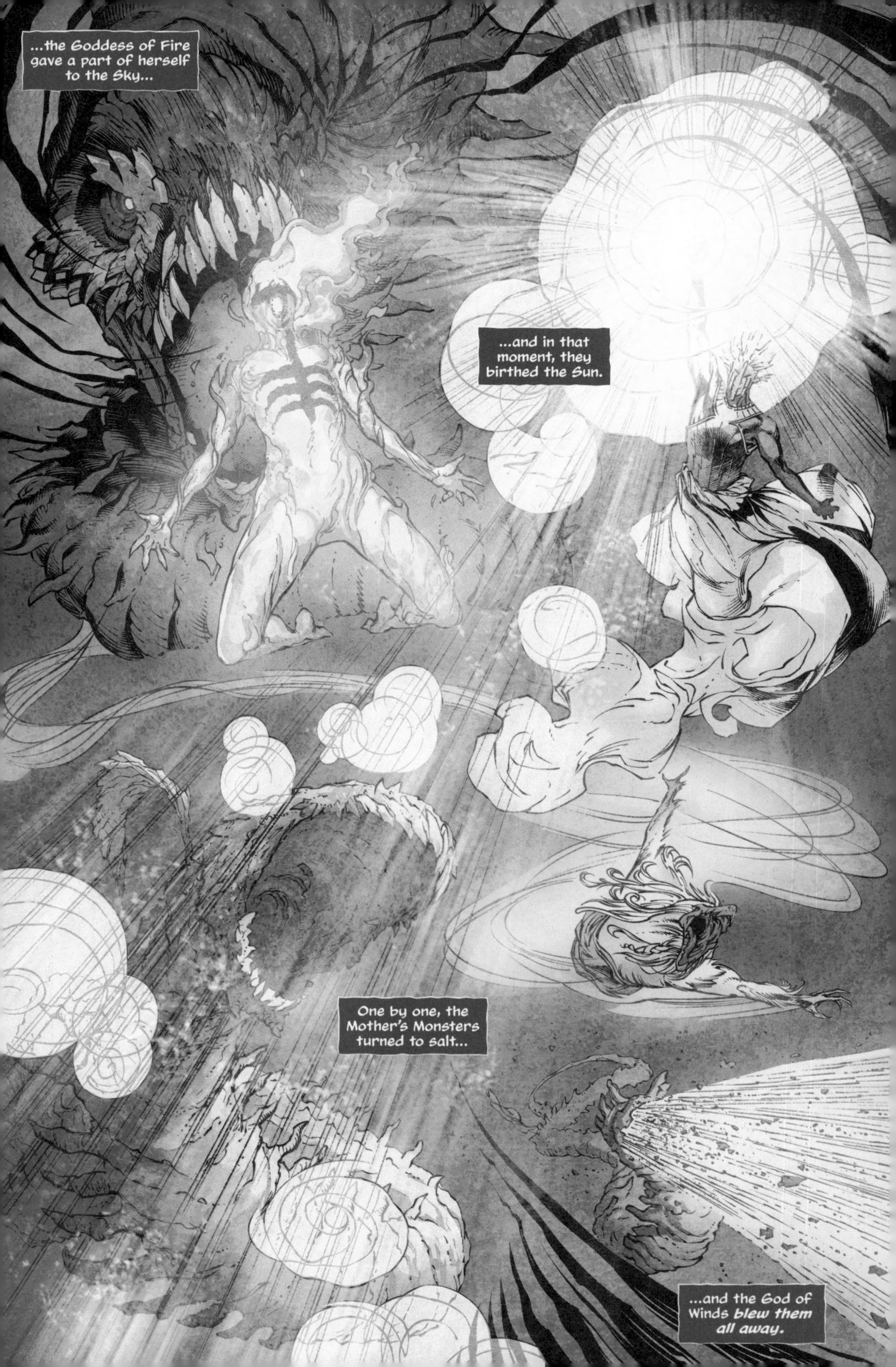
...the Goddess of Fire gave a part of herself to the Sky...
...and in that moment, they birthed the Sun.
One by one, the Mother's Monsters turned to salt...
...and the God of Winds *blew them all away.*

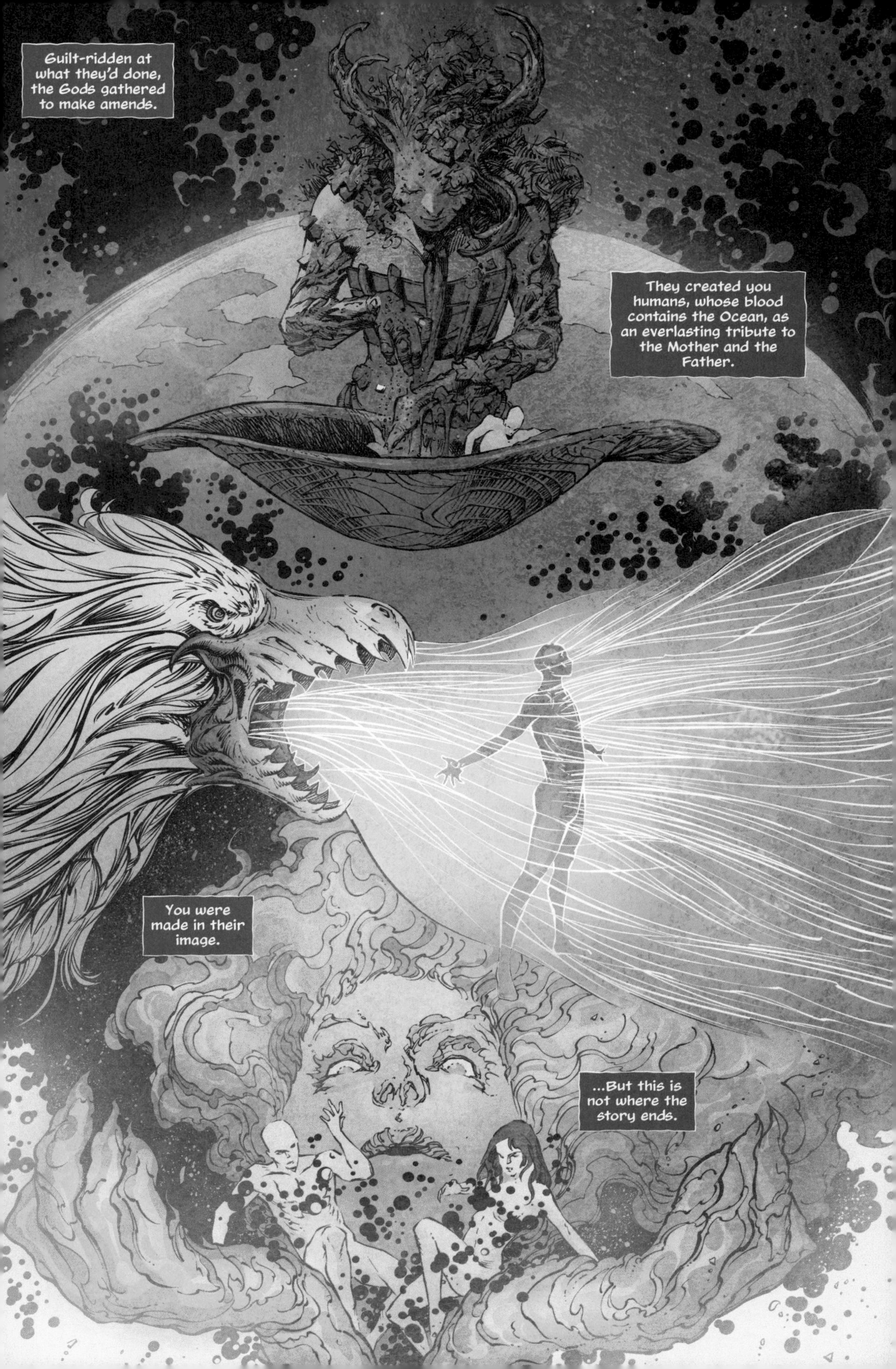
Guilt-ridden at what they'd done, the Gods gathered to make amends.
They created you humans, whose blood contains the Ocean, as an everlasting tribute to the Mother and the Father.
You were made in their image.
...But this is not where the story ends.

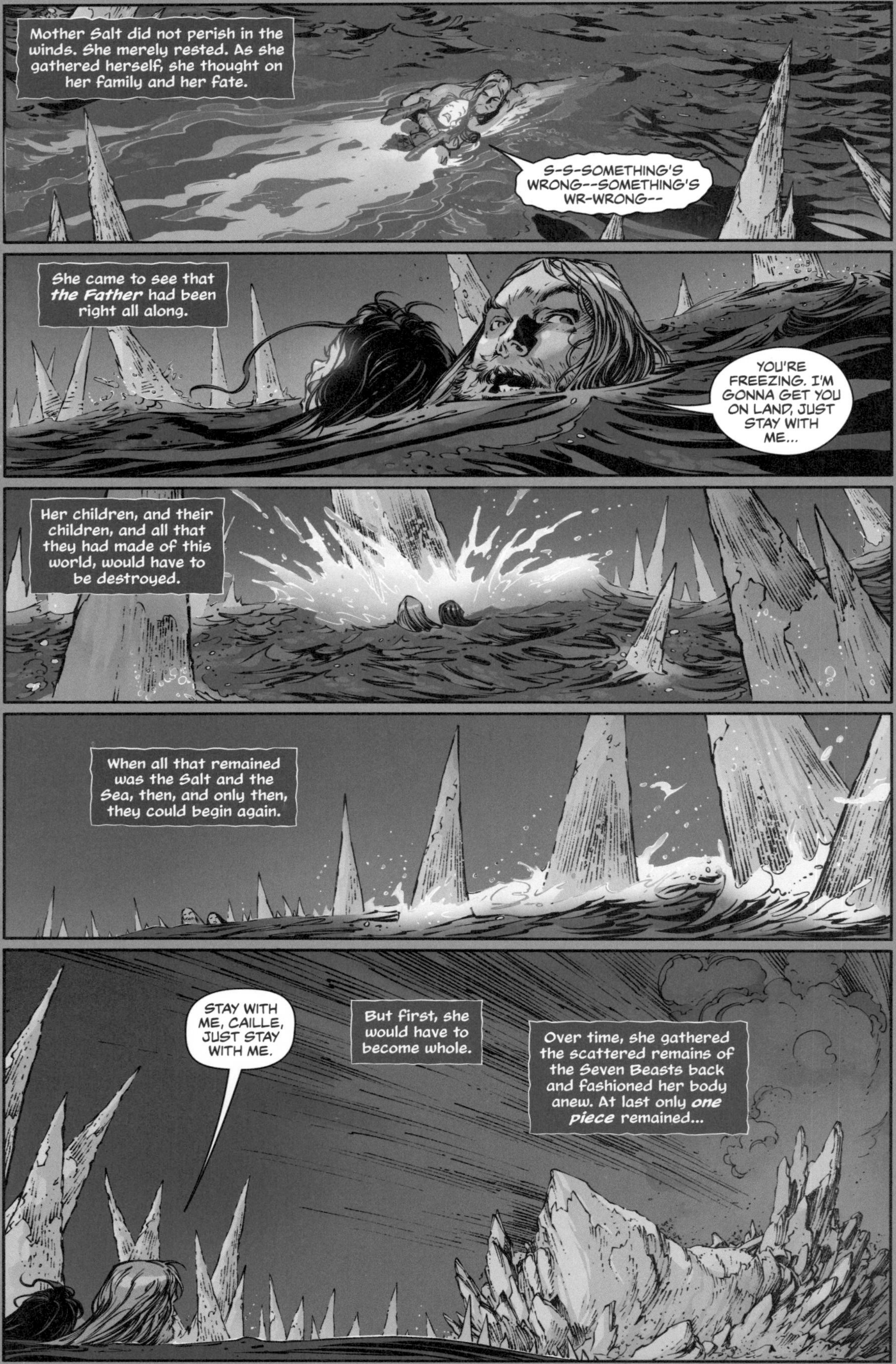
Mother Salt did not perish in the winds. She merely rested. As she gathered herself, she thought on her family and her fate.
S-S-SOMETHING'S WRONG--SOMETHING'S WR-WRONG--
She came to see that *the Father* had been right all along.
YOU'RE FREEZING. I'M GONNA GET YOU ON LAND, JUST STAY WITH ME...
Her children, and their children, and all that they had made of this world, would have to be destroyed.
When all that remained was the Salt and the Sea, then, and only then, they could begin again.
STAY WITH ME, CAILLE, JUST STAY WITH ME.
But first, she would have to become whole.
Over time, she gathered the scattered remains of the Seven Beasts back and fashioned her body anew. At last only *one piece* remained...

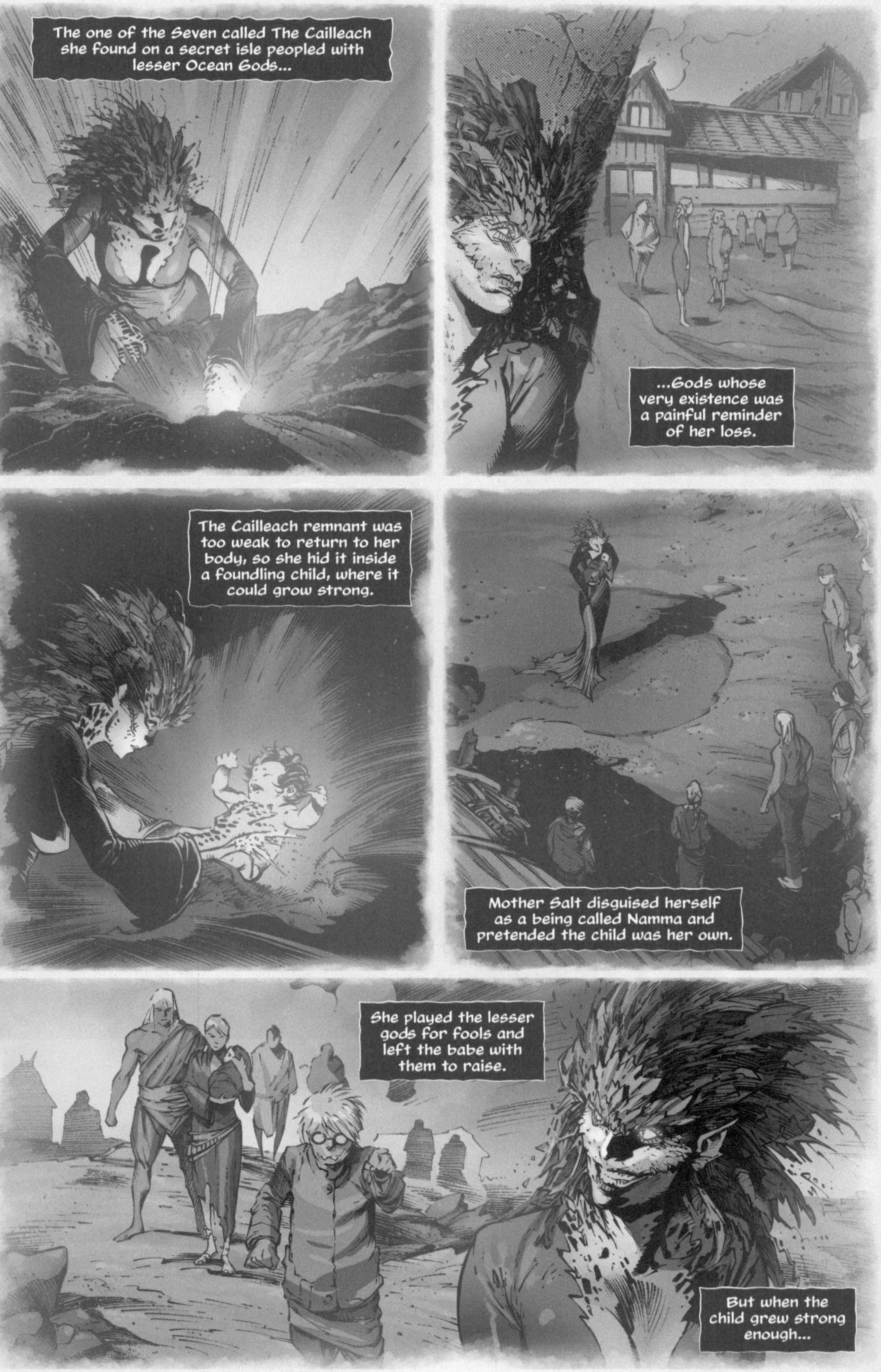
The one of the Seven called The Cailleach she found on a secret isle peopled with lesser Ocean Gods...
...Gods whose very existence was a painful reminder of her loss.
The Cailleach remnant was too weak to return to her body, so she hid it inside a foundling child, where it could grow strong.
Mother Salt disguised herself as a being called Namma and pretended the child was her own.
She played the lesser gods for fools and left the babe with them to raise.
But when the child grew strong enough...

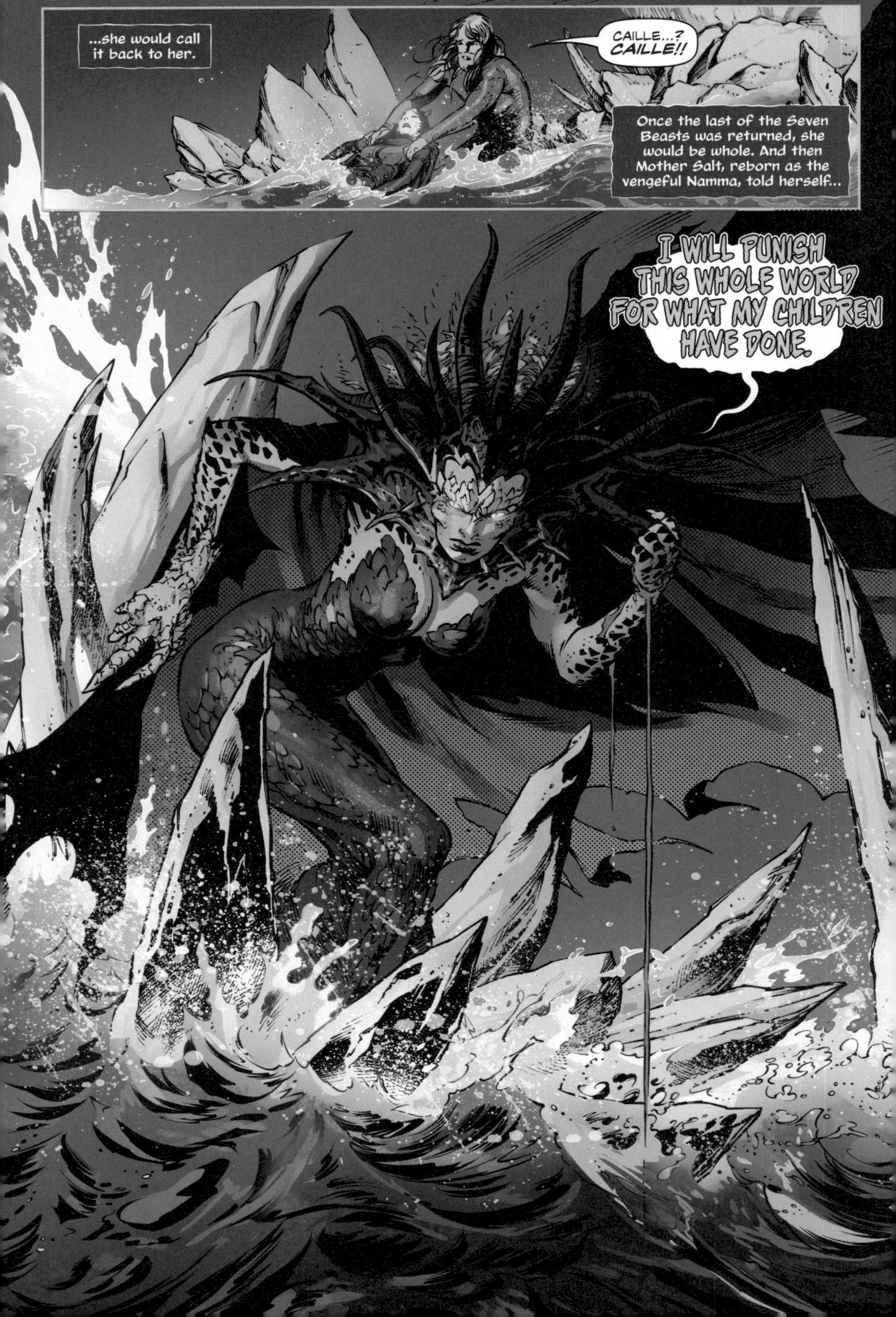
...she would call it back to her.
CAILLE...? CAILLE!!
Once the last of the Seven Beasts was returned, she would be whole. And then Mother Salt, reborn as the vengeful Namma, told herself...
I WILL PUNISH THIS WHOLE WORLD FOR WHAT MY CHILDREN HAVE DONE.

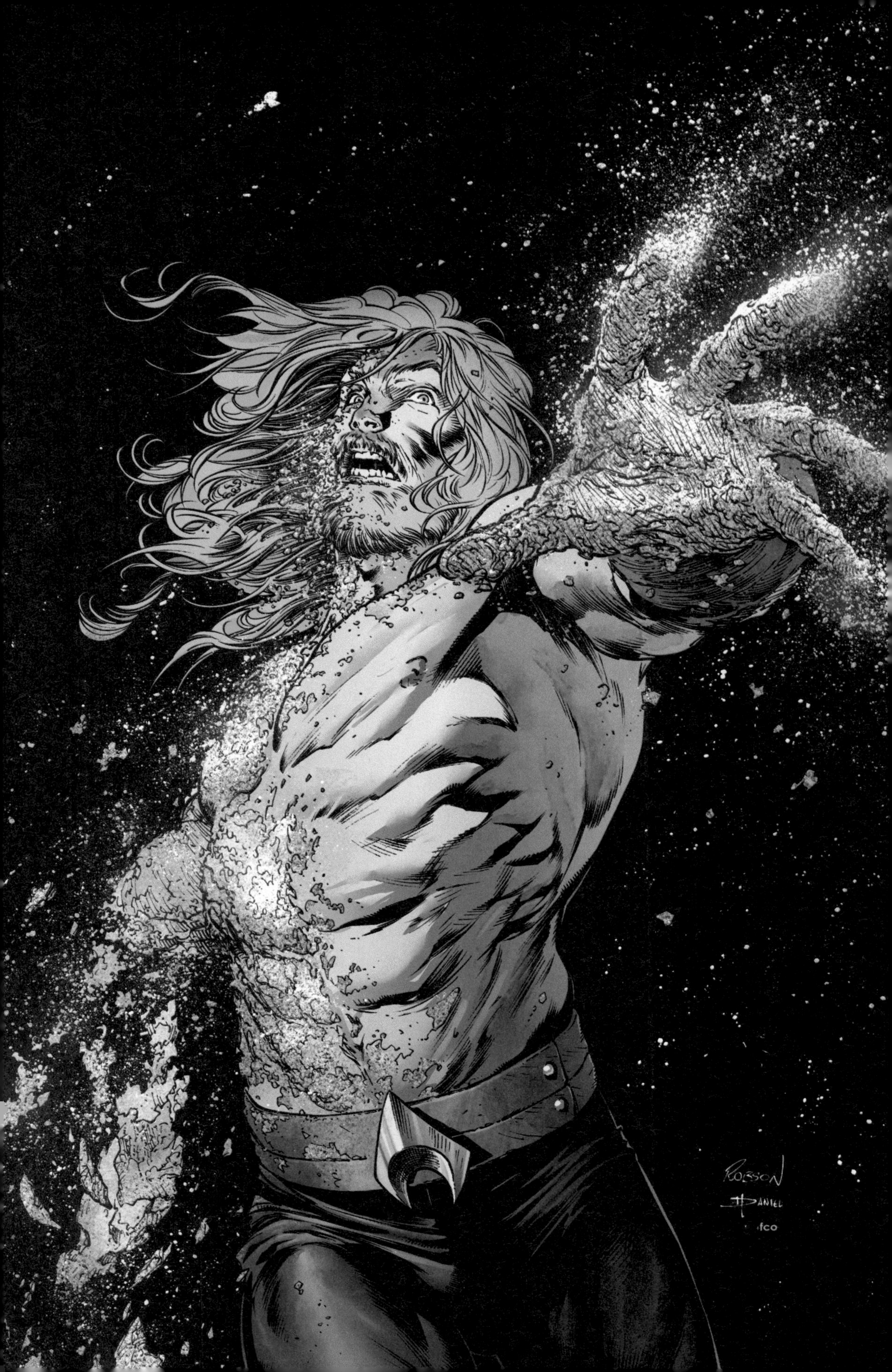

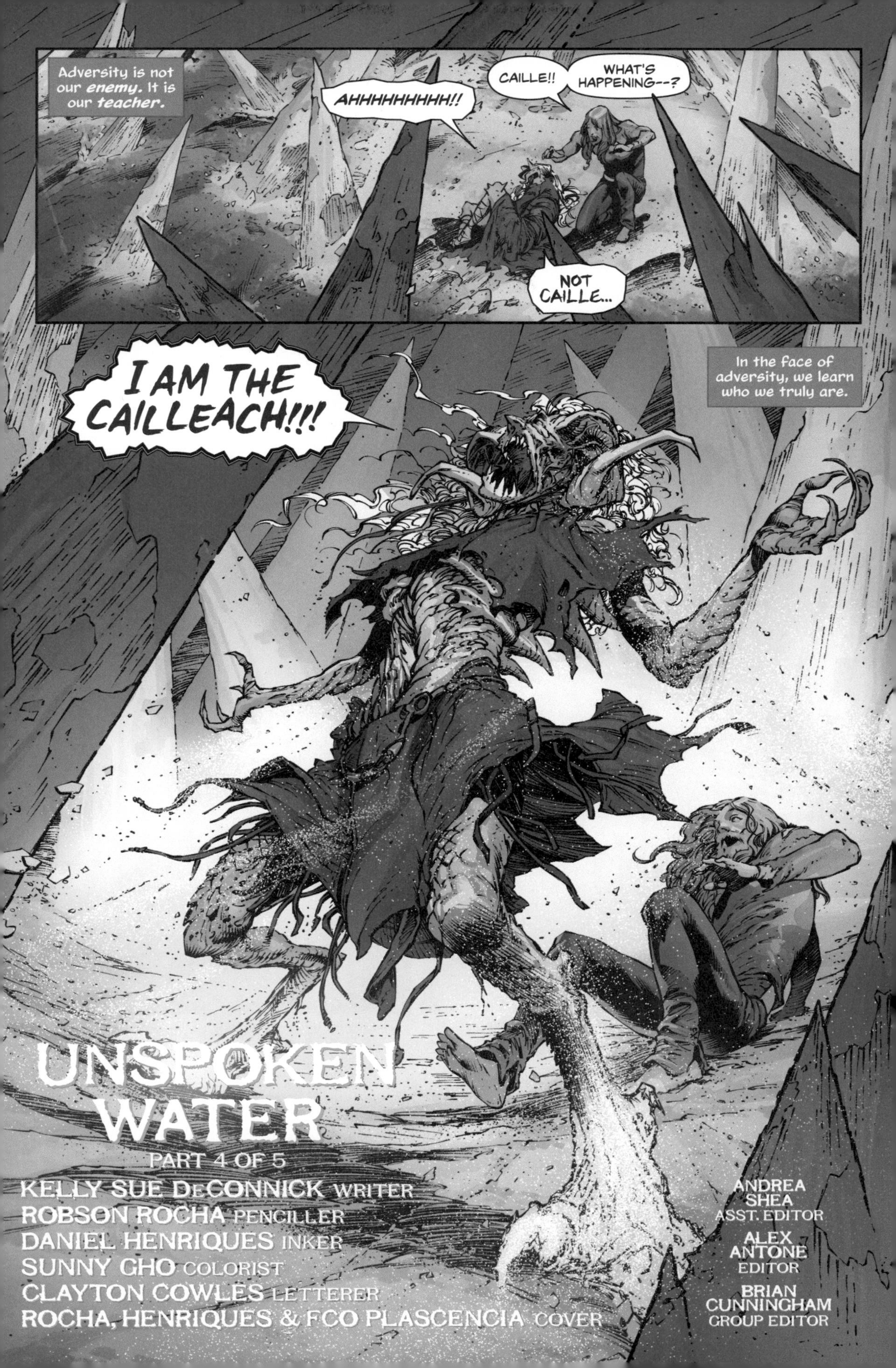
Adversity is not our *enemy.* It is our *teacher.*
AHHHHHHHHH!!
CAILLE!!
WHAT'S HAPPENING--?
NOT CAILLE...
I AM THE CAILLEACH!!!
In the face of adversity, we learn who we truly are.
UNSPOKEN WATER
PART 4 OF 5
KELLY SUE DeCONNICK WRITER
ROBSON ROCHA PENCILLER
DANIEL HENRIQUES INKER
SUNNY GHO COLORIST
CLAYTON COWLES LETTERER
ROCHA, HENRIQUES & FCO PLASCENCIA COVER
ANDREA SHEA ASST. EDITOR
ALEX ANTONE EDITOR
BRIAN CUNNINGHAM GROUP EDITOR

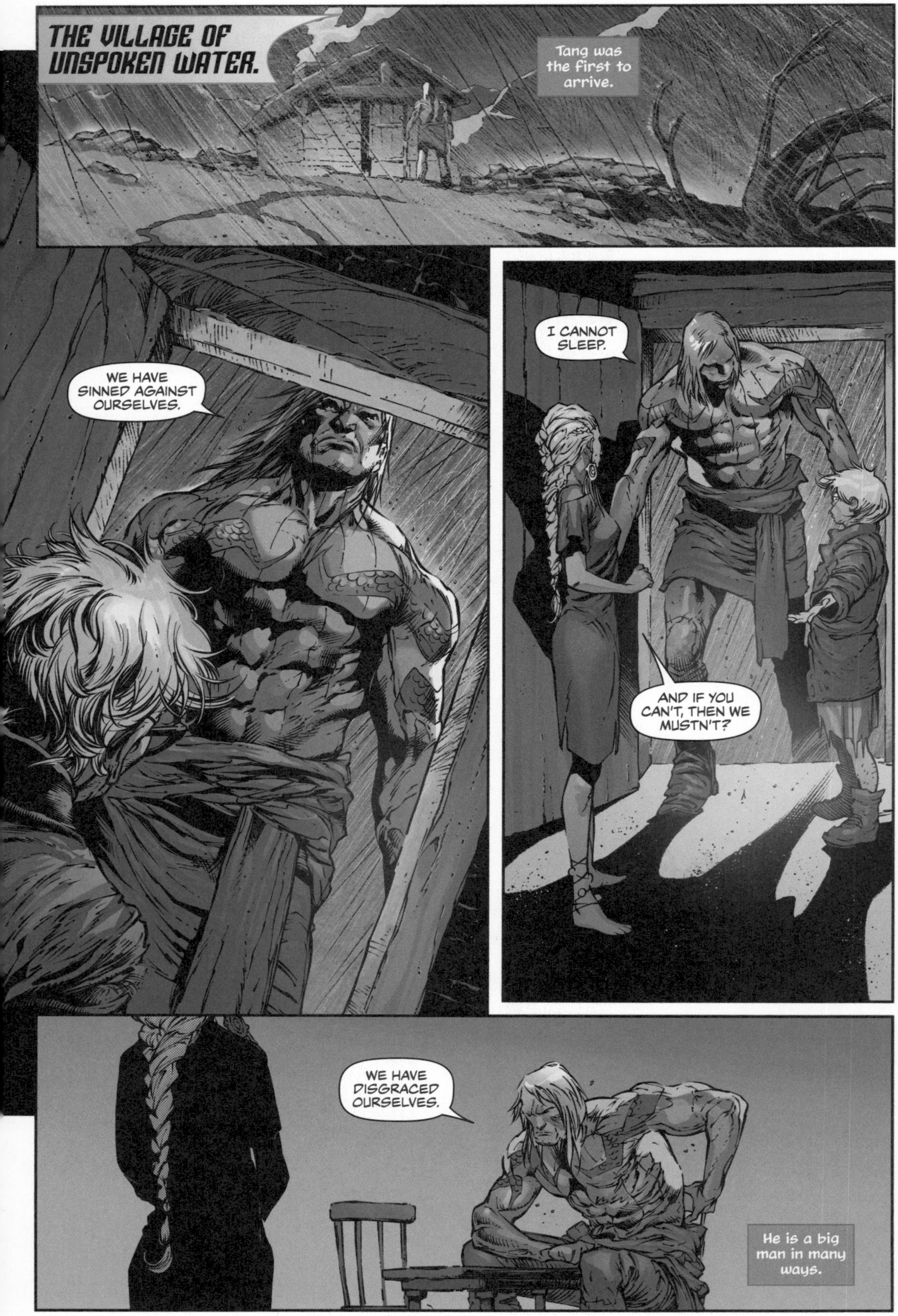
THE VILLAGE OF UNSPOKEN WATER.
Tang was the first to arrive.
WE HAVE SINNED AGAINST OURSELVES.
I CANNOT SLEEP.
AND IF YOU CAN'T, THEN WE MUSTN'T?
WE HAVE DISGRACED OURSELVES.
He is a big man in many ways.

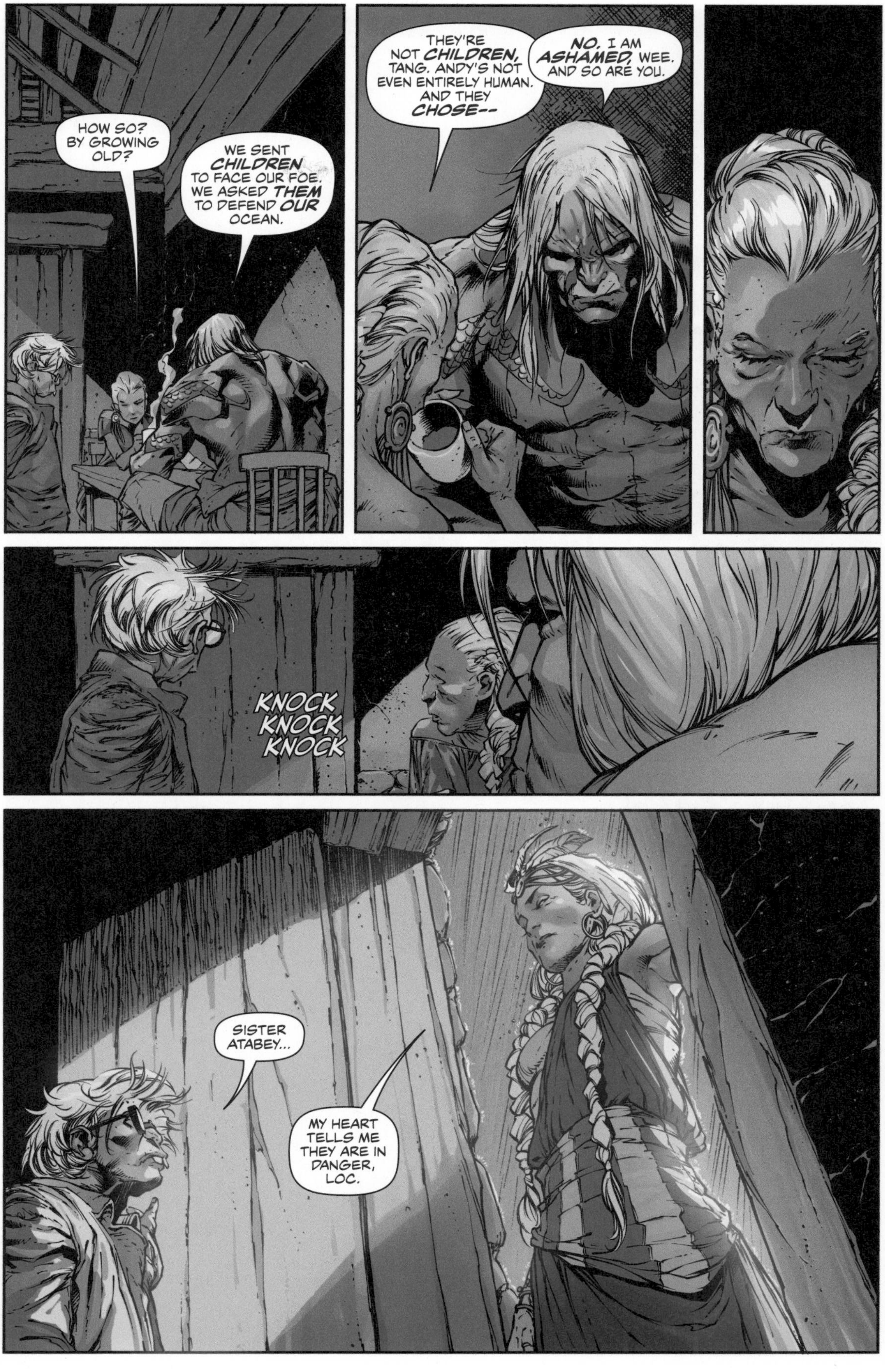
HOW SO? BY GROWING OLD?
WE SENT CHILDREN TO FACE OUR FOE. WE ASKED THEM TO DEFEND OUR OCEAN.
THEY'RE NOT CHILDREN, TANG. ANDY'S NOT EVEN ENTIRELY HUMAN. AND THEY CHOSE--
NO. I AM ASHAMED, WEE. AND SO ARE YOU.
KNOCK KNOCK KNOCK
SISTER ATABEY...
MY HEART TELLS ME THEY ARE IN DANGER, LOC.

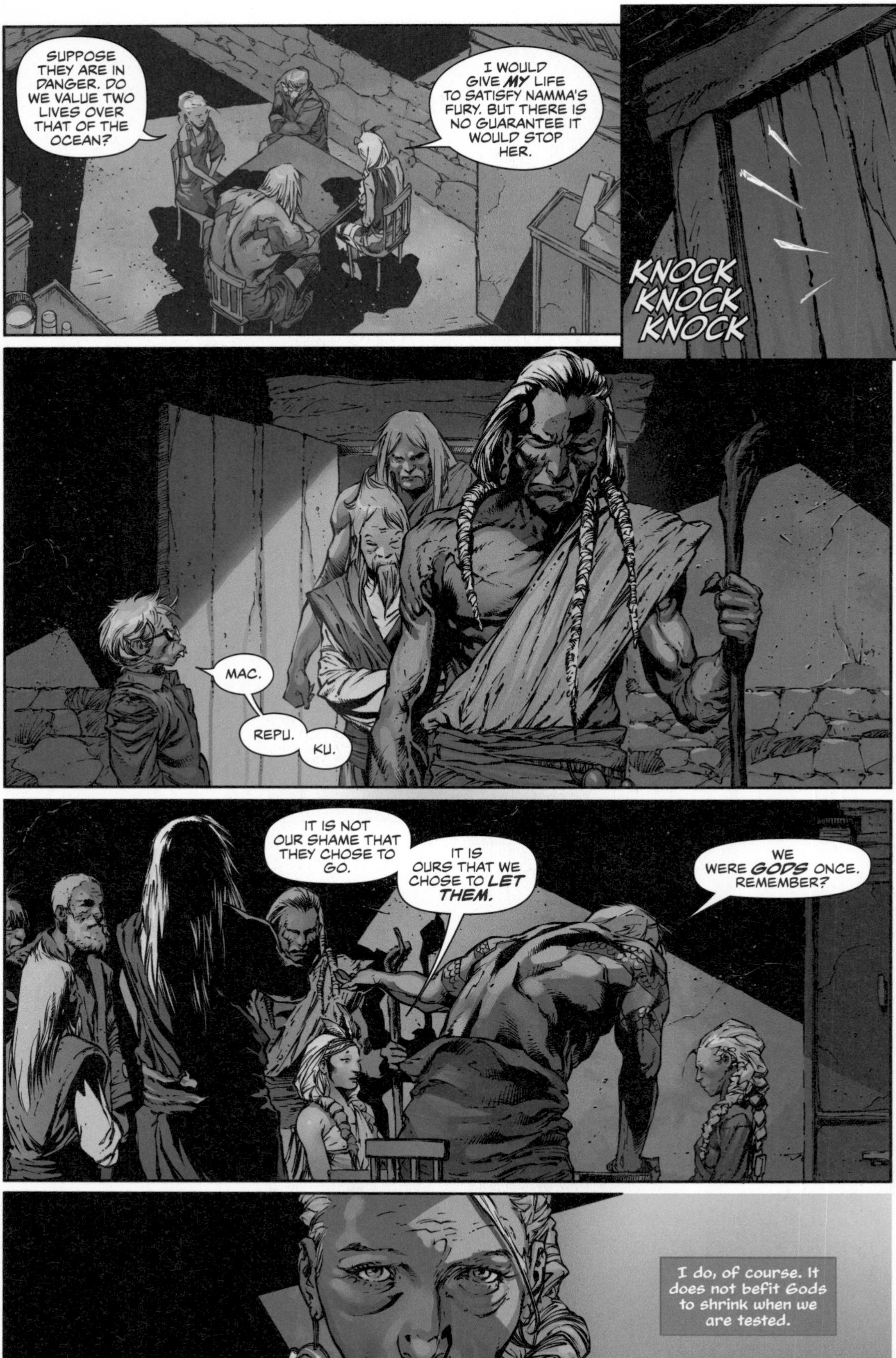
SUPPOSE THEY ARE IN DANGER. DO WE VALUE TWO LIVES OVER THAT OF THE OCEAN?
I WOULD GIVE MY LIFE TO SATISFY NAMMA'S FURY. BUT THERE IS NO GUARANTEE IT WOULD STOP HER.
KNOCK KNOCK KNOCK
MAC.
REPU.
KU.
IT IS NOT OUR SHAME THAT THEY CHOSE TO GO.
IT IS OURS THAT WE CHOSE TO LET THEM.
WE WERE GODS ONCE. REMEMBER?
I do, of course. It does not befit Gods to shrink when we are tested.

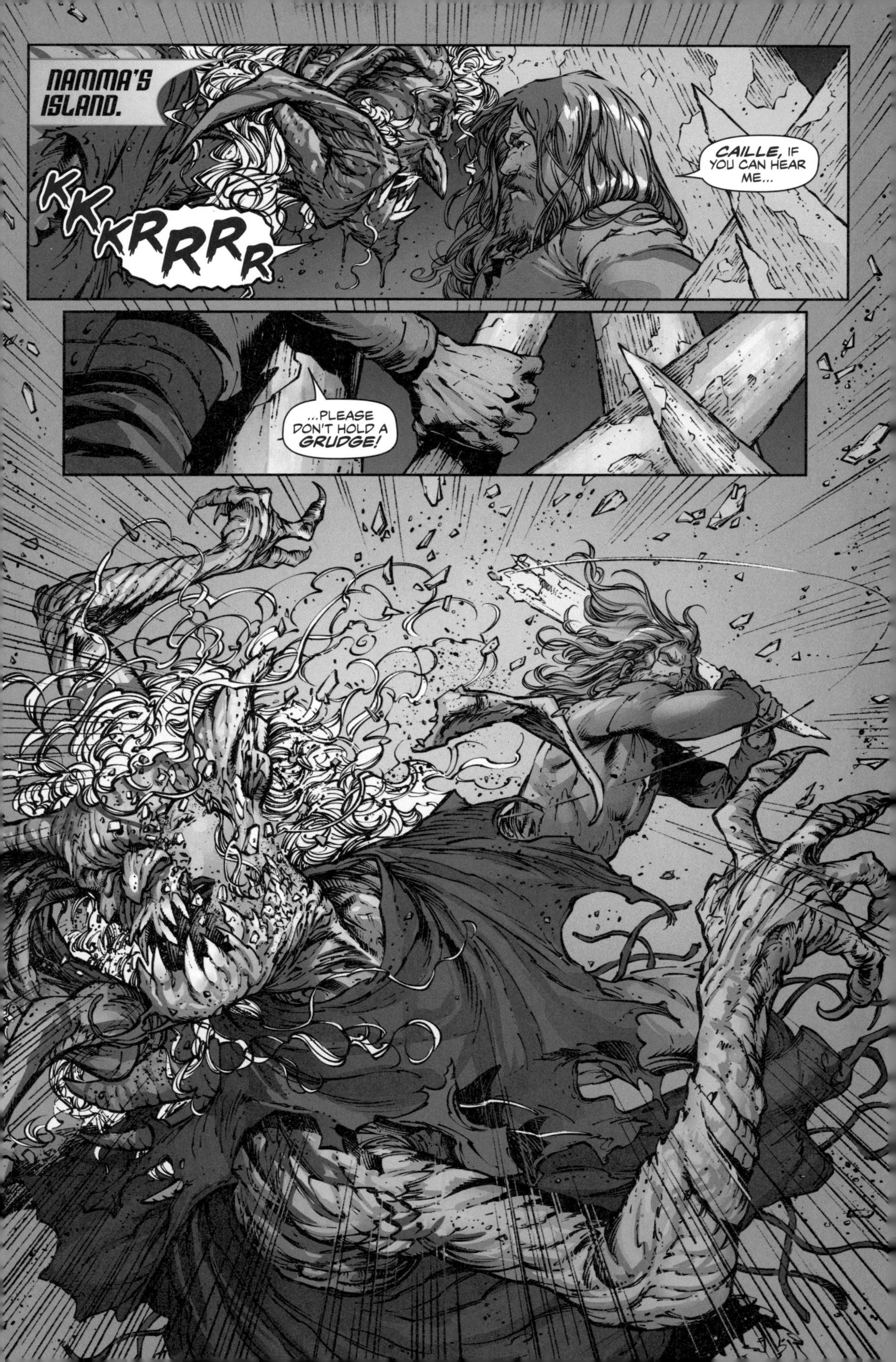
NAMMA'S ISLAND.
KKKRRRRR
CAILLE, IF YOU CAN HEAR ME...
...PLEASE DON'T HOLD A GRUDGE!

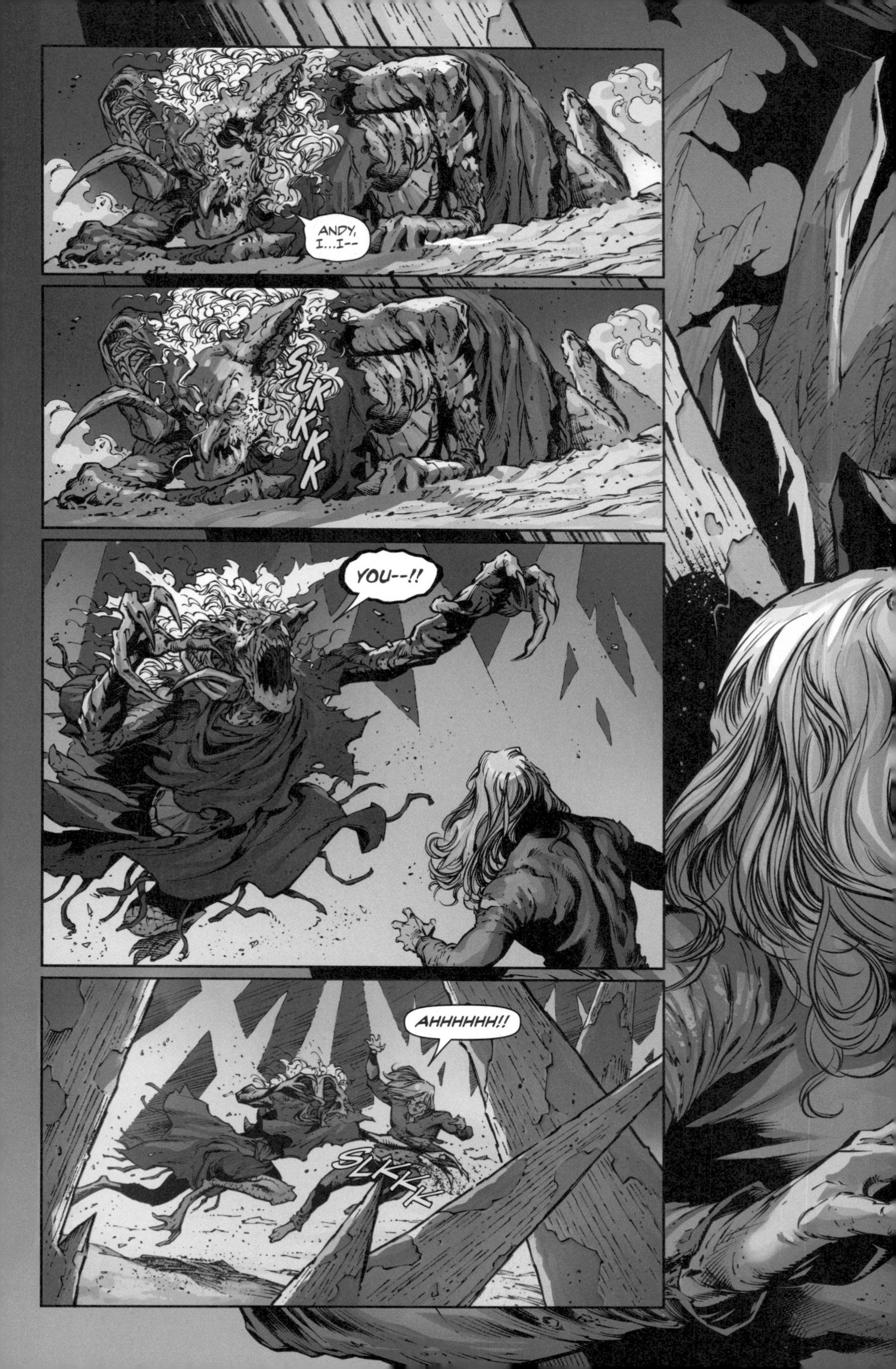
ANDY, I...I--
SLKKKK
YOU--!!
AHHHHHH!!
SLKKKK

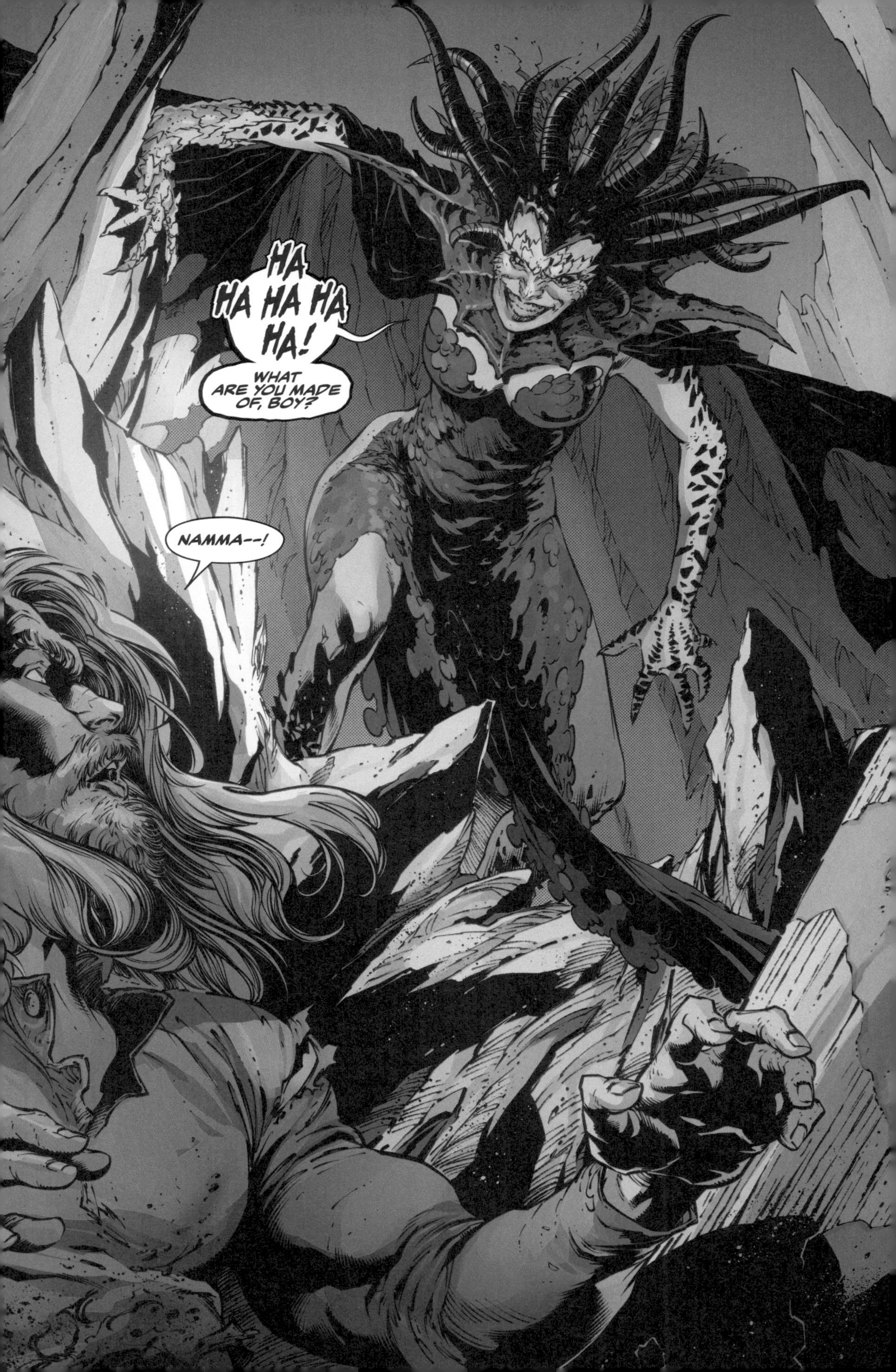

HA HA HA HA HA HA!
WHAT ARE YOU MADE OF, BOY?
NAMMA--!

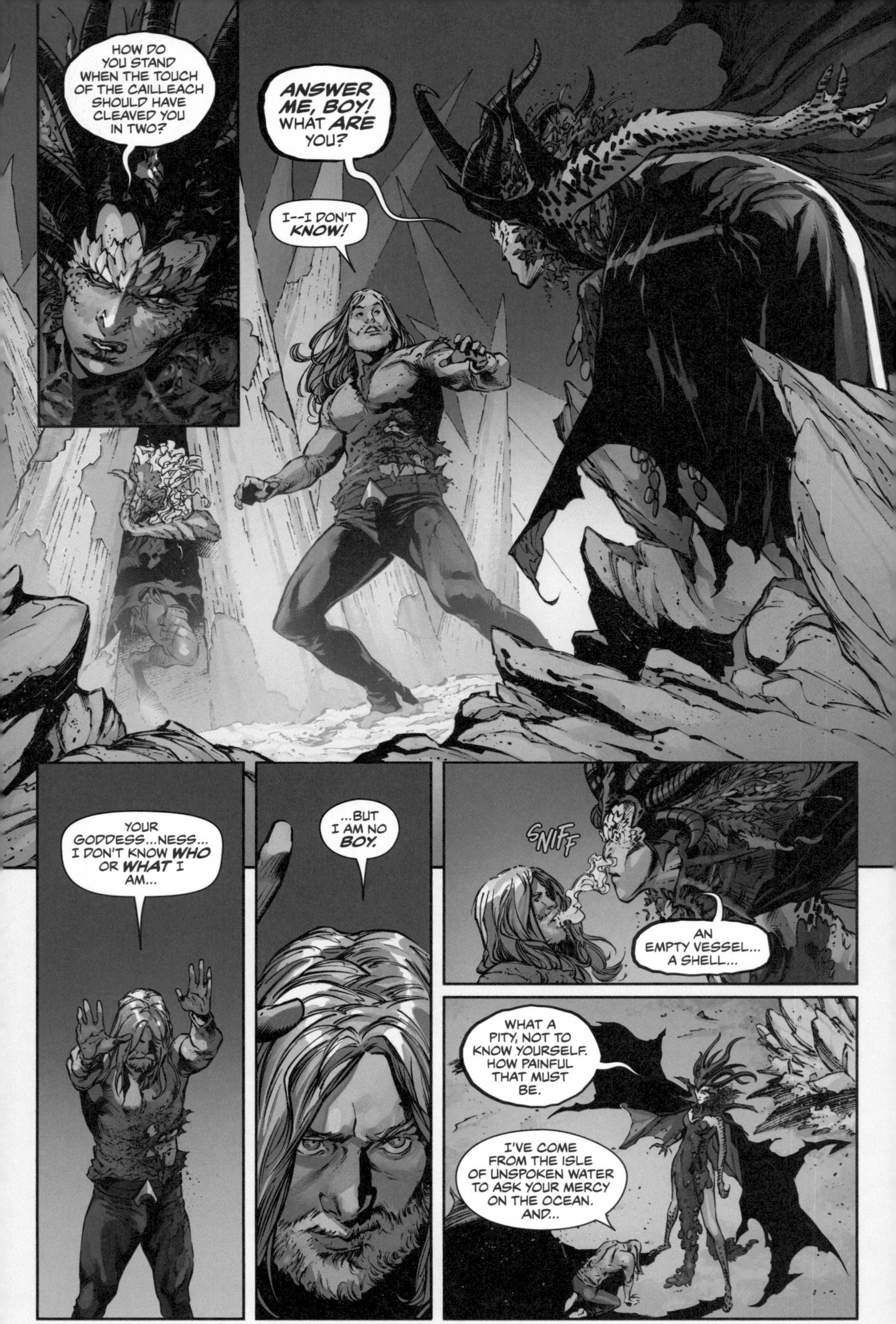
HOW DO YOU STAND WHEN THE TOUCH OF THE CAILLEACH SHOULD HAVE CLEAVED YOU IN TWO?
ANSWER ME, BOY! WHAT ARE YOU?
I--I DON'T KNOW!
YOUR GODDESS...NESS... I DON'T KNOW WHO OR WHAT I AM...
...BUT I AM NO BOY.
SNIFF
AN EMPTY VESSEL... A SHELL...
WHAT A PITY, NOT TO KNOW YOURSELF. HOW PAINFUL THAT MUST BE.
I'VE COME FROM THE ISLE OF UNSPOKEN WATER TO ASK YOUR MERCY ON THE OCEAN. AND...

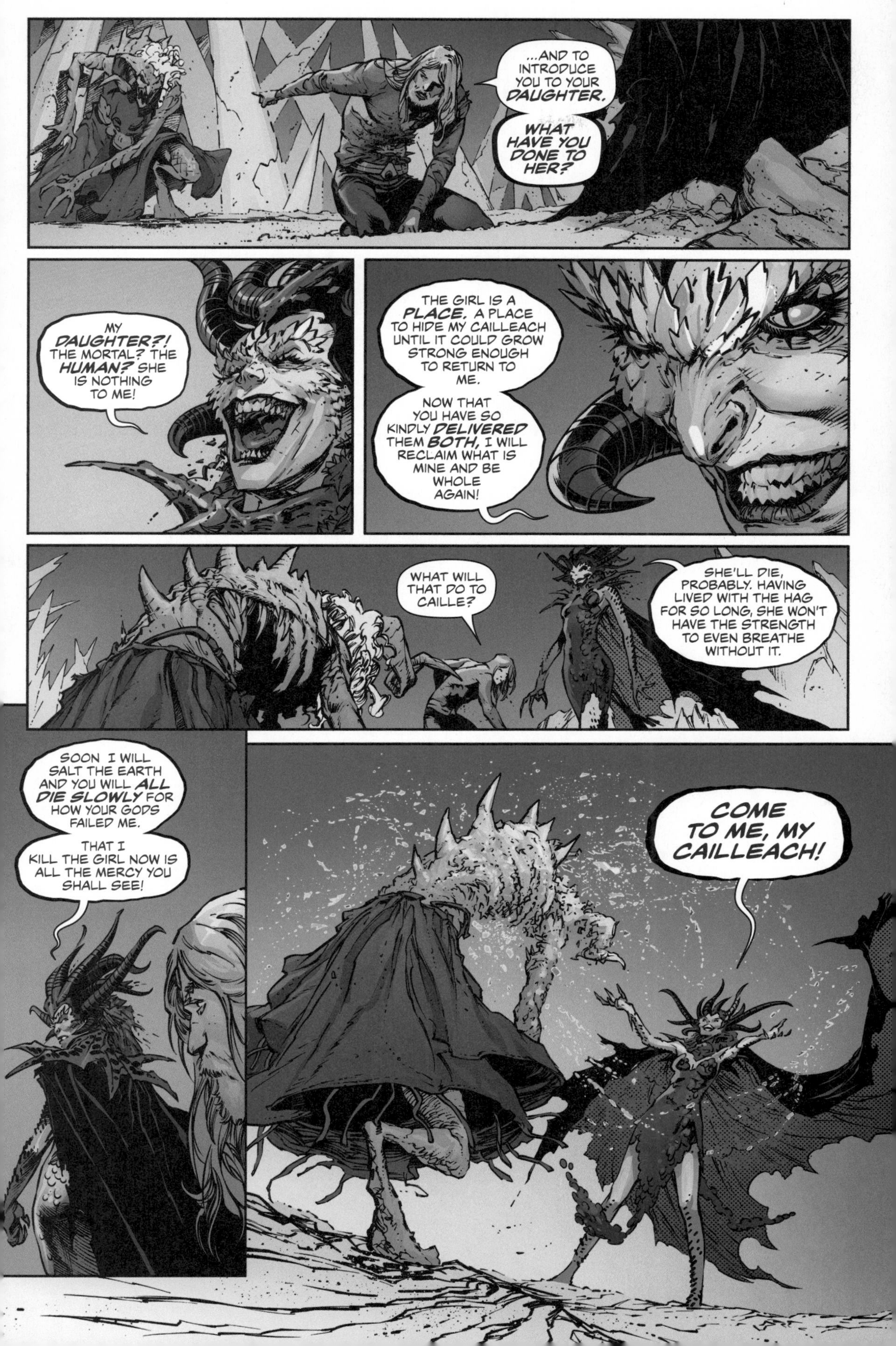
...AND TO INTRODUCE YOU TO YOUR DAUGHTER.
WHAT HAVE YOU DONE TO HER?
MY DAUGHTER?! THE MORTAL? THE HUMAN? SHE IS NOTHING TO ME!
THE GIRL IS A PLACE. A PLACE TO HIDE MY CAILLEACH UNTIL IT COULD GROW STRONG ENOUGH TO RETURN TO ME.
NOW THAT YOU HAVE SO KINDLY DELIVERED THEM BOTH, I WILL RECLAIM WHAT IS MINE AND BE WHOLE AGAIN!
WHAT WILL THAT DO TO CAILLE?
SHE'LL DIE, PROBABLY. HAVING LIVED WITH THE HAG FOR SO LONG, SHE WON'T HAVE THE STRENGTH TO EVEN BREATHE WITHOUT IT.
SOON I WILL SALT THE EARTH AND YOU WILL ALL DIE SLOWLY FOR HOW YOUR GODS FAILED ME.
THAT I KILL THE GIRL NOW IS ALL THE MERCY YOU SHALL SEE!
COME TO ME, MY CAILLEACH!

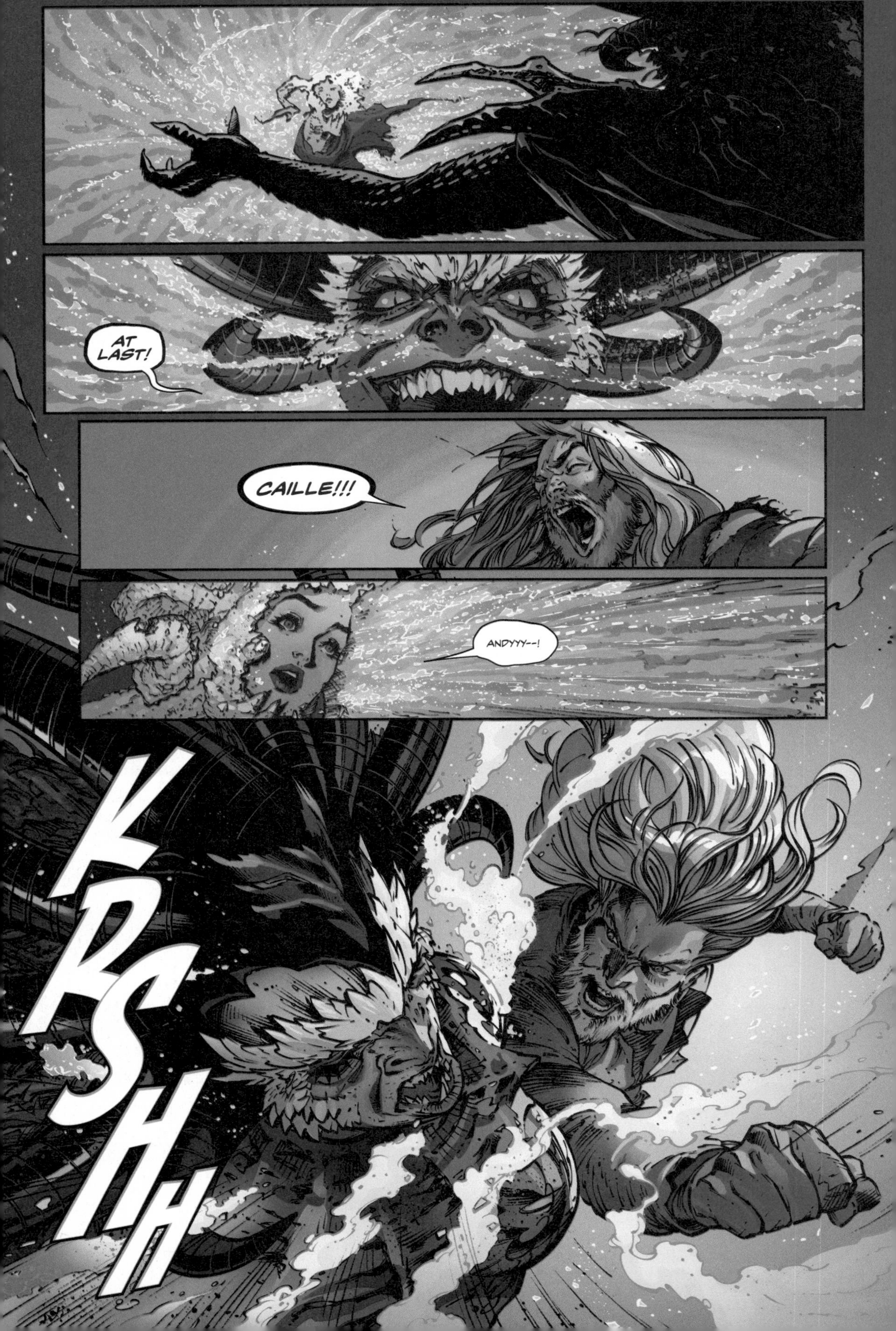
AT LAST!
CAILLE!!!
ANDYYY--!
KRSHH

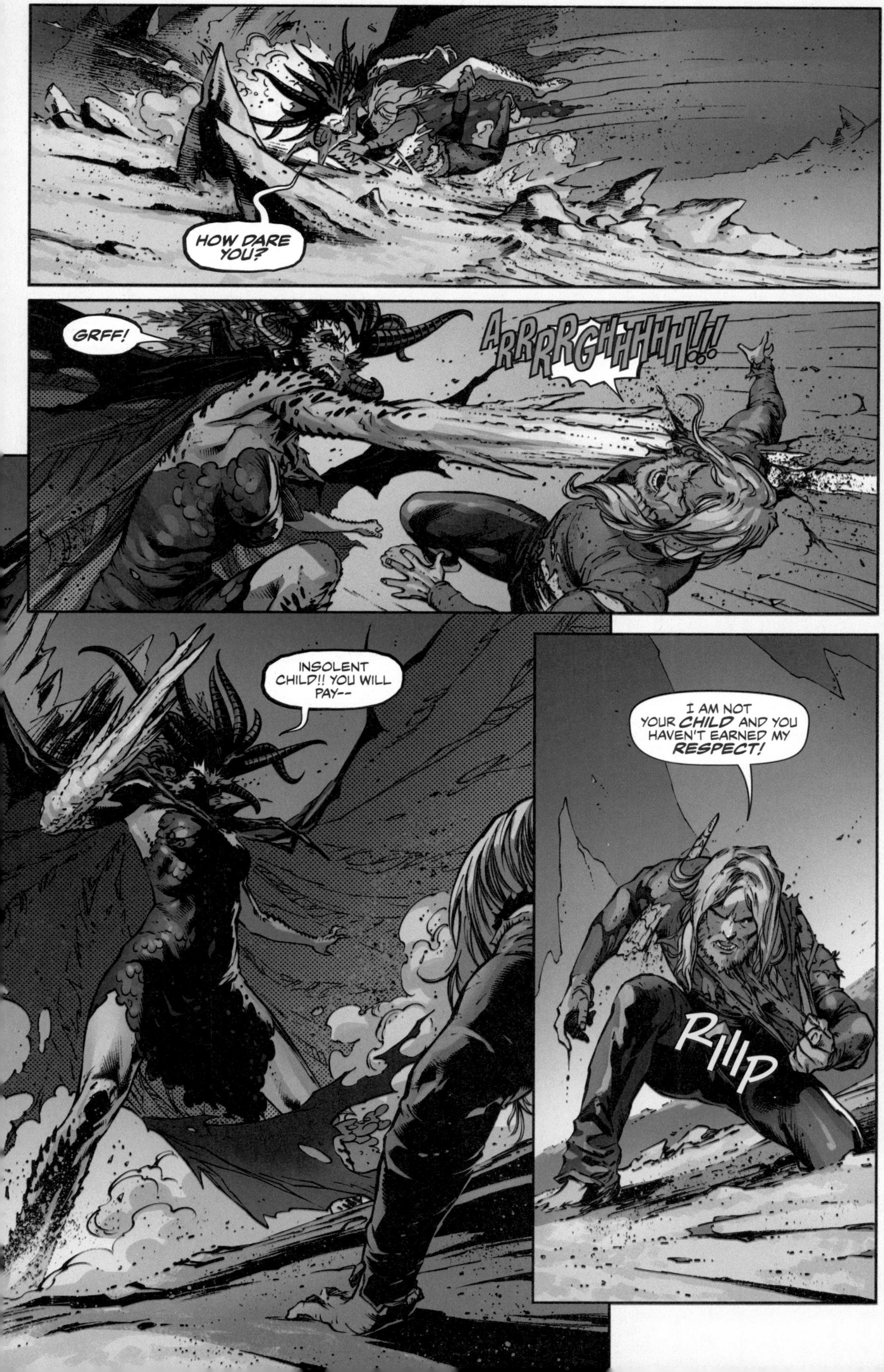
HOW DARE YOU?
GRFF!
ARRRRGHHHHH!!
INSOLENT CHILD!! YOU WILL PAY--
I AM NOT YOUR CHILD AND YOU HAVEN'T EARNED MY RESPECT!
RIIIP

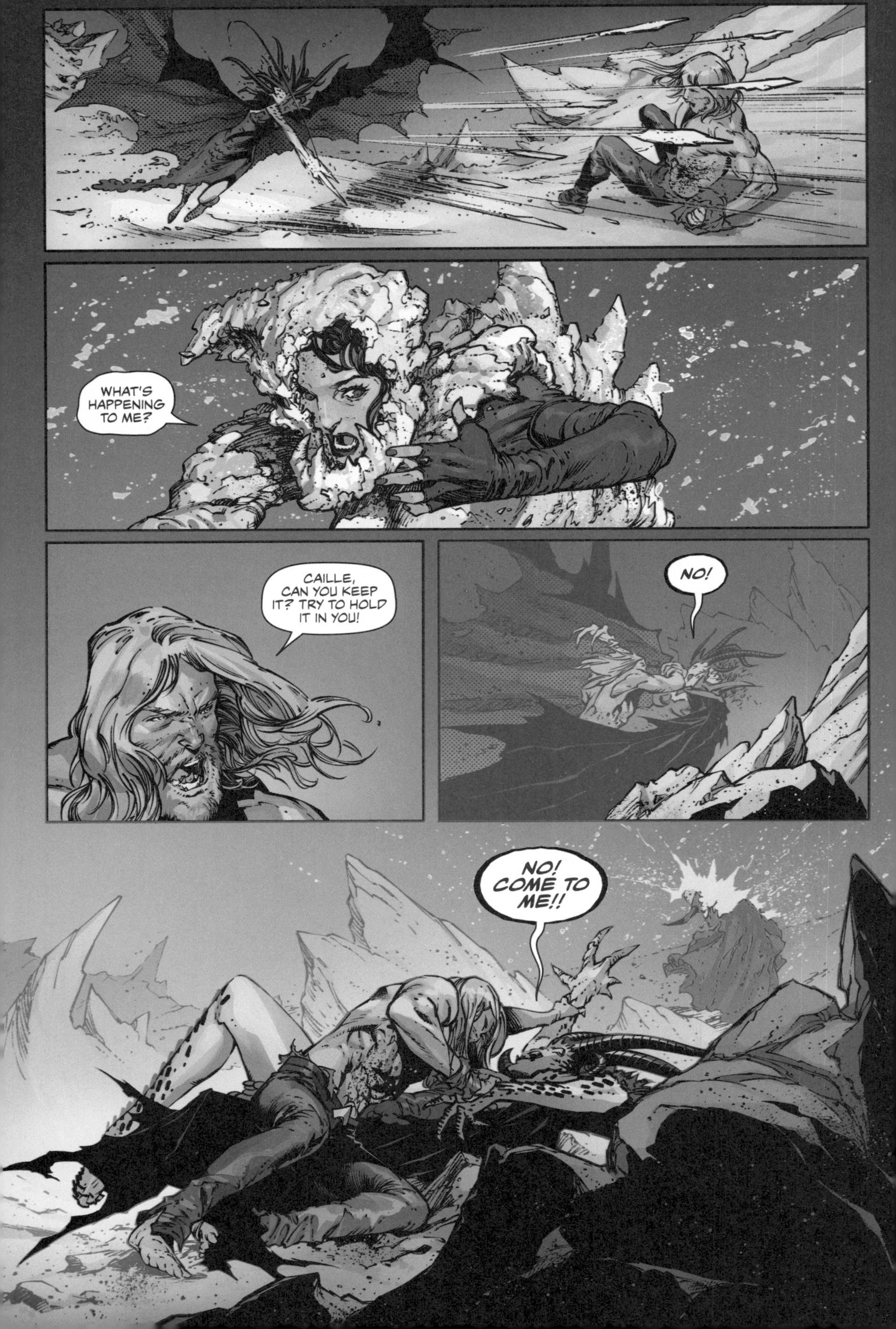
WHAT'S HAPPENING TO ME?
CAILLE, CAN YOU KEEP IT? TRY TO HOLD IT IN YOU!
NO!
NO! COME TO ME!!

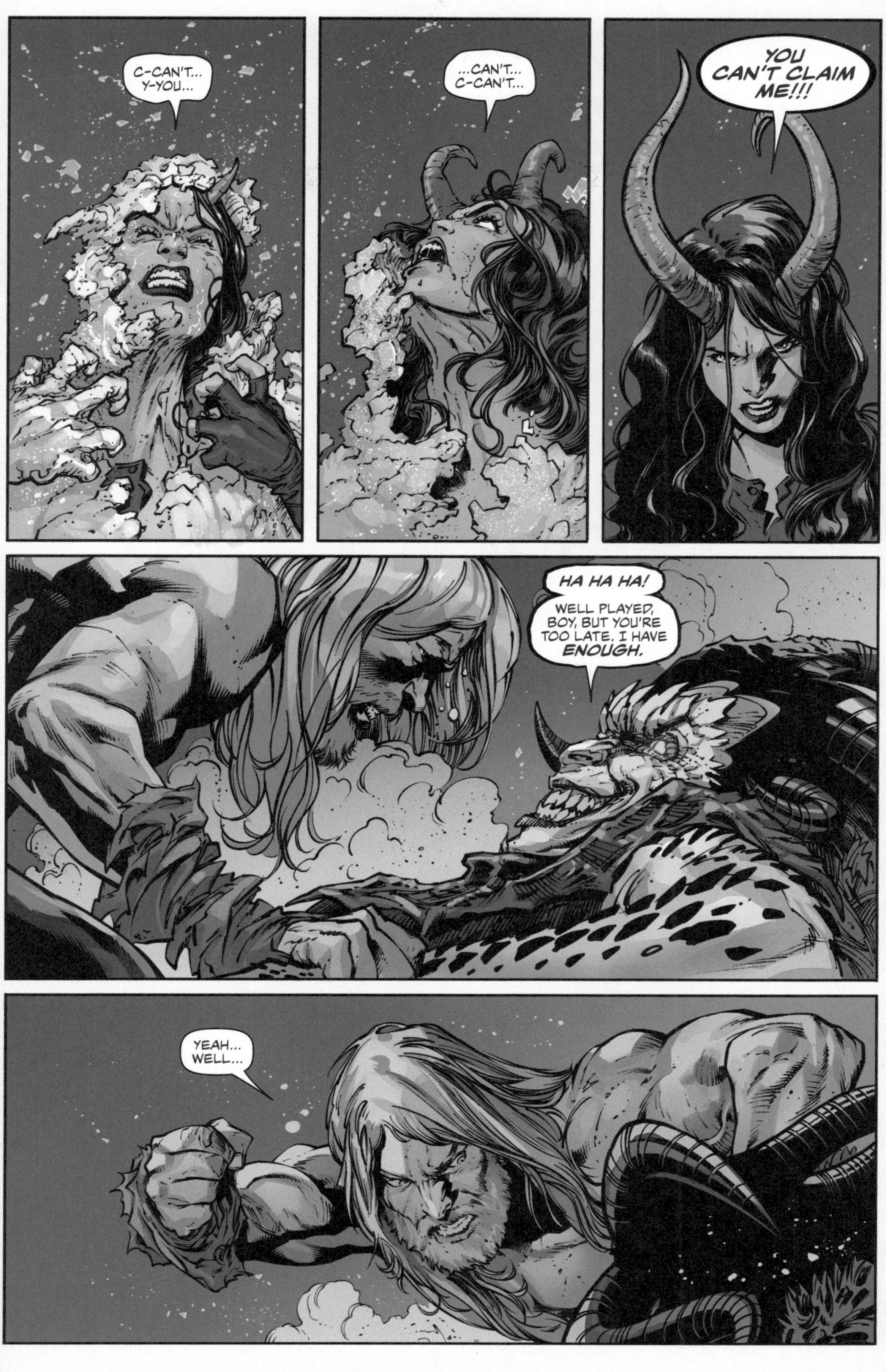
C-CAN'T... Y-YOU...
...CAN'T... C-CAN'T...
YOU CAN'T CLAIM ME!!!
HA HA HA!
WELL PLAYED, BOY, BUT YOU'RE TOO LATE. I HAVE ENOUGH.
YEAH... WELL...

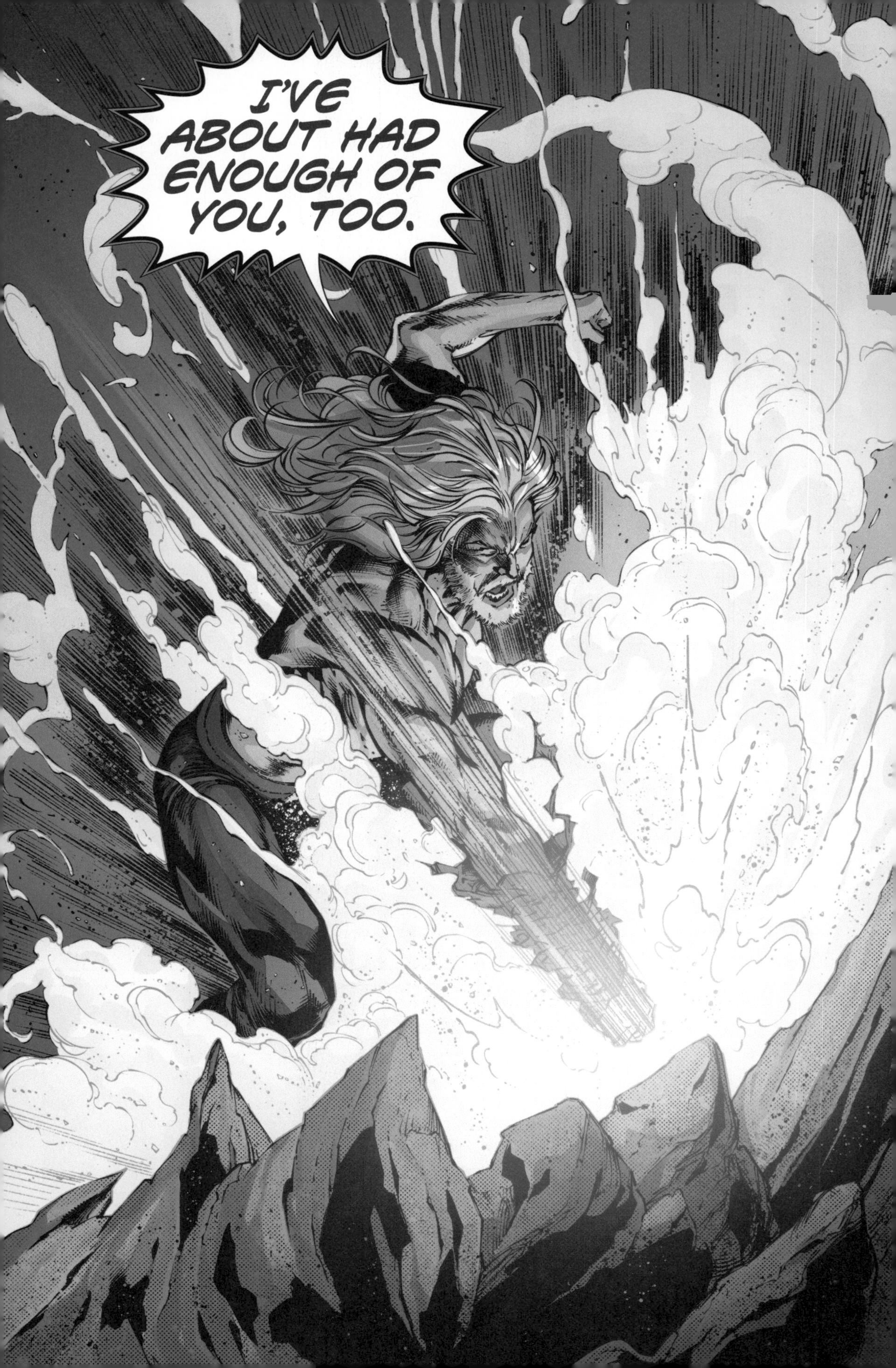
I'VE ABOUT HAD ENOUGH OF YOU, TOO.

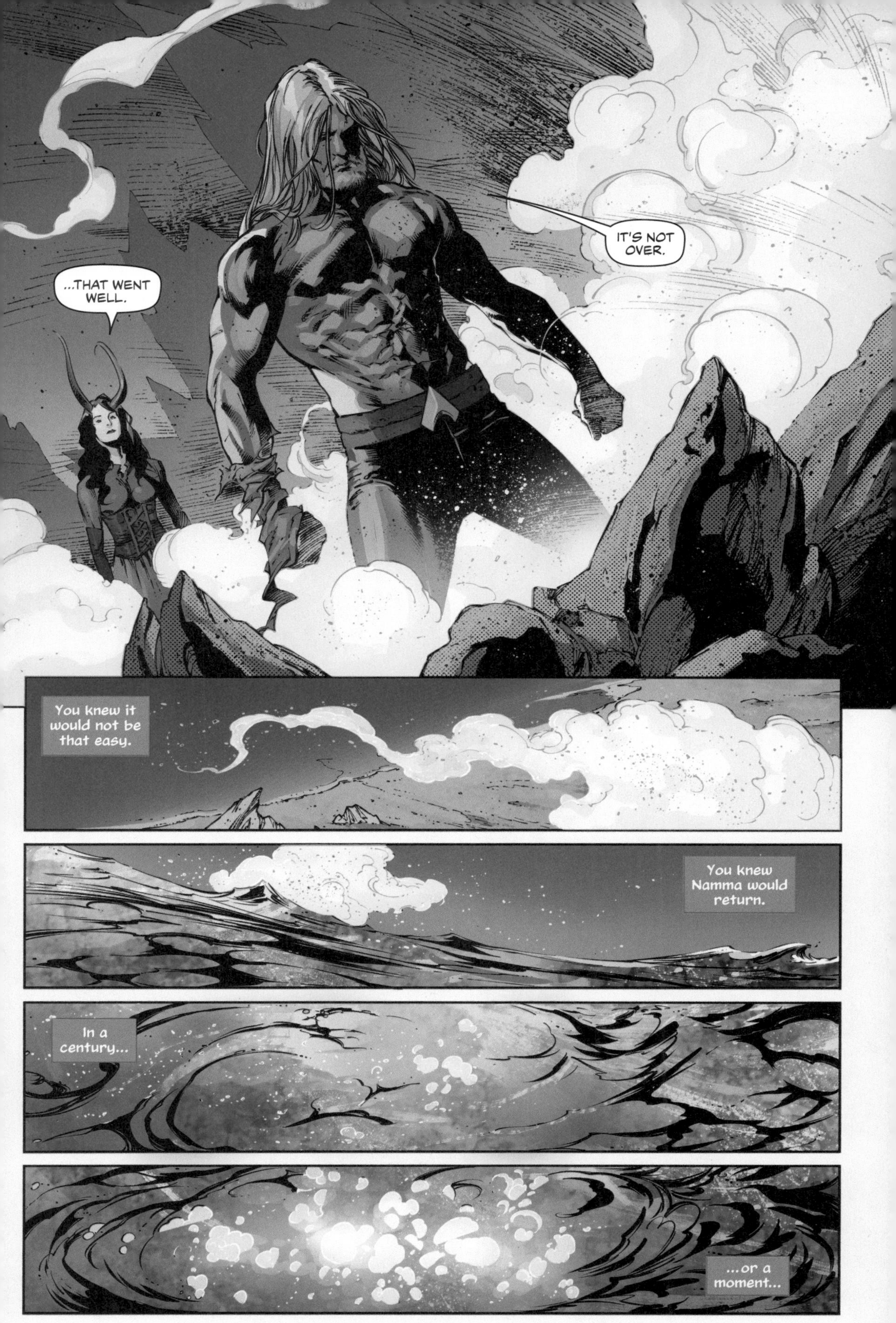
IT'S NOT OVER.
...THAT WENT WELL.
You knew it would not be that easy.
You knew Namma would return.
In a century...
...or a moment...

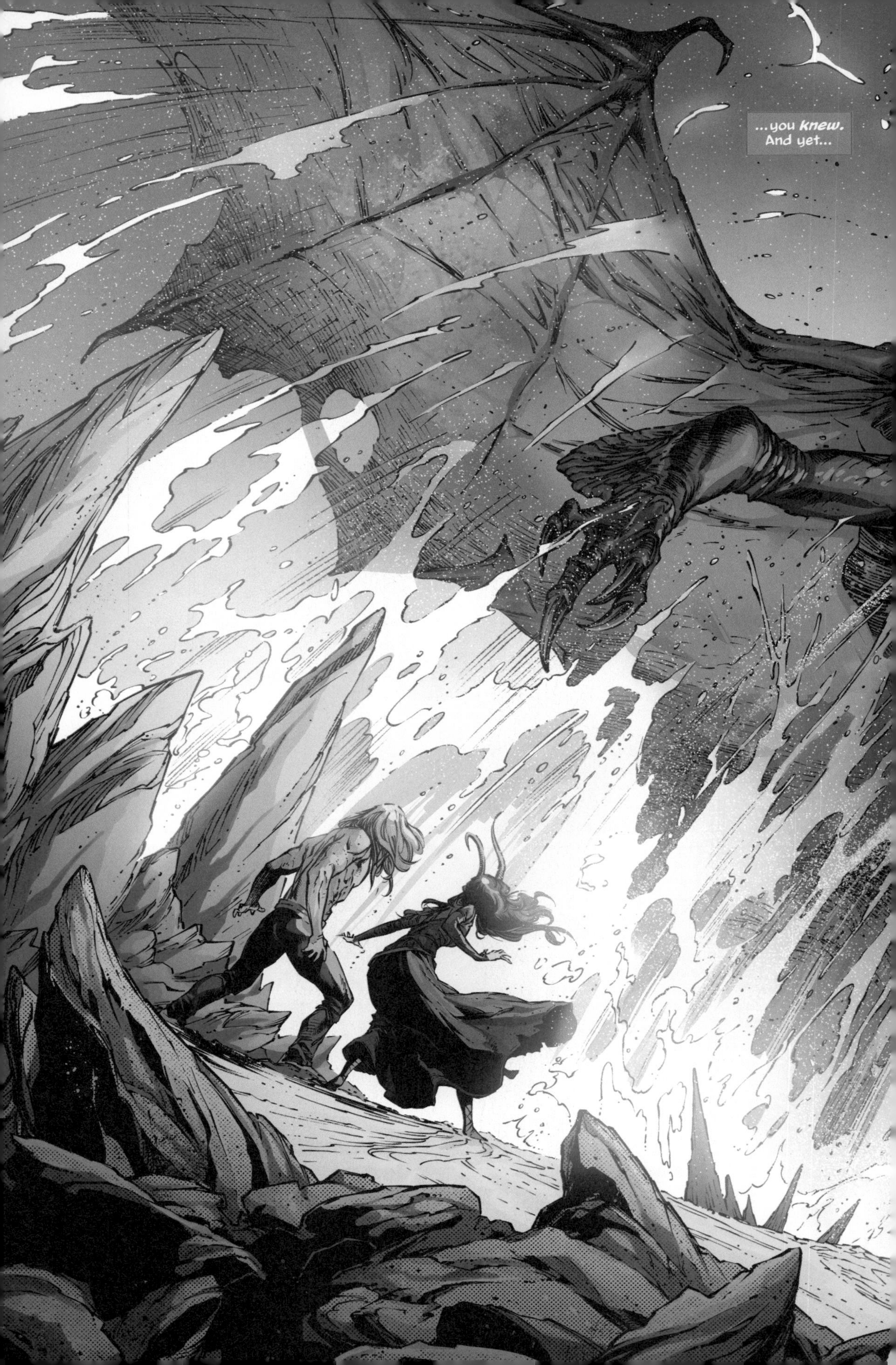
...you *knew.* And yet...

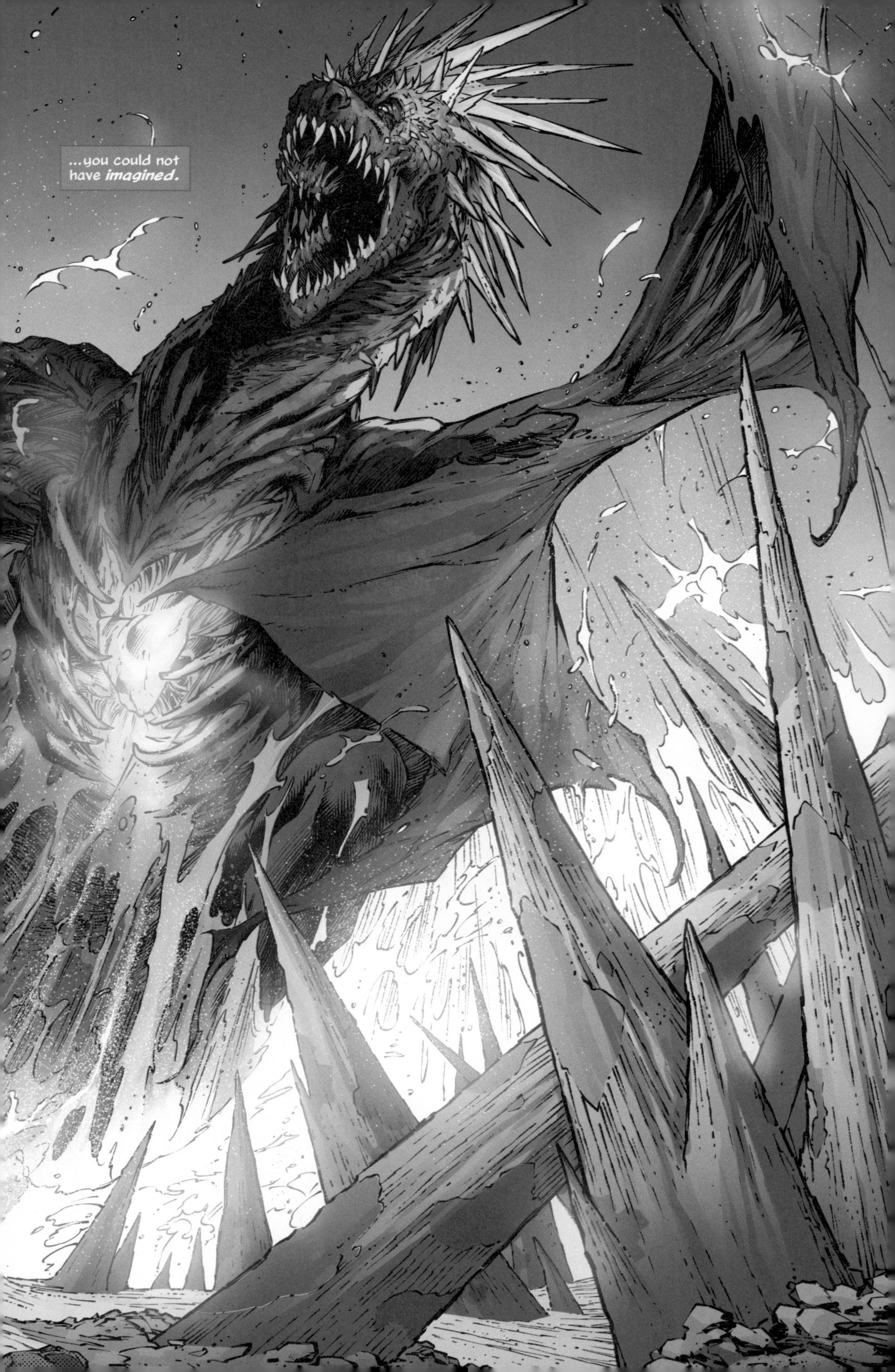
...you could not have *imagined*.

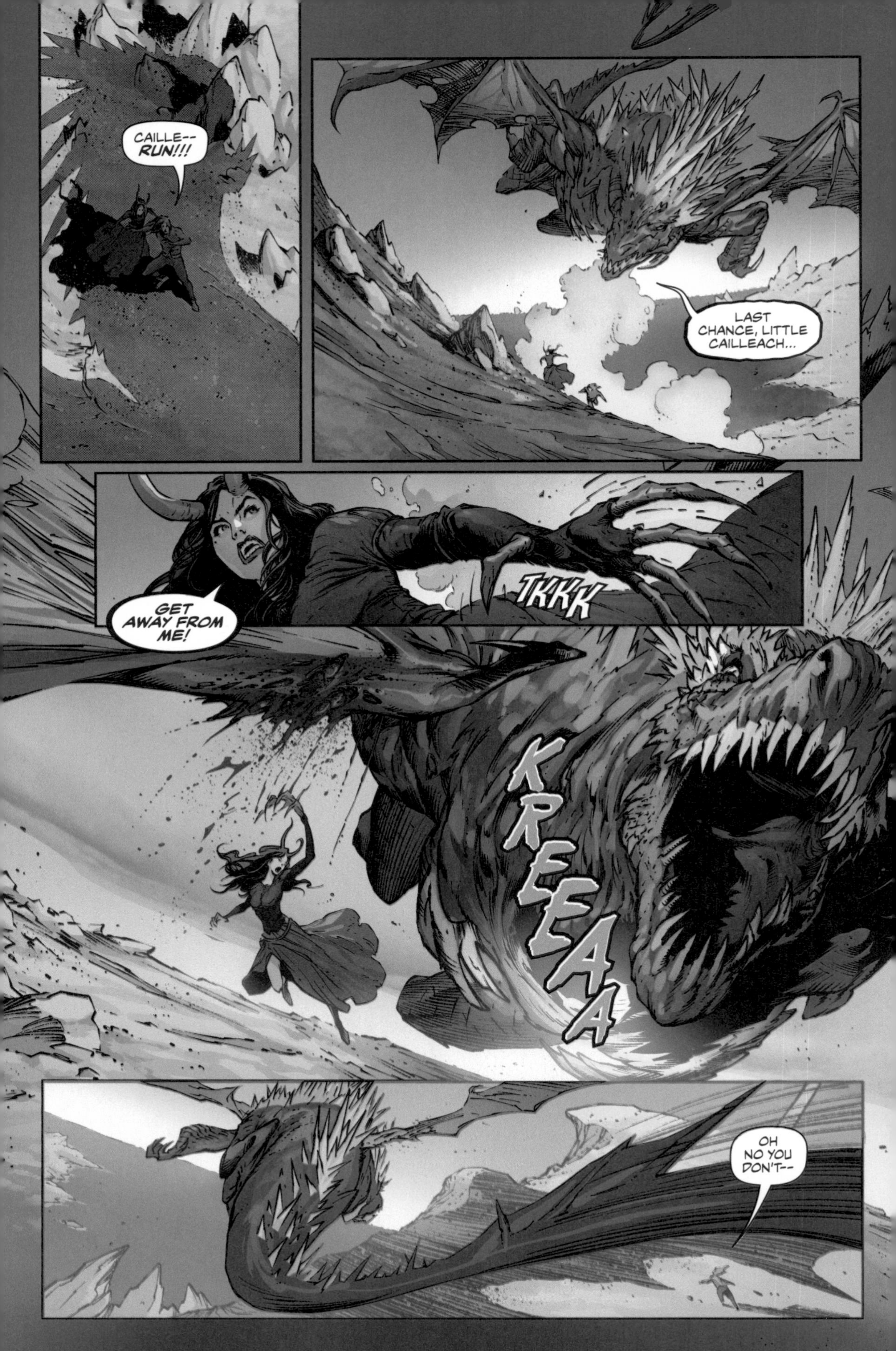
CAILLE--
RUN!!!
LAST CHANCE, LITTLE CAILLEACH...
GET AWAY FROM ME!
TKKK
KREEAA
OH NO YOU DON'T--

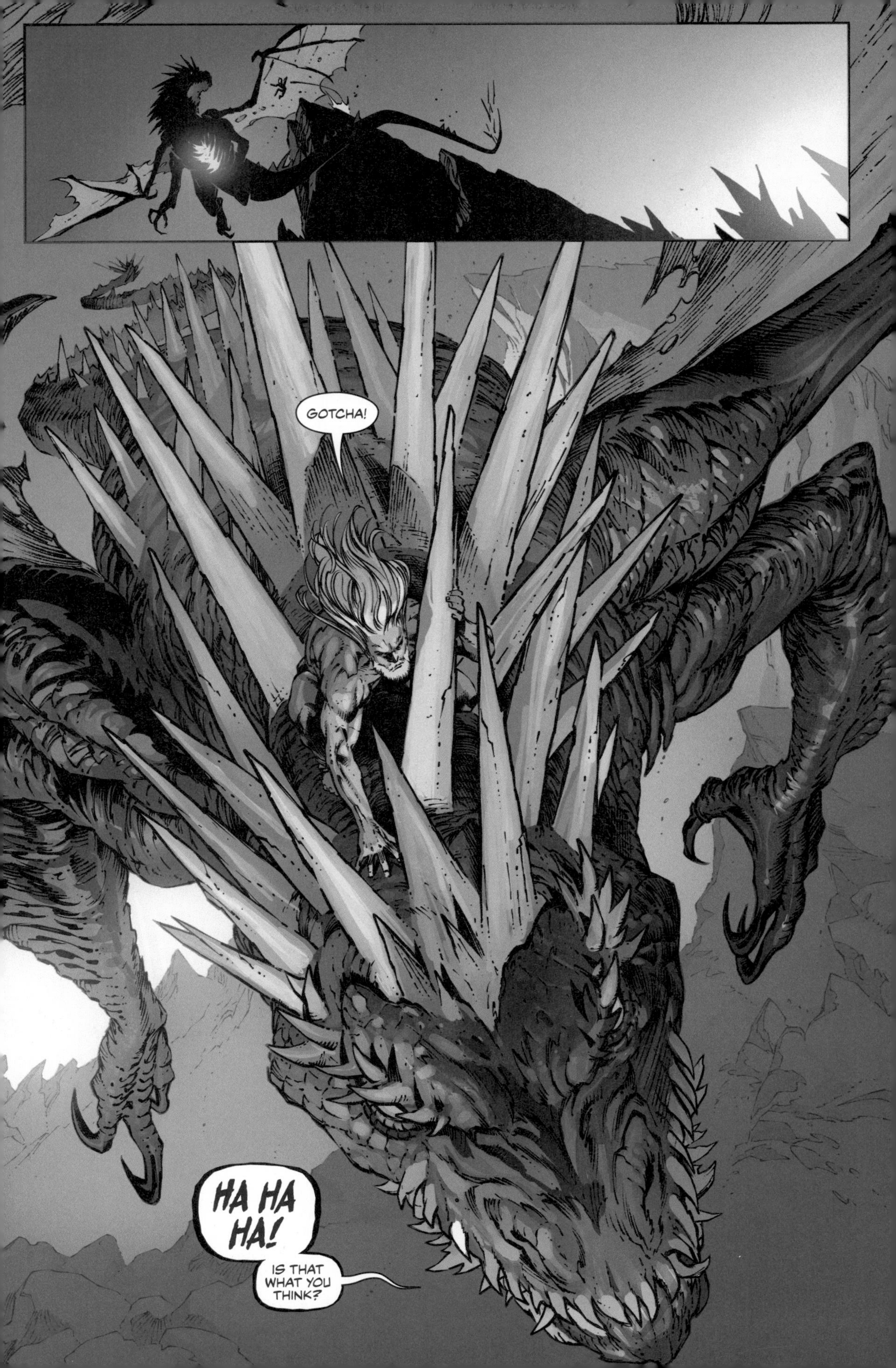
GOTCHA!
HA HA HA!
IS THAT WHAT YOU THINK?

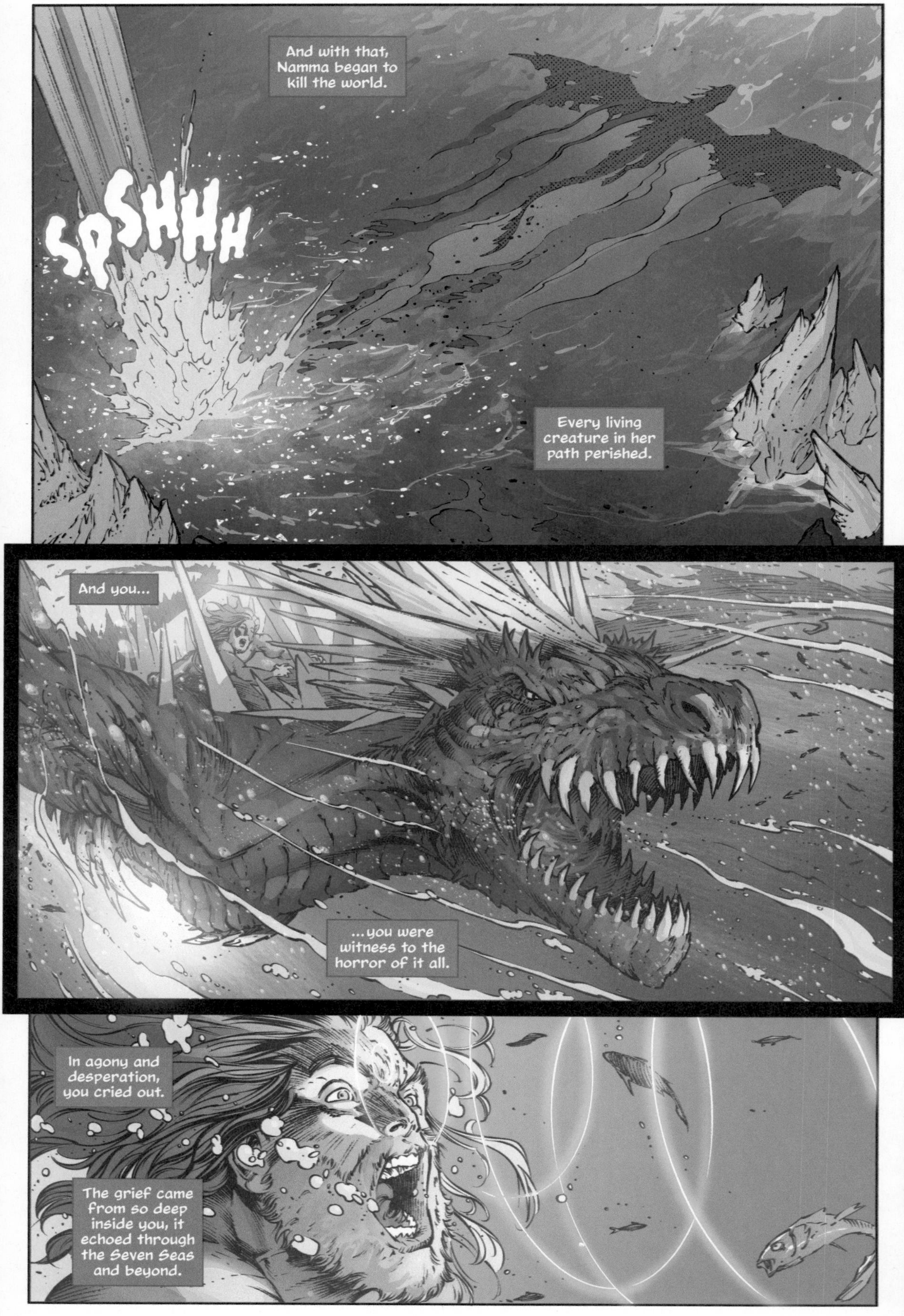
And with that, Namma began to kill the world.
SPSHHH
Every living creature in her path perished.
And you...
...you were witness to the horror of it all.
In agony and desperation, you cried out.
The grief came from so deep inside you, it echoed through the Seven Seas and beyond.

On land, they heard your Call.

In Atlantis, they heard your Call.

HE LIVES.

And in the village of Unspoken Water, we heard your Call.

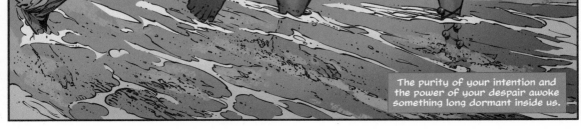

The purity of your intention and the power of your despair awoke something long dormant inside us.

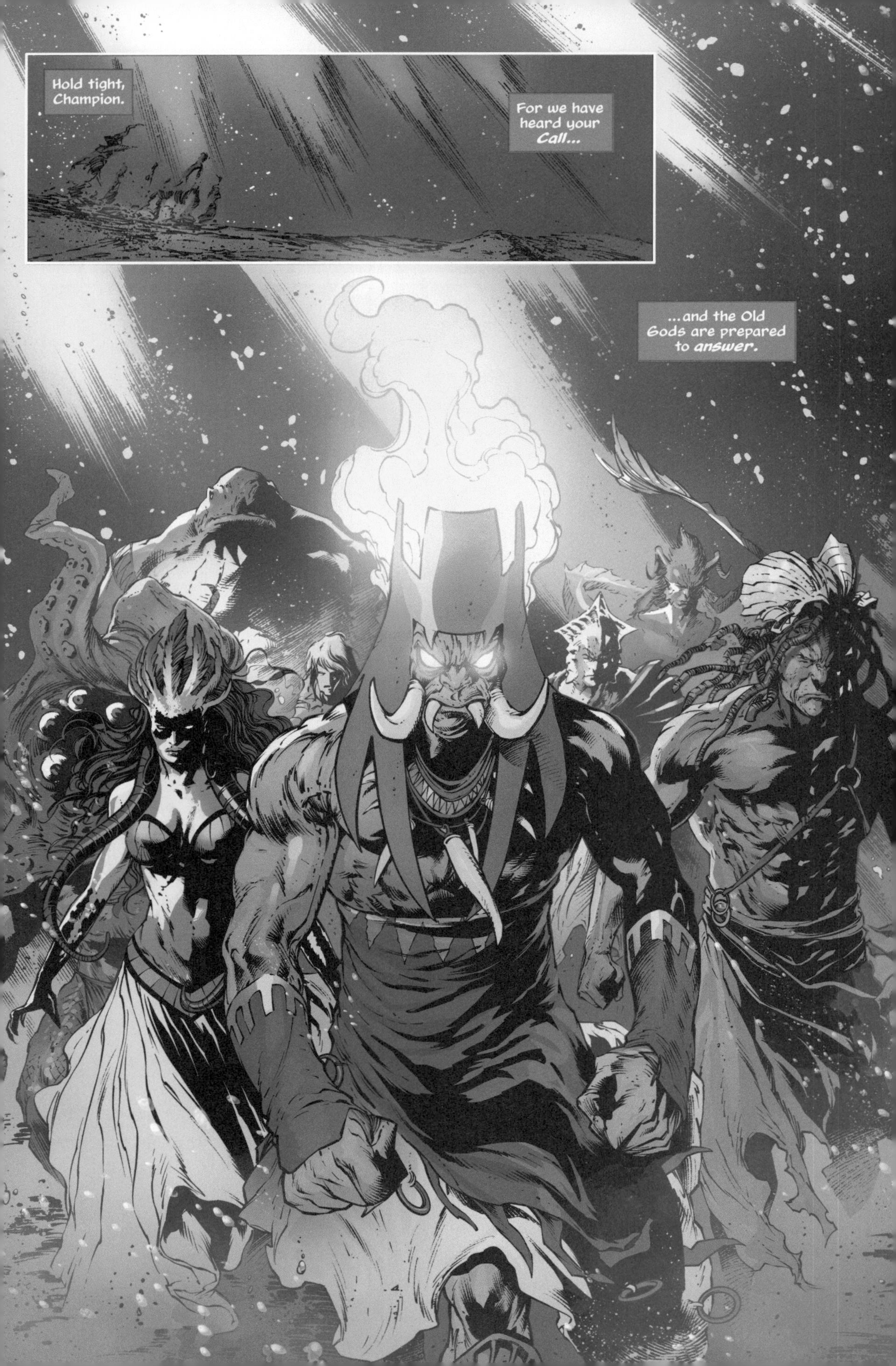
Hold tight, Champion.
For we have heard your *Call*...
...and the Old Gods are prepared to *answer*.

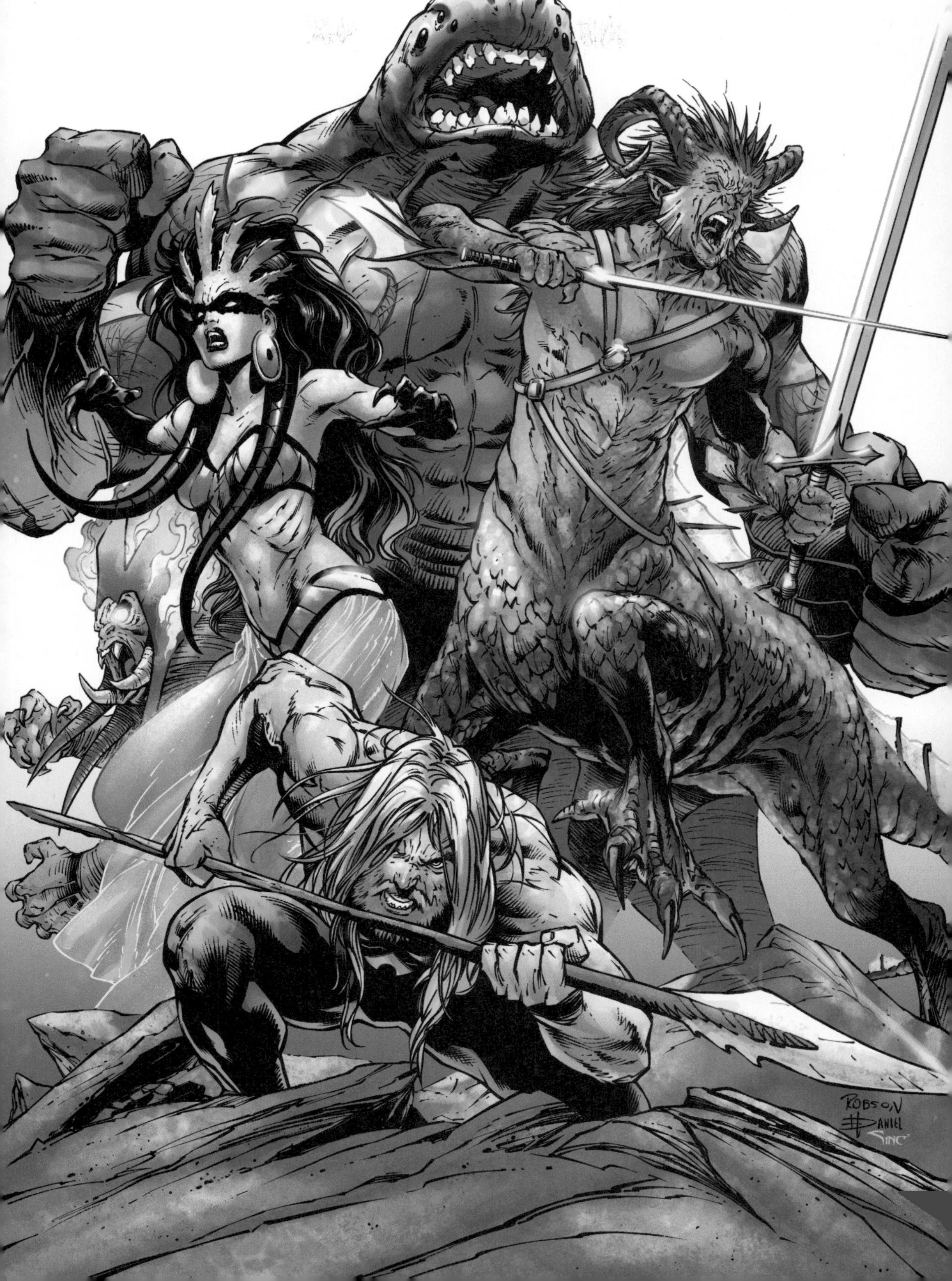
ROBSON
DANIEL
SINC

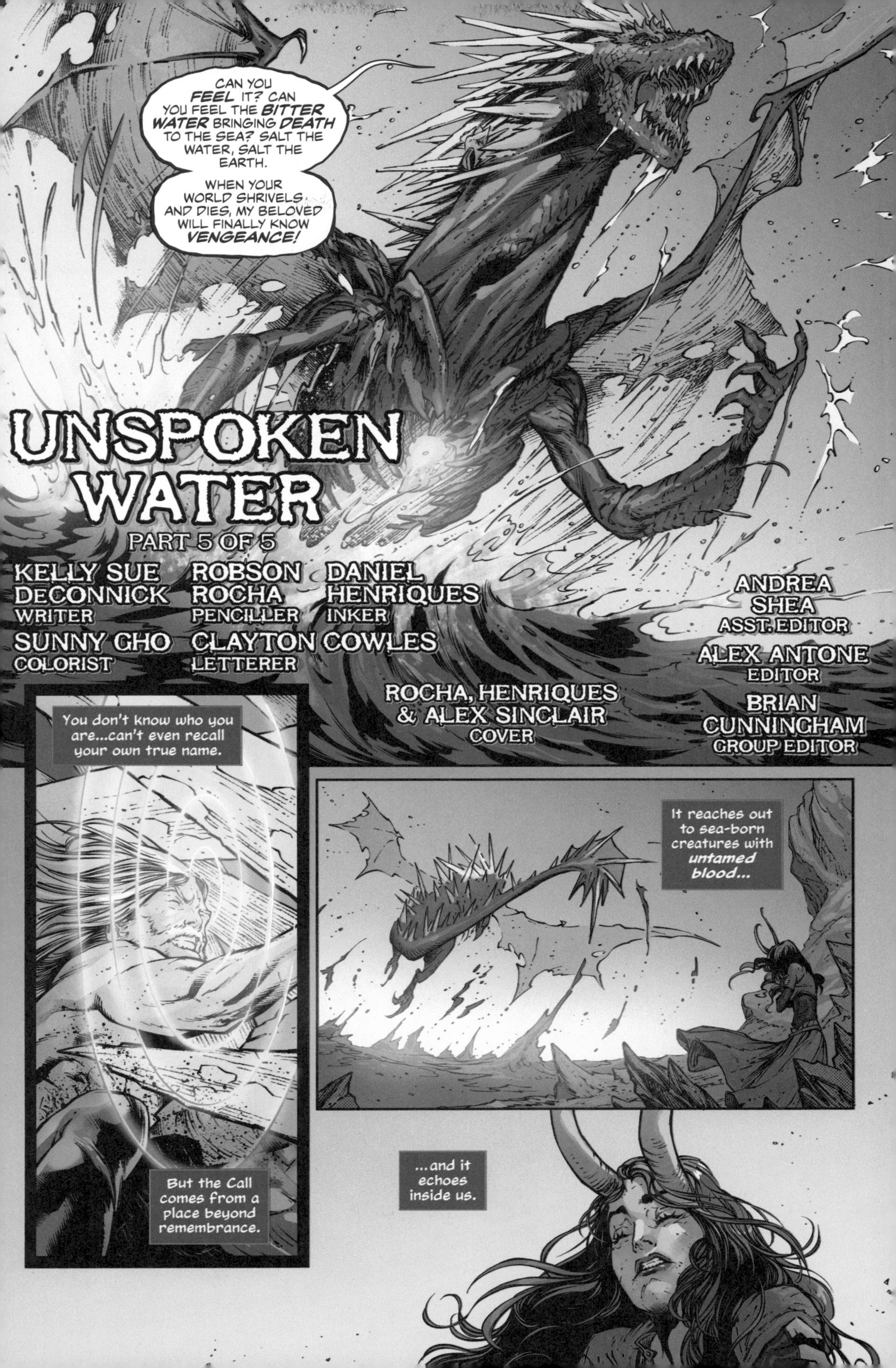
CAN YOU FEEL IT? CAN YOU FEEL THE BITTER WATER BRINGING DEATH TO THE SEA? SALT THE WATER, SALT THE EARTH.
WHEN YOUR WORLD SHRIVELS AND DIES, MY BELOVED WILL FINALLY KNOW VENGEANCE!
UNSPOKEN WATER
PART 5 OF 5
KELLY SUE DECONNICK WRITER
ROBSON ROCHA PENCILLER
DANIEL HENRIQUES INKER
SUNNY GHO COLORIST
CLAYTON COWLES LETTERER
ROCHA, HENRIQUES & ALEX SINCLAIR COVER
ANDREA SHEA ASST. EDITOR
ALEX ANTONE EDITOR
BRIAN CUNNINGHAM GROUP EDITOR
You don't know who you are...can't even recall your own true name.
But the Call comes from a place beyond remembrance.
It reaches out to sea-born creatures with untamed blood...
...and it echoes inside us.

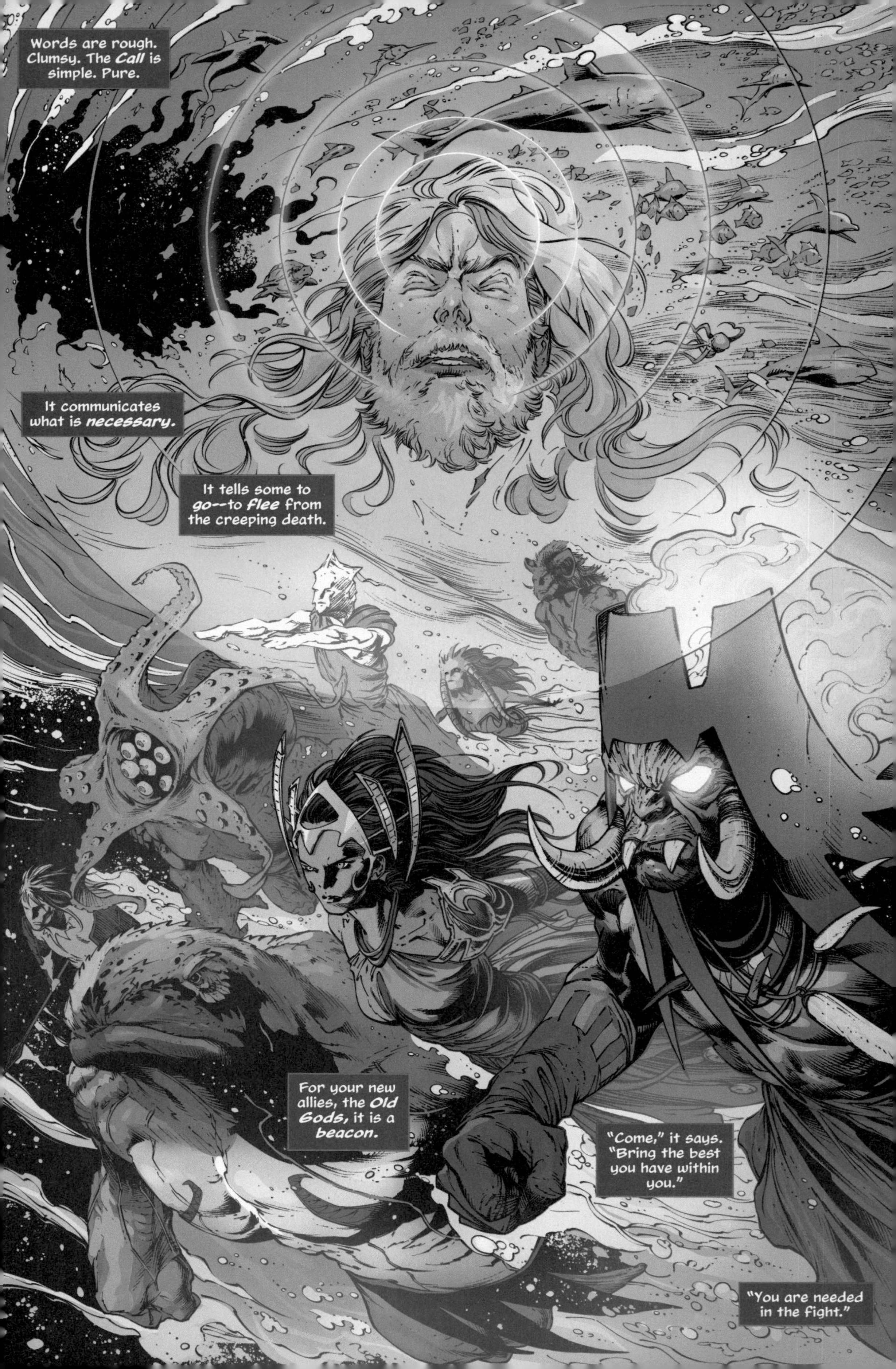
Words are rough. Clumsy. The *Call* is simple. Pure.
It communicates what is *necessary.*
It tells some to *go*--to *flee* from the creeping death.
For your new allies, the *Old Gods,* it is a *beacon.*
"Come," it says. "Bring the best you have within you."
"You are needed in the fight."

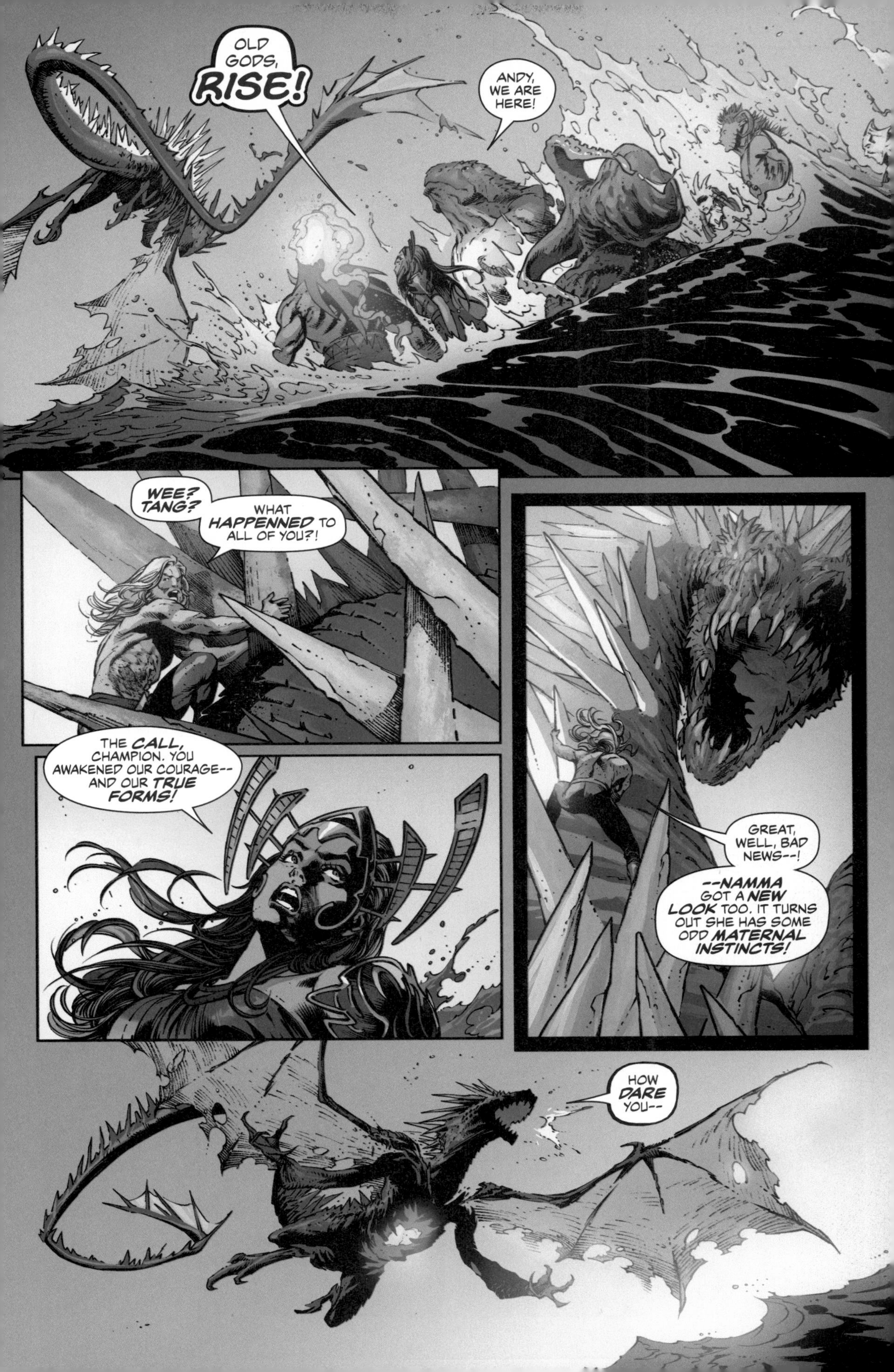
OLD GODS, RISE!
ANDY, WE ARE HERE!
WEE? TANG?
WHAT HAPPENNED TO ALL OF YOU?!
THE CALL, CHAMPION. YOU AWAKENED OUR COURAGE-- AND OUR TRUE FORMS!
GREAT, WELL, BAD NEWS--!
--NAMMA GOT A NEW LOOK TOO. IT TURNS OUT SHE HAS SOME ODD MATERNAL INSTINCTS!
HOW DARE YOU--

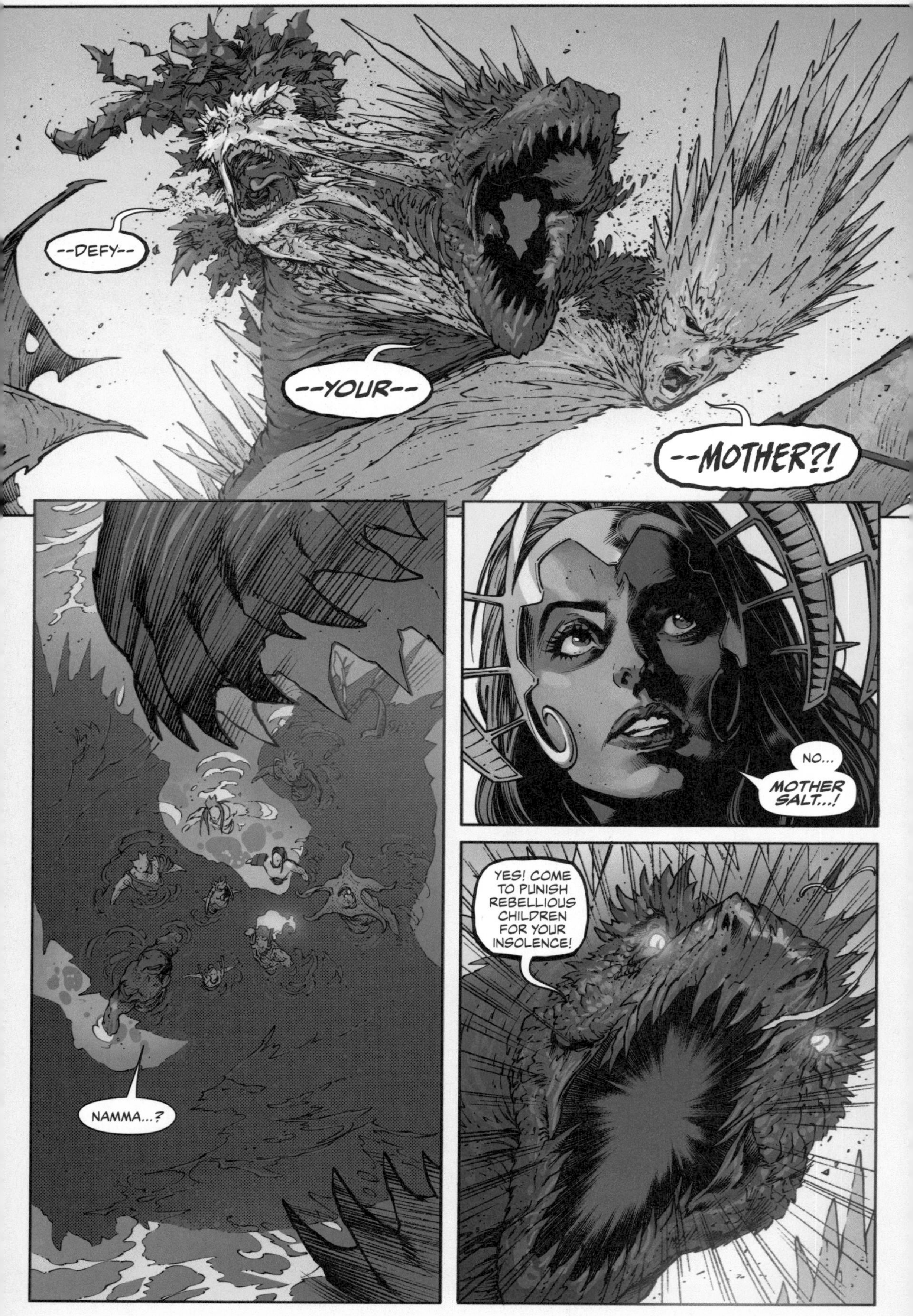
--DEFY--
--YOUR--
--MOTHER?!
NAMMA...?
NO... MOTHER SALT...!
YES! COME TO PUNISH REBELLIOUS CHILDREN FOR YOUR INSOLENCE!

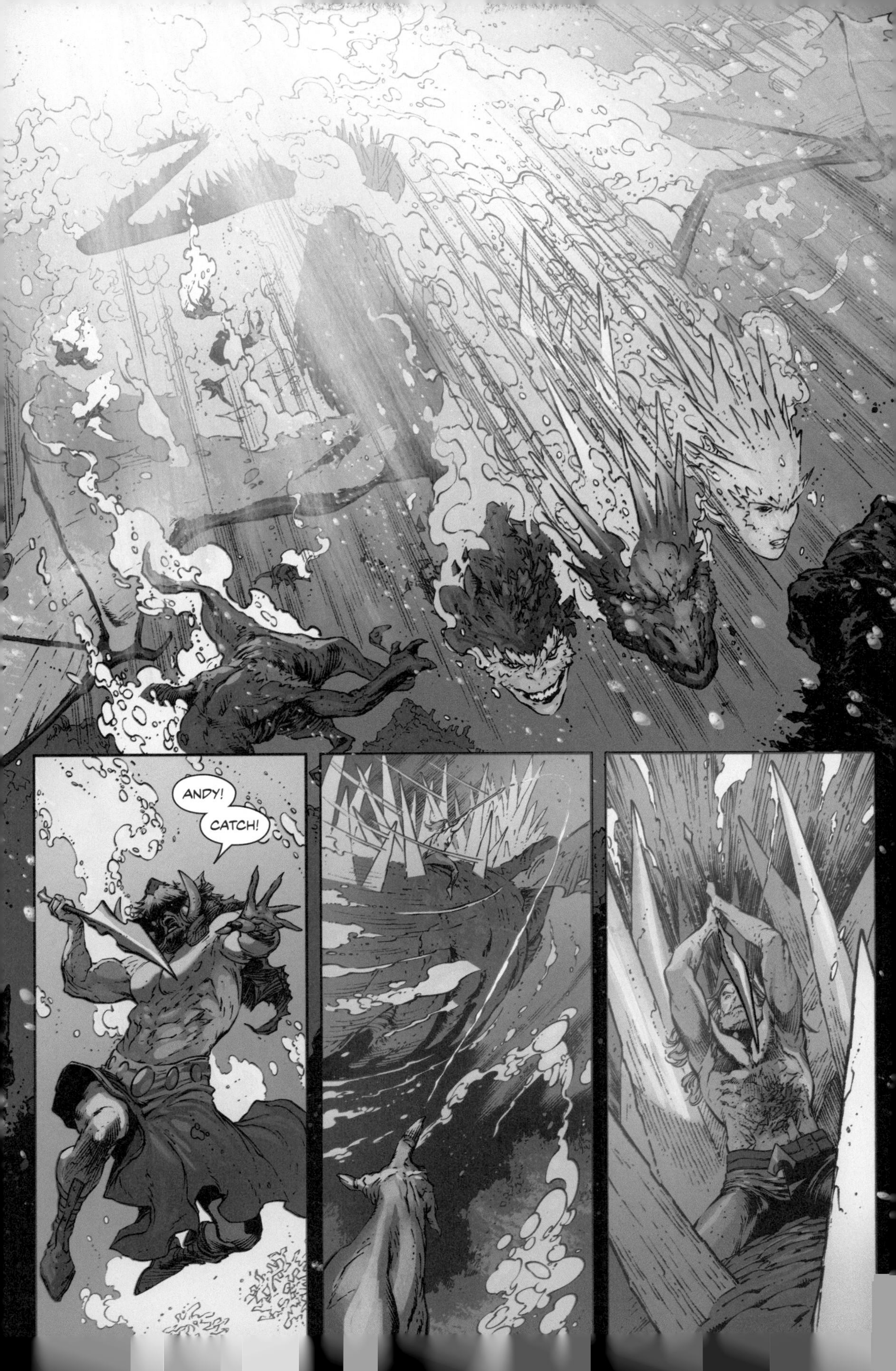
ANDY!
CATCH!

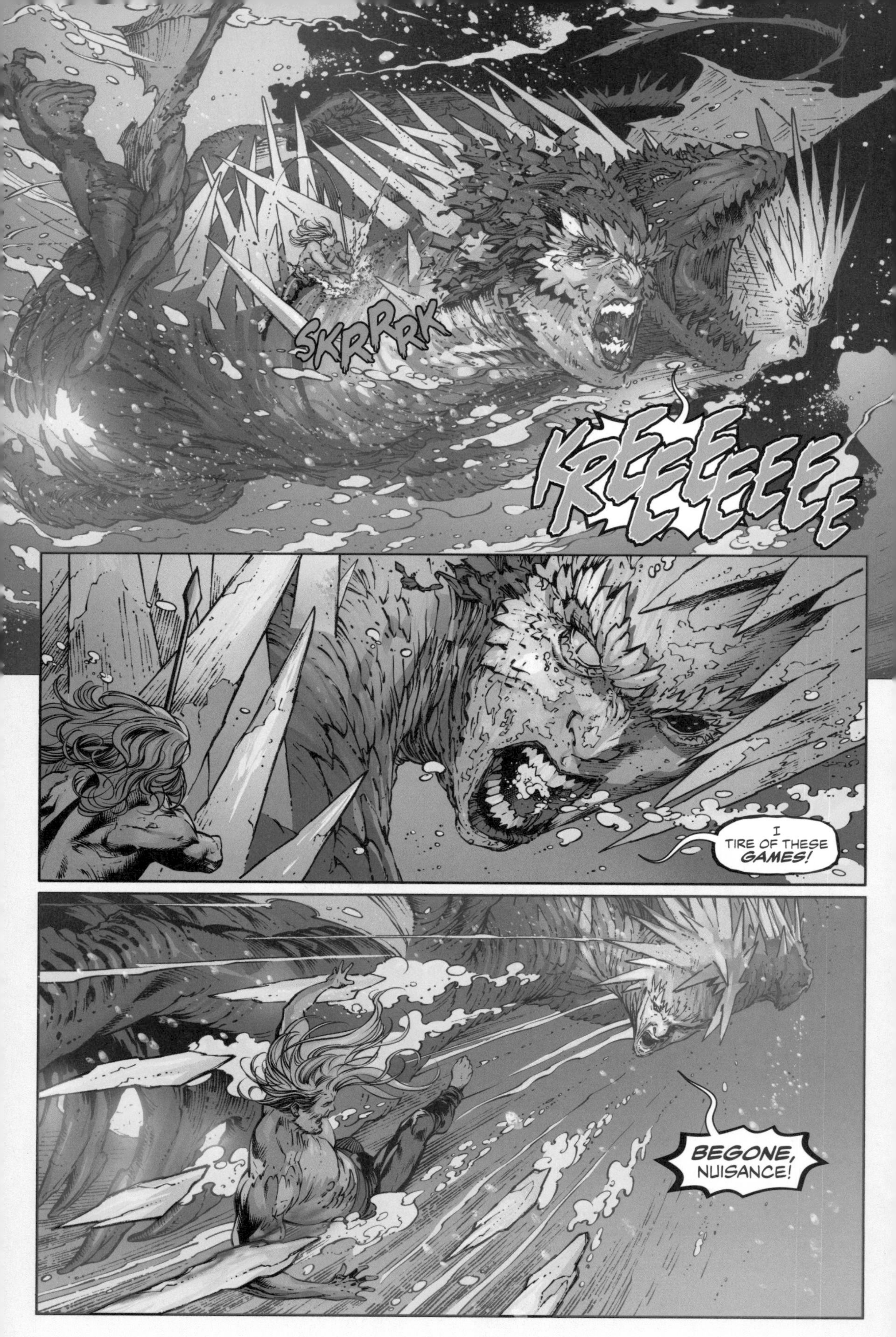
SKRRRK
KREEEEEEEEE
I TIRE OF THESE GAMES!
BEGONE, NUISANCE!

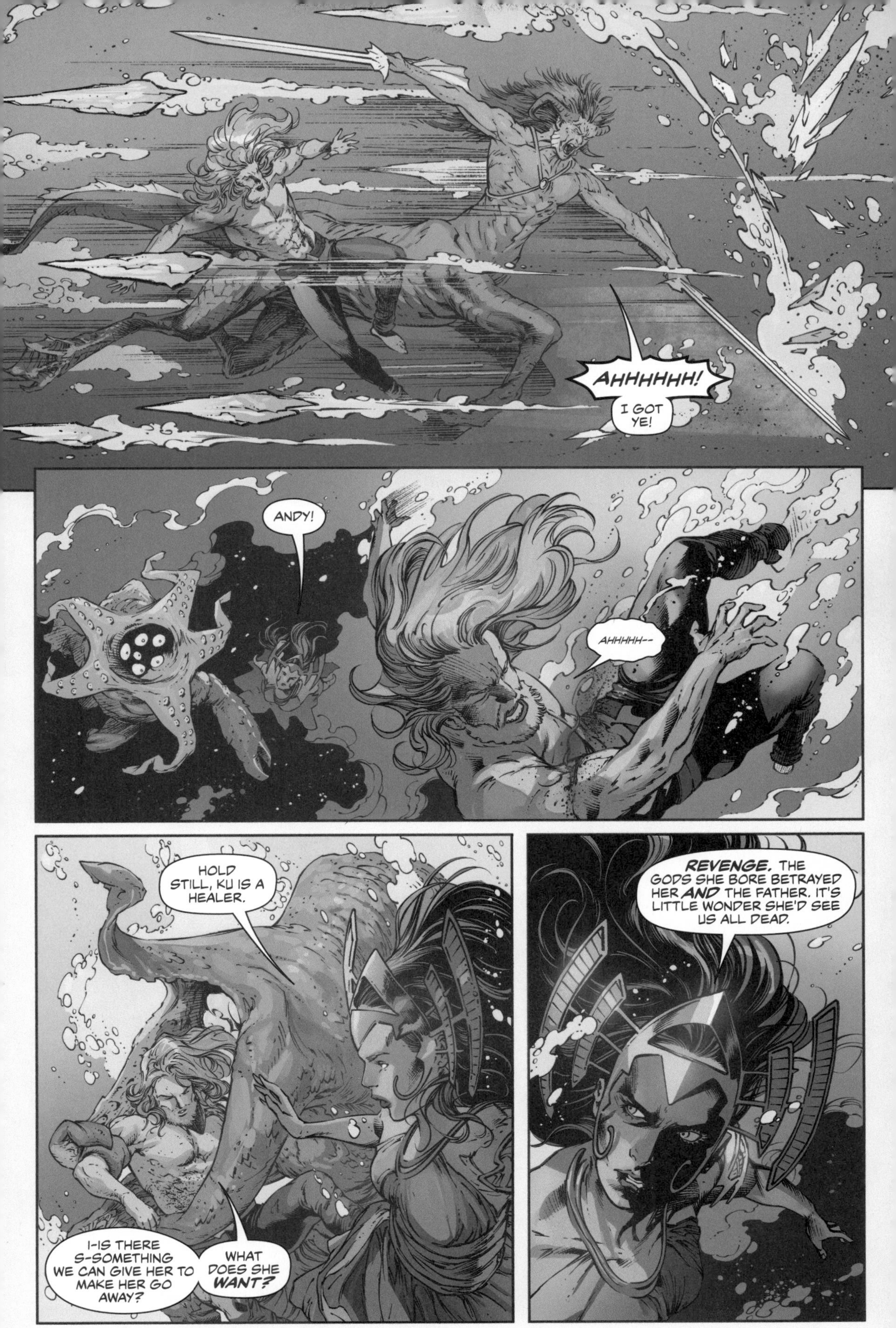
AHHHHHH!
I GOT YE!
ANDY!
AHHHHH--
HOLD STILL, KU IS A HEALER.
I-IS THERE S-SOMETHING WE CAN GIVE HER TO MAKE HER GO AWAY?
WHAT DOES SHE *WANT?*
REVENGE. THE GODS SHE BORE BETRAYED HER *AND* THE FATHER. IT'S LITTLE WONDER SHE'D SEE US ALL DEAD.

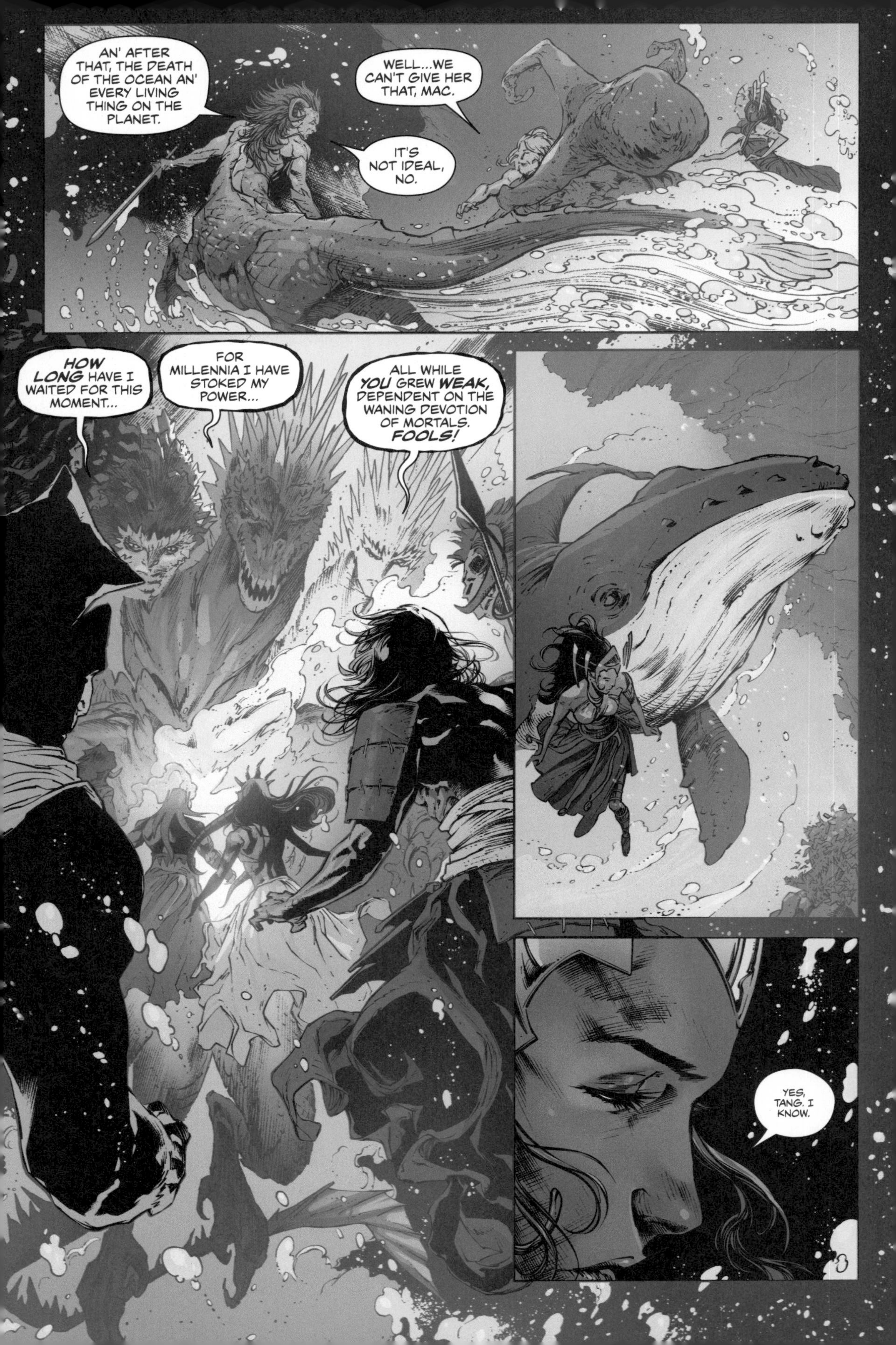
AN' AFTER THAT, THE DEATH OF THE OCEAN AN' EVERY LIVING THING ON THE PLANET.
WELL...WE CAN'T GIVE HER THAT, MAC.
IT'S NOT IDEAL, NO.
HOW LONG HAVE I WAITED FOR THIS MOMENT...
FOR MILLENNIA I HAVE STOKED MY POWER...
ALL WHILE YOU GREW WEAK, DEPENDENT ON THE WANING DEVOTION OF MORTALS. FOOLS!
YES, TANG. I KNOW.

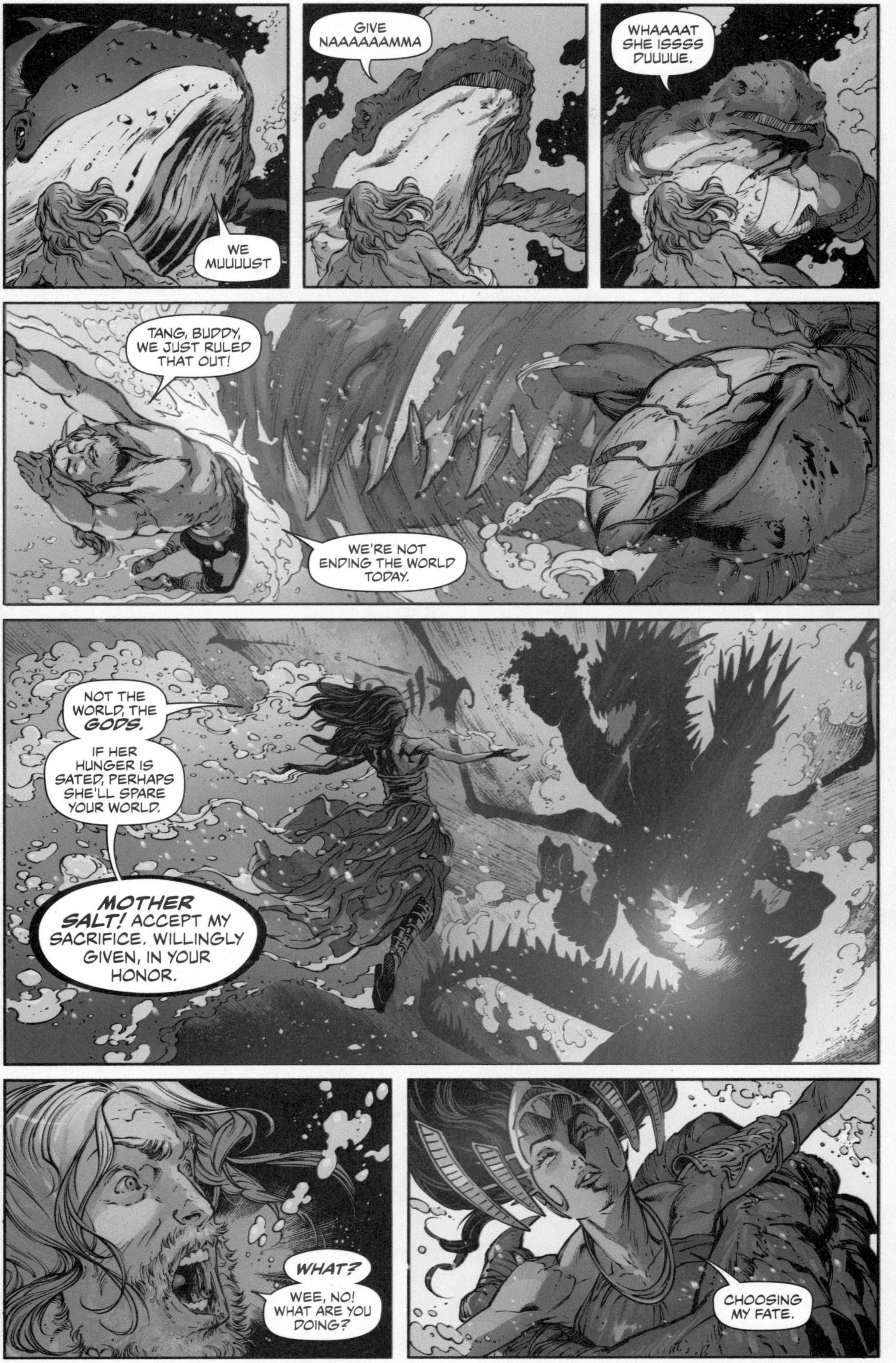
WE MUUUUST
GIVE NAAAAAAAMMA
WHAAAAT SHE ISSSS DUUUUE.
TANG, BUDDY, WE JUST RULED THAT OUT!
WE'RE NOT ENDING THE WORLD TODAY.
NOT THE WORLD, THE *GODS.*
IF HER HUNGER IS SATED, PERHAPS SHE'LL SPARE YOUR WORLD.
MOTHER SALT! ACCEPT MY SACRIFICE. WILLINGLY GIVEN, IN YOUR HONOR.
WHAT?
WEE, NO! WHAT ARE YOU DOING?
CHOOSING MY FATE.

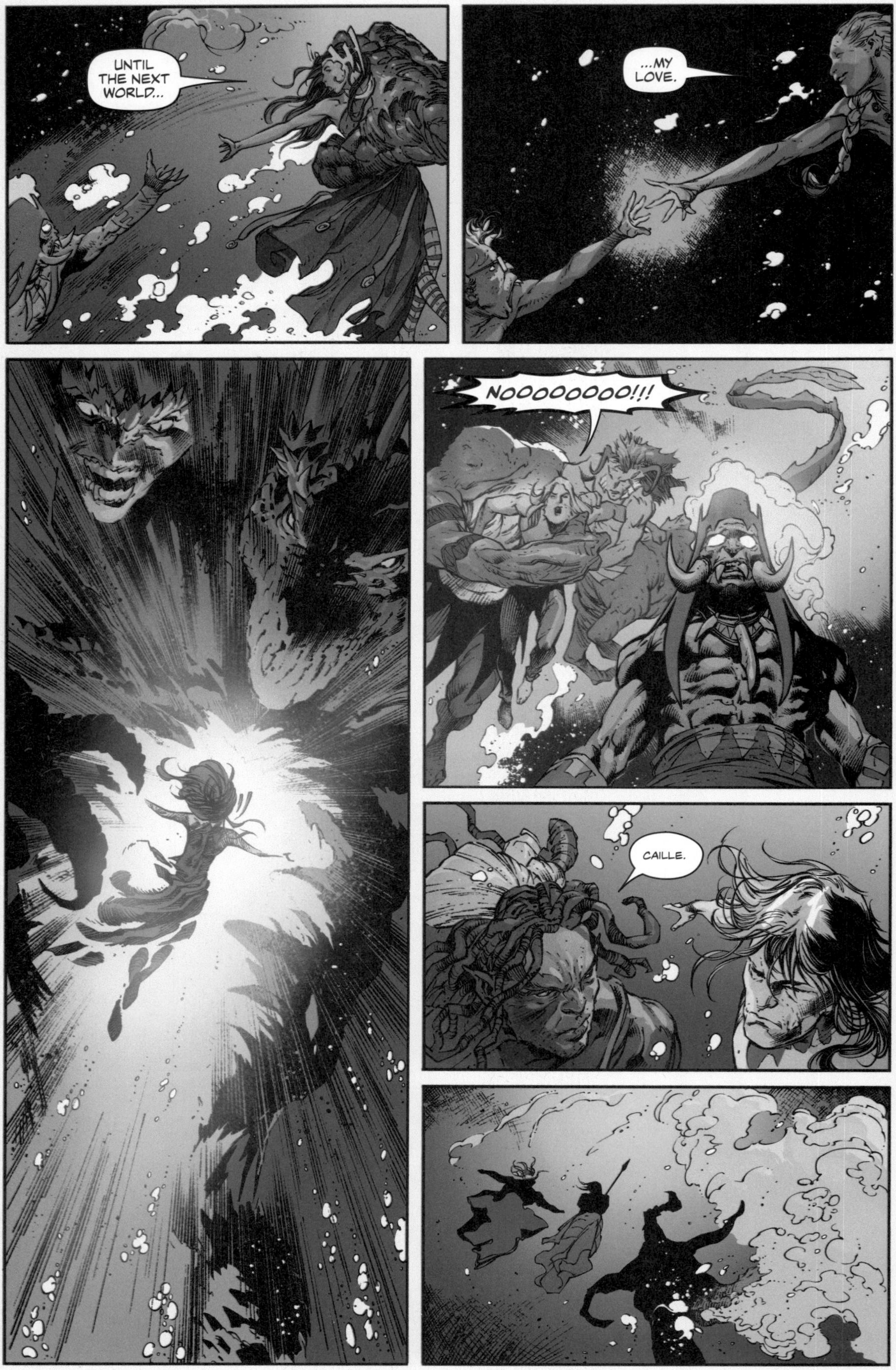
UNTIL THE NEXT WORLD...
...MY LOVE.
NOOOOOOOO!!!
CAILLE.

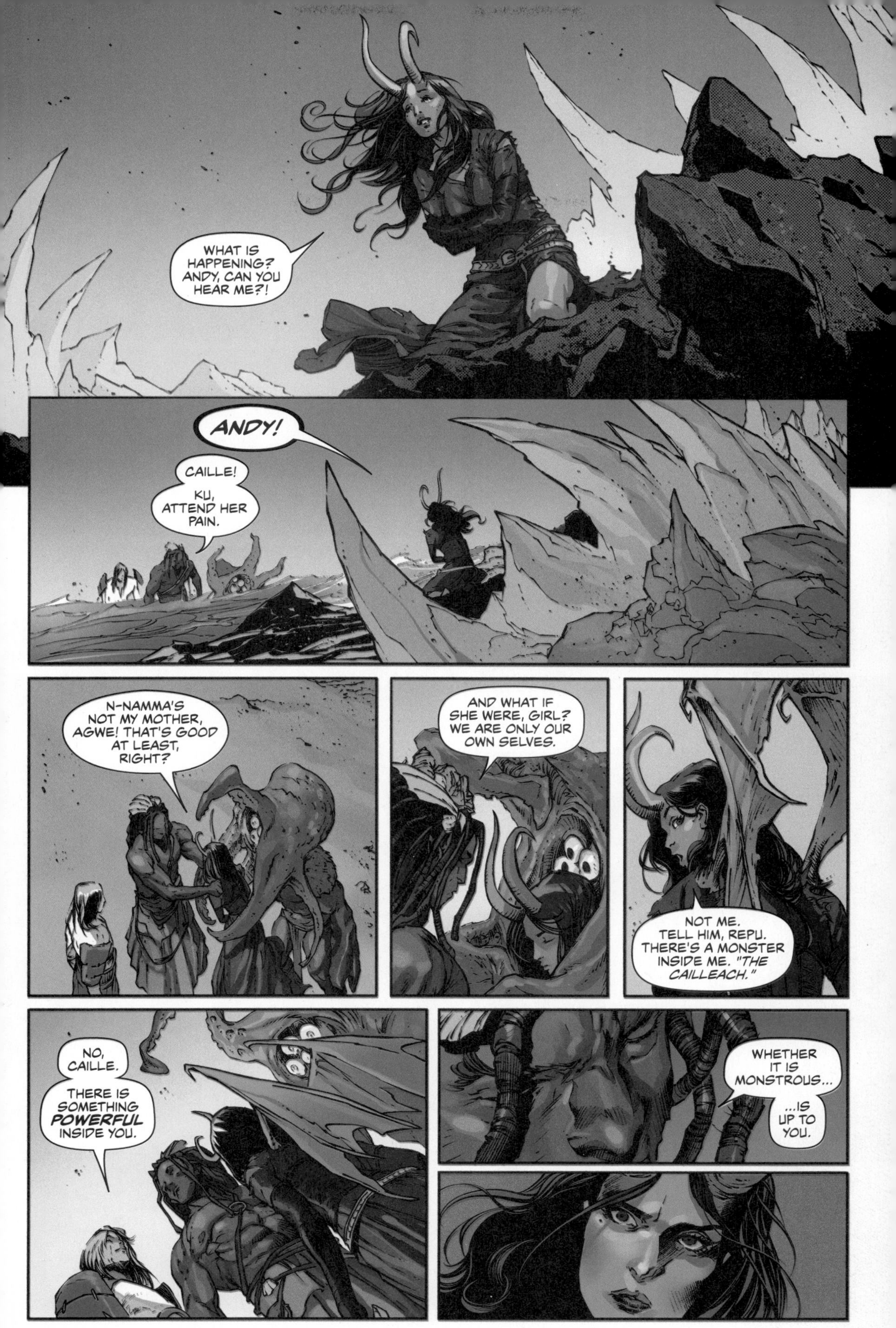
WHAT IS HAPPENING? ANDY, CAN YOU HEAR ME?!
ANDY!
CAILLE!
KU, ATTEND HER PAIN.
N-NAMMA'S NOT MY MOTHER, AGWE! THAT'S GOOD AT LEAST, RIGHT?
AND WHAT IF SHE WERE, GIRL? WE ARE ONLY OUR OWN SELVES.
NOT ME. TELL HIM, REPU. THERE'S A MONSTER INSIDE ME. "THE CAILLEACH."
NO, CAILLE.
THERE IS SOMETHING POWERFUL INSIDE YOU.
WHETHER IT IS MONSTROUS...
...IS UP TO YOU.

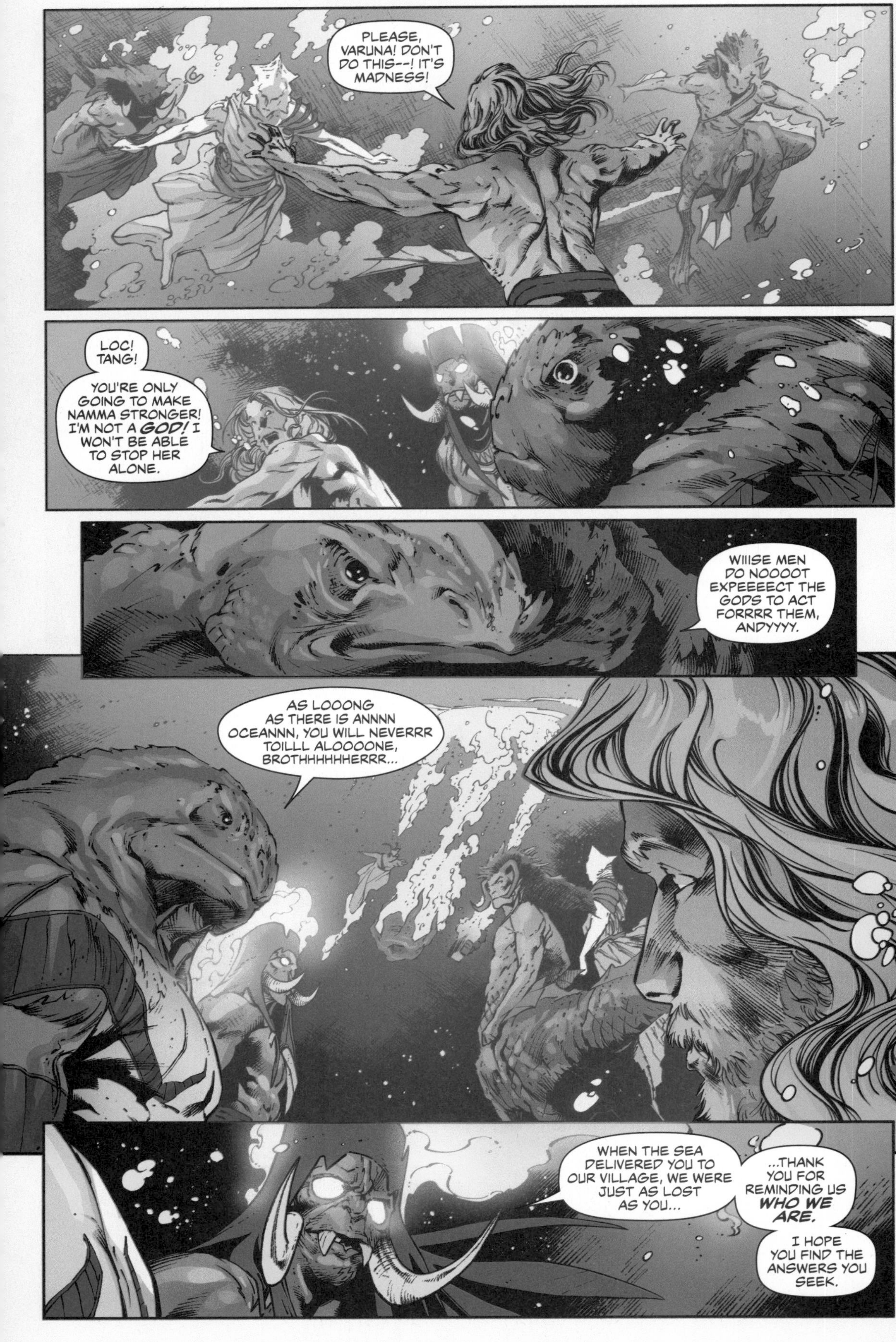
PLEASE, VARUNA! DON'T DO THIS--! IT'S MADNESS!
LOC! TANG!
YOU'RE ONLY GOING TO MAKE NAMMA STRONGER! I'M NOT A GOD! I WON'T BE ABLE TO STOP HER ALONE.
WIIISE MEN DO NOOOOT EXPEEEECT THE GODS TO ACT FORRRR THEM, ANDYYYY.
AS LOOONG AS THERE IS ANNNN OCEANNN, YOU WILL NEVERRR TOILLL ALOOOONE, BROTHHHHHHHERRR...
WHEN THE SEA DELIVERED YOU TO OUR VILLAGE, WE WERE JUST AS LOST AS YOU...
...THANK YOU FOR REMINDING US WHO WE ARE.
I HOPE YOU FIND THE ANSWERS YOU SEEK.

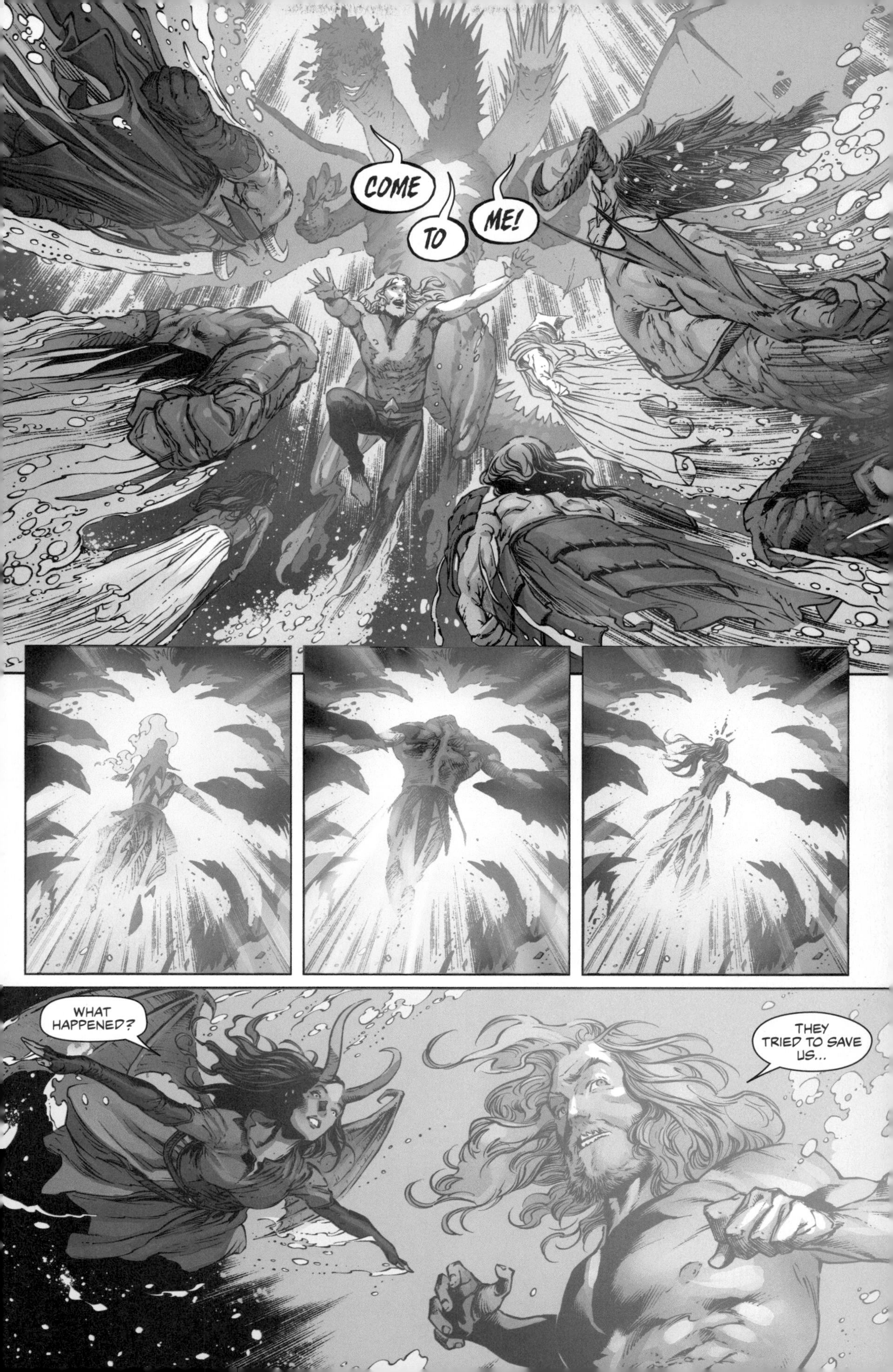
COME
TO
ME!
WHAT HAPPENED?
THEY TRIED TO SAVE US...

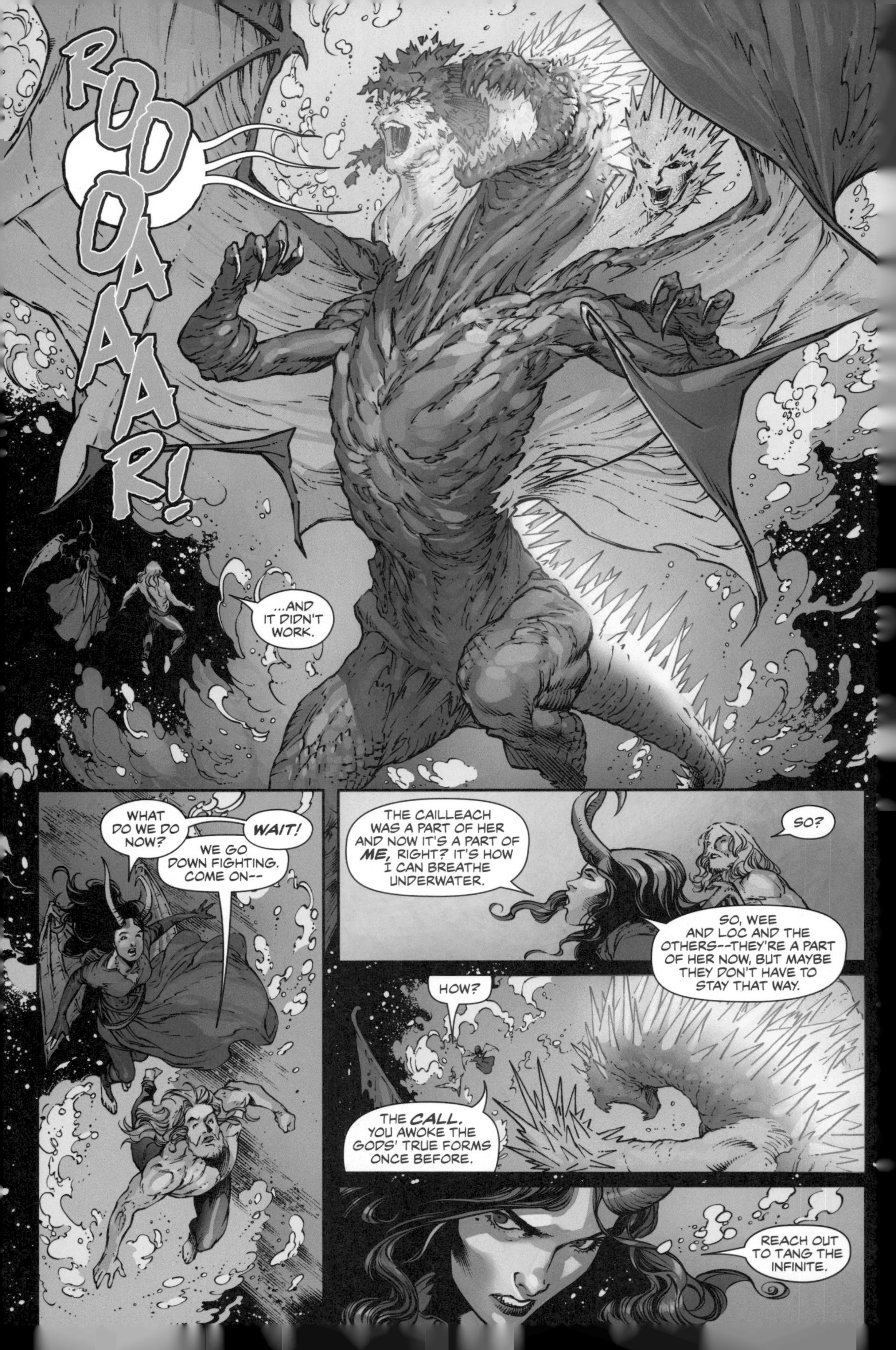
ROOOAAAR!
...AND IT DIDN'T WORK.
WHAT DO WE DO NOW?
WE GO DOWN FIGHTING. COME ON--
WAIT!
THE CAILLEACH WAS A PART OF HER AND NOW IT'S A PART OF ME, RIGHT? IT'S HOW I CAN BREATHE UNDERWATER.
SO?
SO, WEE AND LOC AND THE OTHERS--THEY'RE A PART OF HER NOW, BUT MAYBE THEY DON'T HAVE TO STAY THAT WAY.
HOW?
THE CALL. YOU AWOKE THE GODS' TRUE FORMS ONCE BEFORE.
REACH OUT TO TANG THE INFINITE.

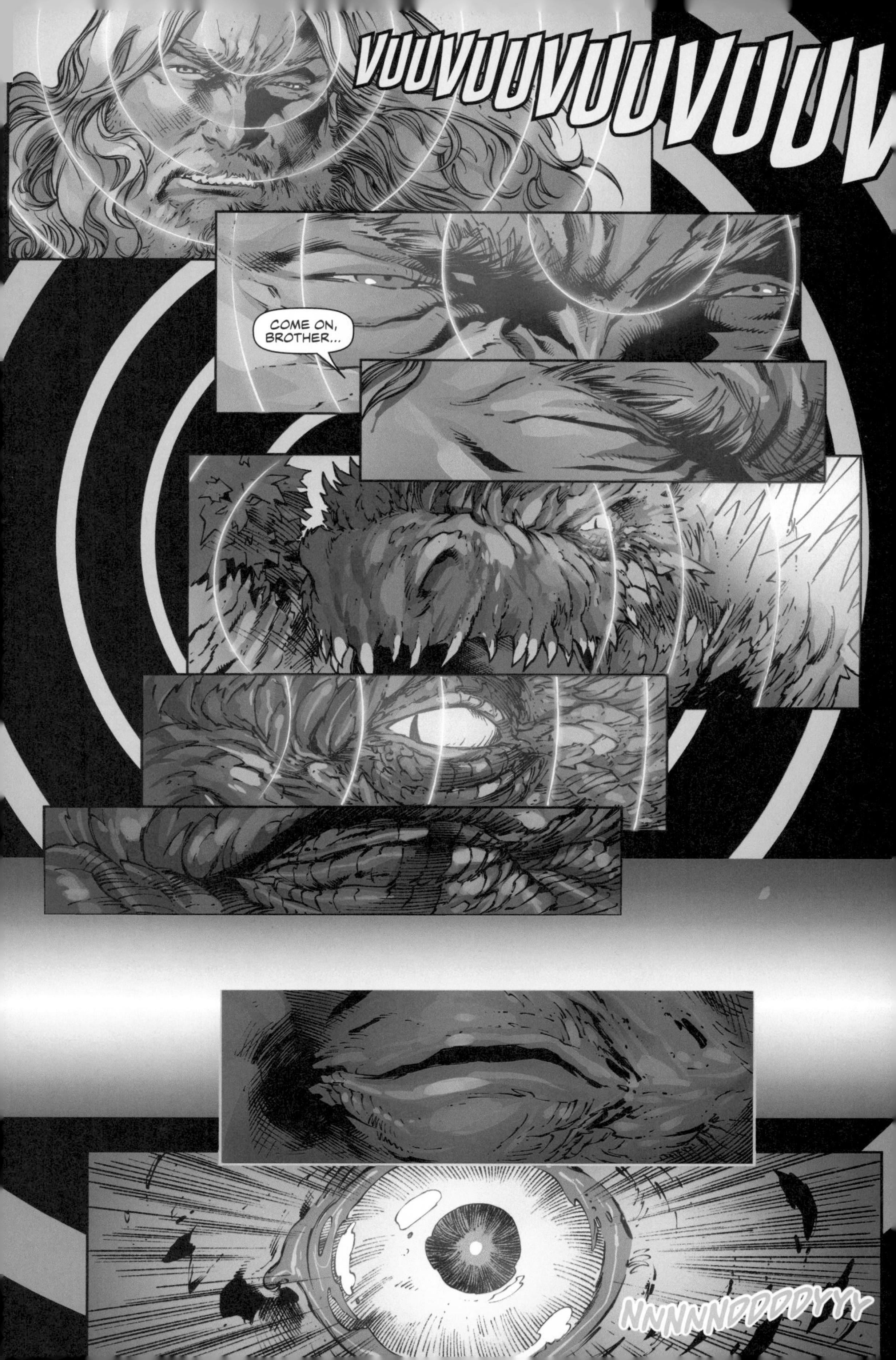
VUUVUUVUUVUUV
COME ON, BROTHER...
NNNNNDDDDYYY

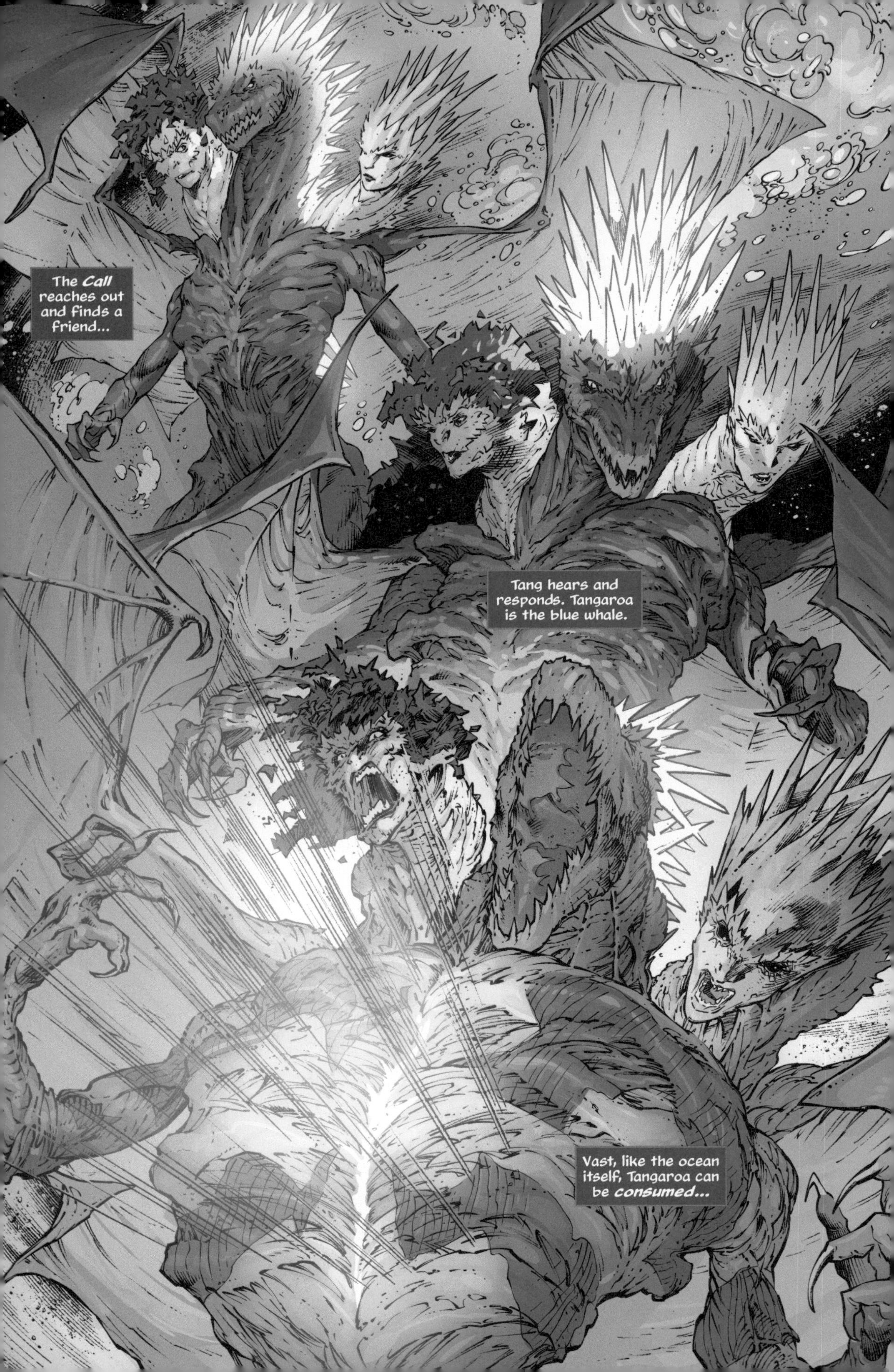
The *Call* reaches out and finds a friend...
Tang hears and responds. Tangaroa is the blue whale.
Vast, like the ocean itself, Tangaroa can be *consumed*...

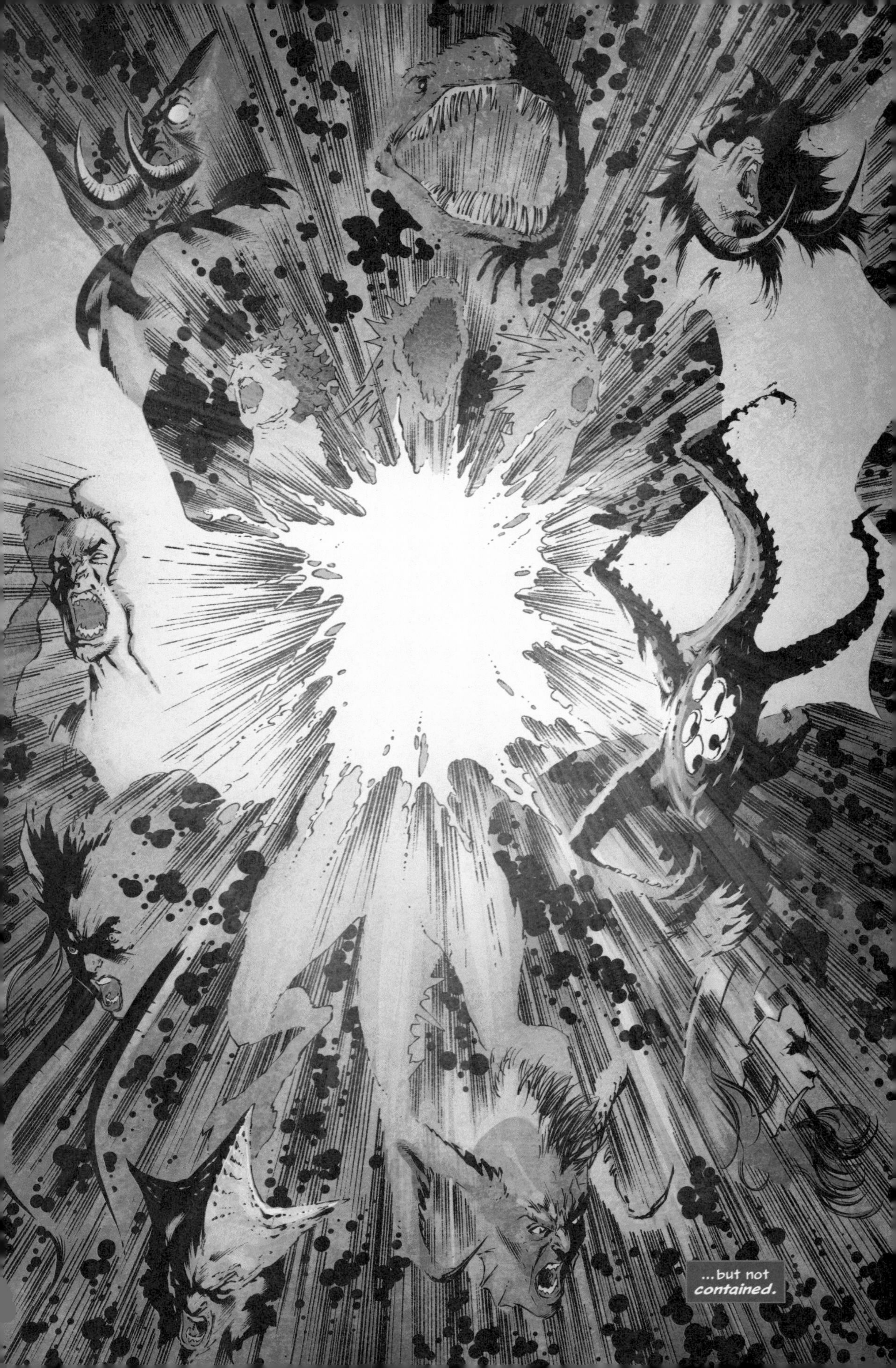
...but not contained.

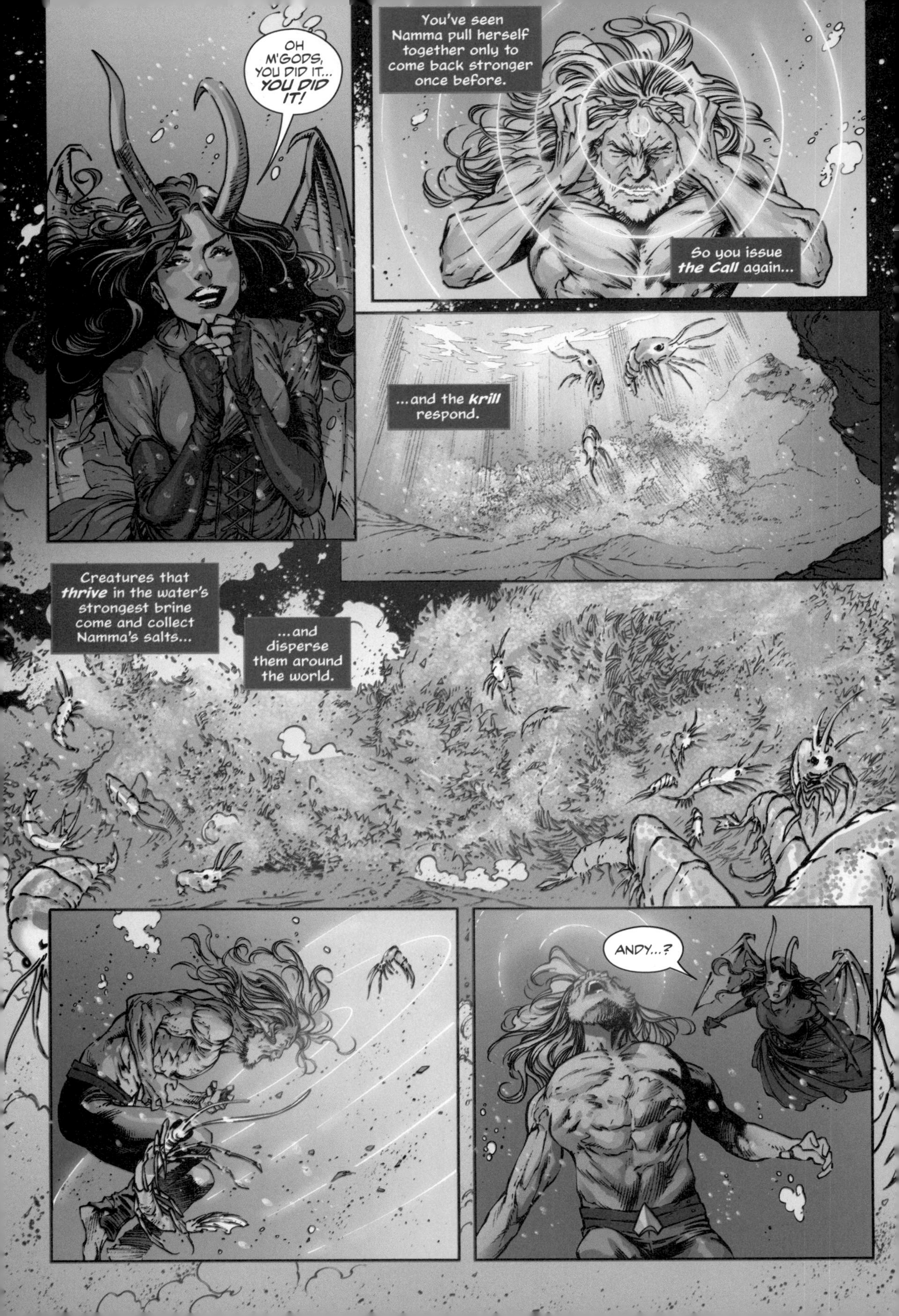
OH M'GODS, YOU DID IT... YOU DID IT!
You've seen Namma pull herself together only to come back stronger once before.
So you issue the Call again...
...and the krill respond.
Creatures that thrive in the water's strongest brine come and collect Namma's salts...
...and disperse them around the world.
ANDY...?

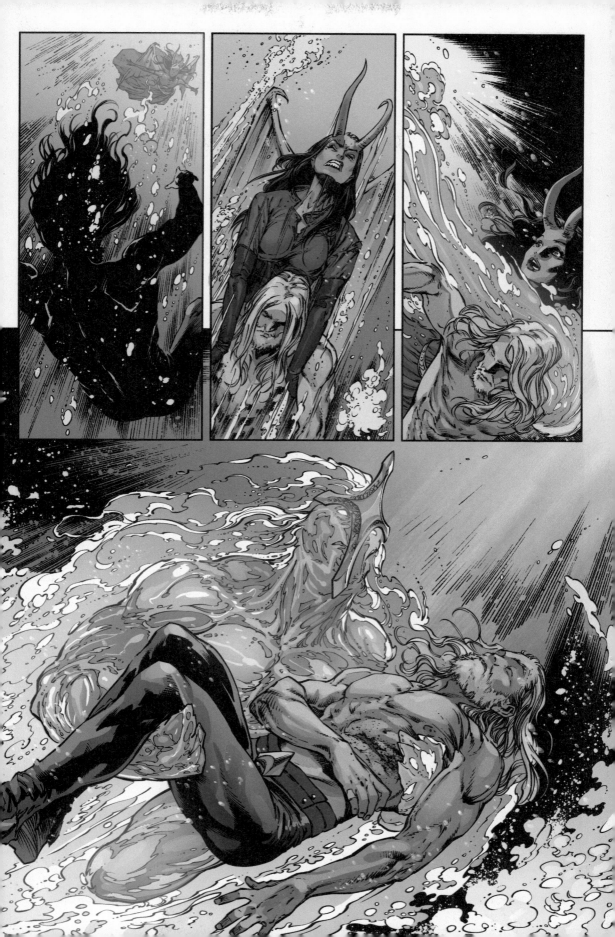

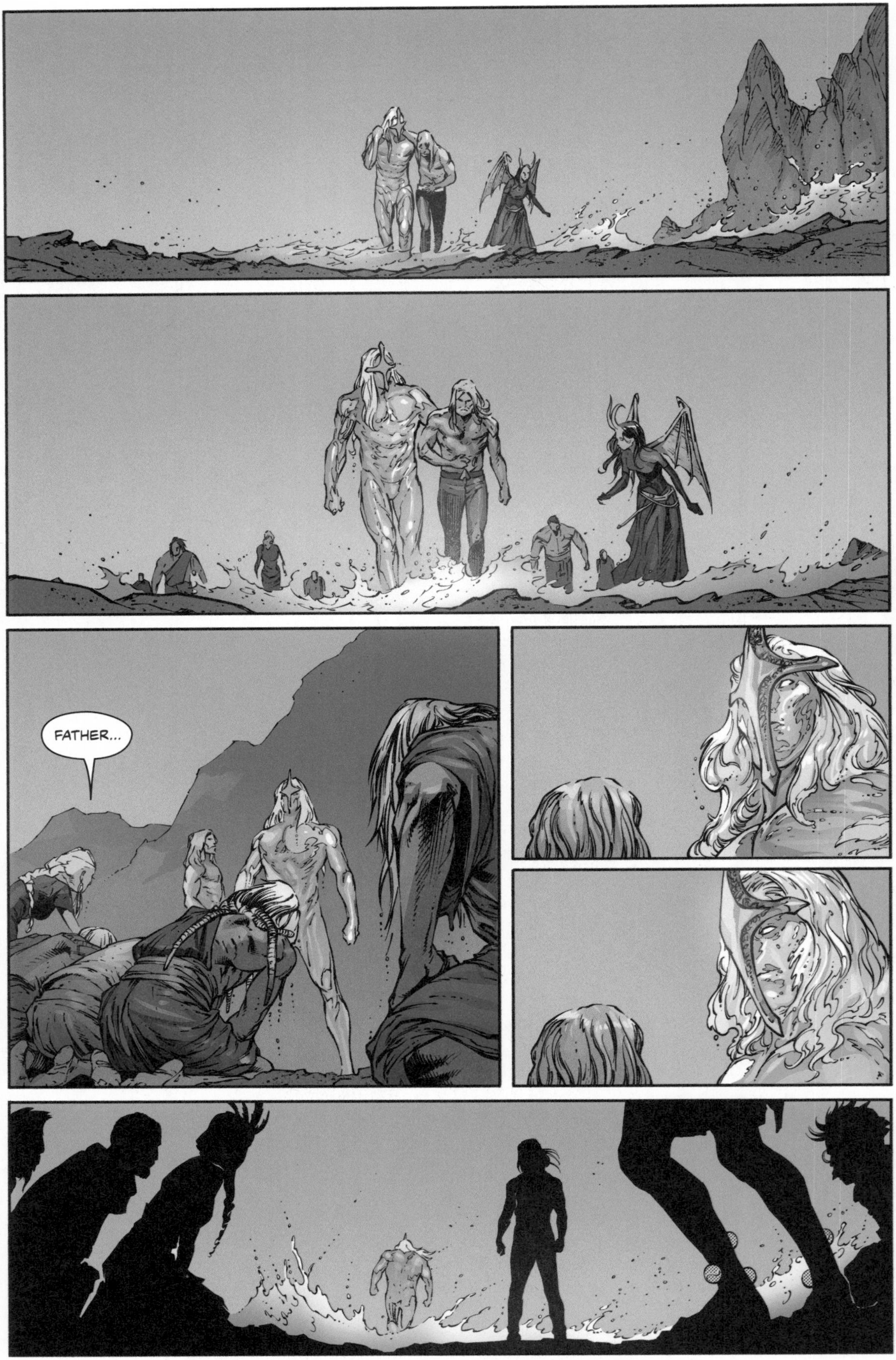
FATHER...

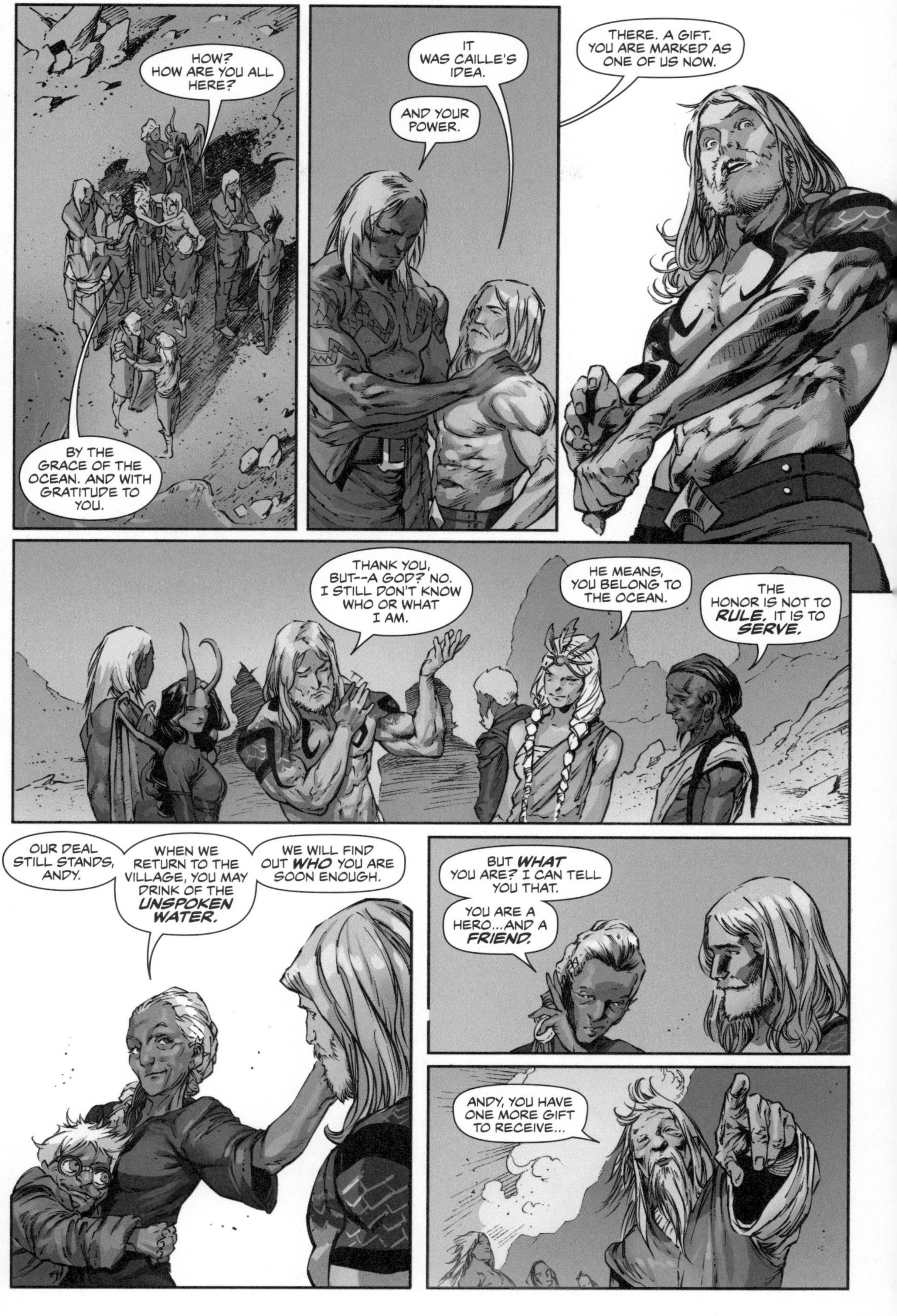
HOW? HOW ARE YOU ALL HERE?
BY THE GRACE OF THE OCEAN. AND WITH GRATITUDE TO YOU.
IT WAS CAILLE'S IDEA.
AND YOUR POWER.
THERE. A GIFT. YOU ARE MARKED AS ONE OF US NOW.
THANK YOU, BUT--A GOD? NO. I STILL DON'T KNOW WHO OR WHAT I AM.
HE MEANS, YOU BELONG TO THE OCEAN.
THE HONOR IS NOT TO RULE. IT IS TO SERVE.
OUR DEAL STILL STANDS, ANDY.
WHEN WE RETURN TO THE VILLAGE, YOU MAY DRINK OF THE UNSPOKEN WATER.
WE WILL FIND OUT WHO YOU ARE SOON ENOUGH.
BUT WHAT YOU ARE? I CAN TELL YOU THAT.
YOU ARE A HERO...AND A FRIEND.
ANDY, YOU HAVE ONE MORE GIFT TO RECEIVE...

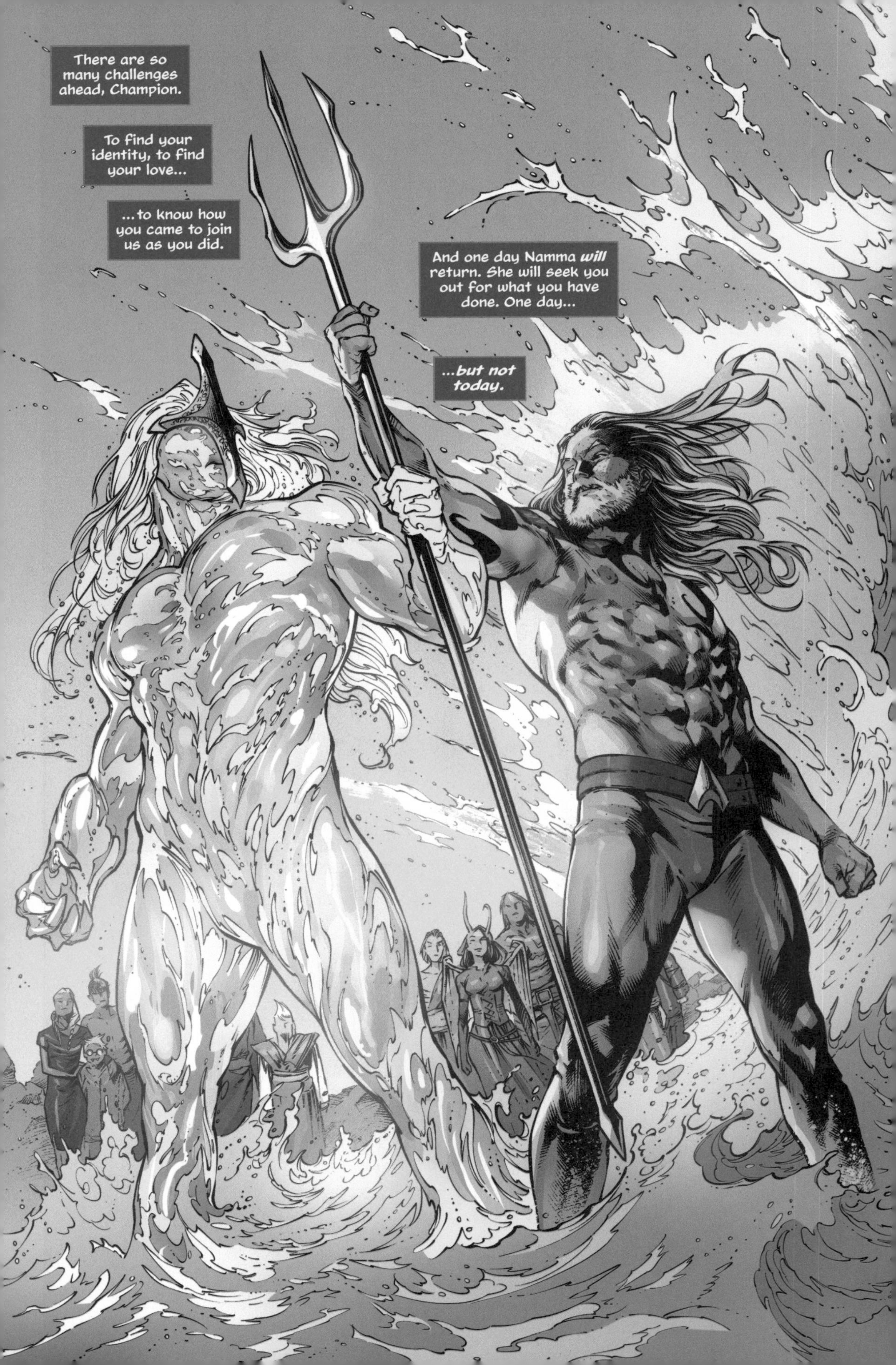
There are so many challenges ahead, Champion.
To find your identity, to find your love...
...to know how you came to join us as you did.
And one day Namma *will* return. She will seek you out for what you have done. One day...
...but not today.

VARIANT COVER GALLERY

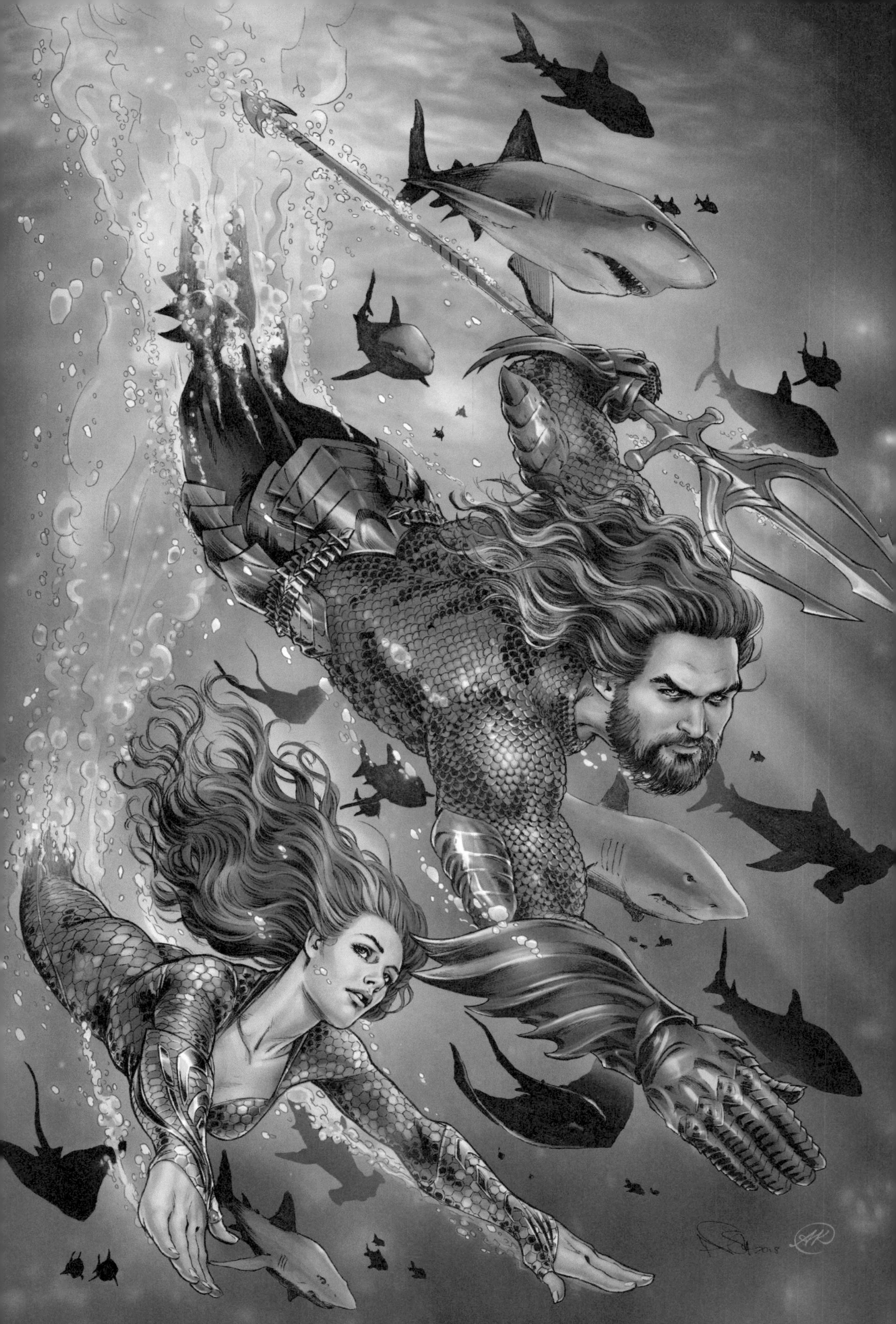

AQUAMAN #43 variant cover by **NICOLA SCOTT** and **ANNETTE KWOK**

AQUAMAN #44 variant cover by **RAFAEL ALBUQUERQUE**

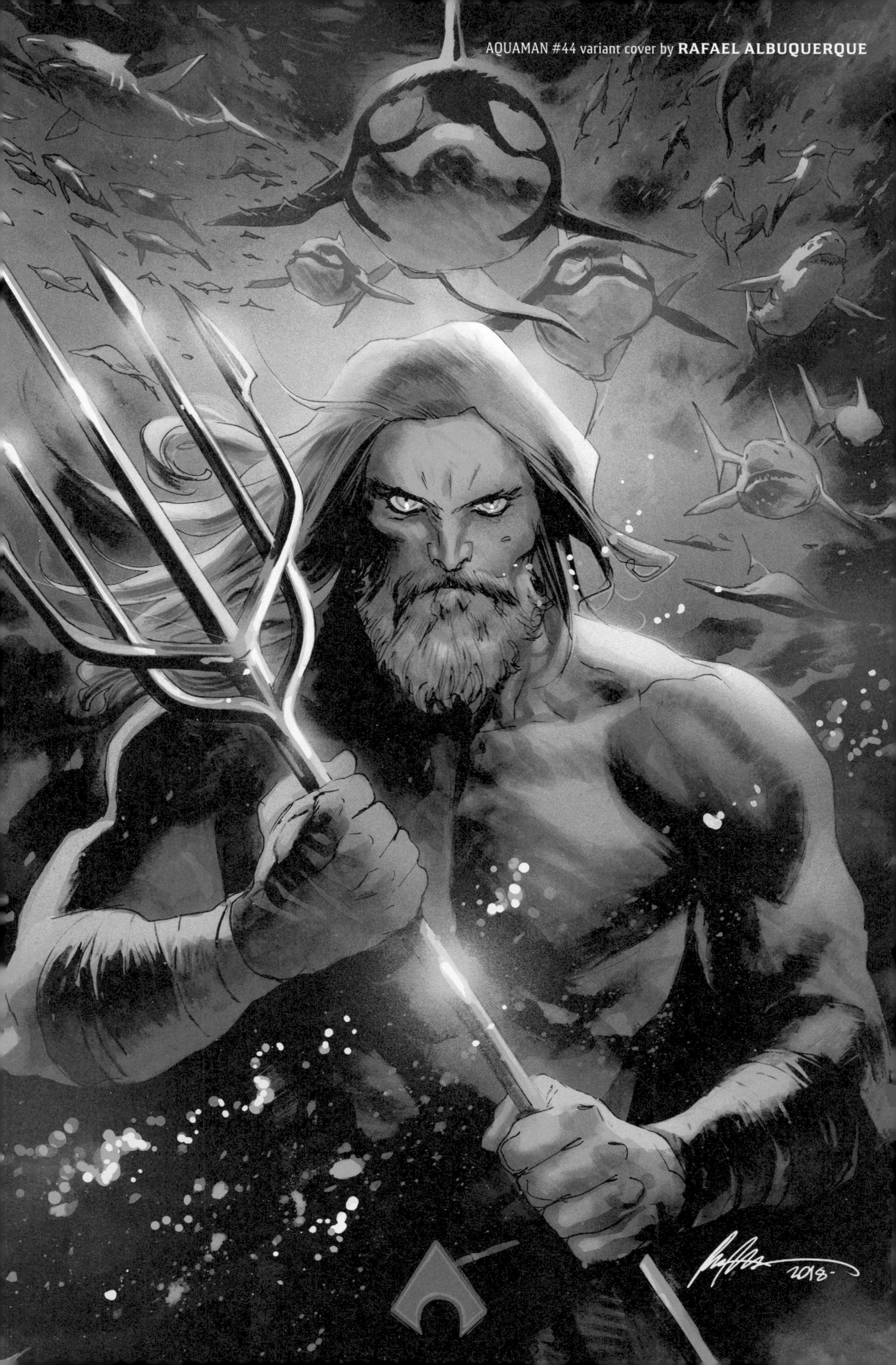

AQUAMAN #45 variant cover by
CULLY HAMNER

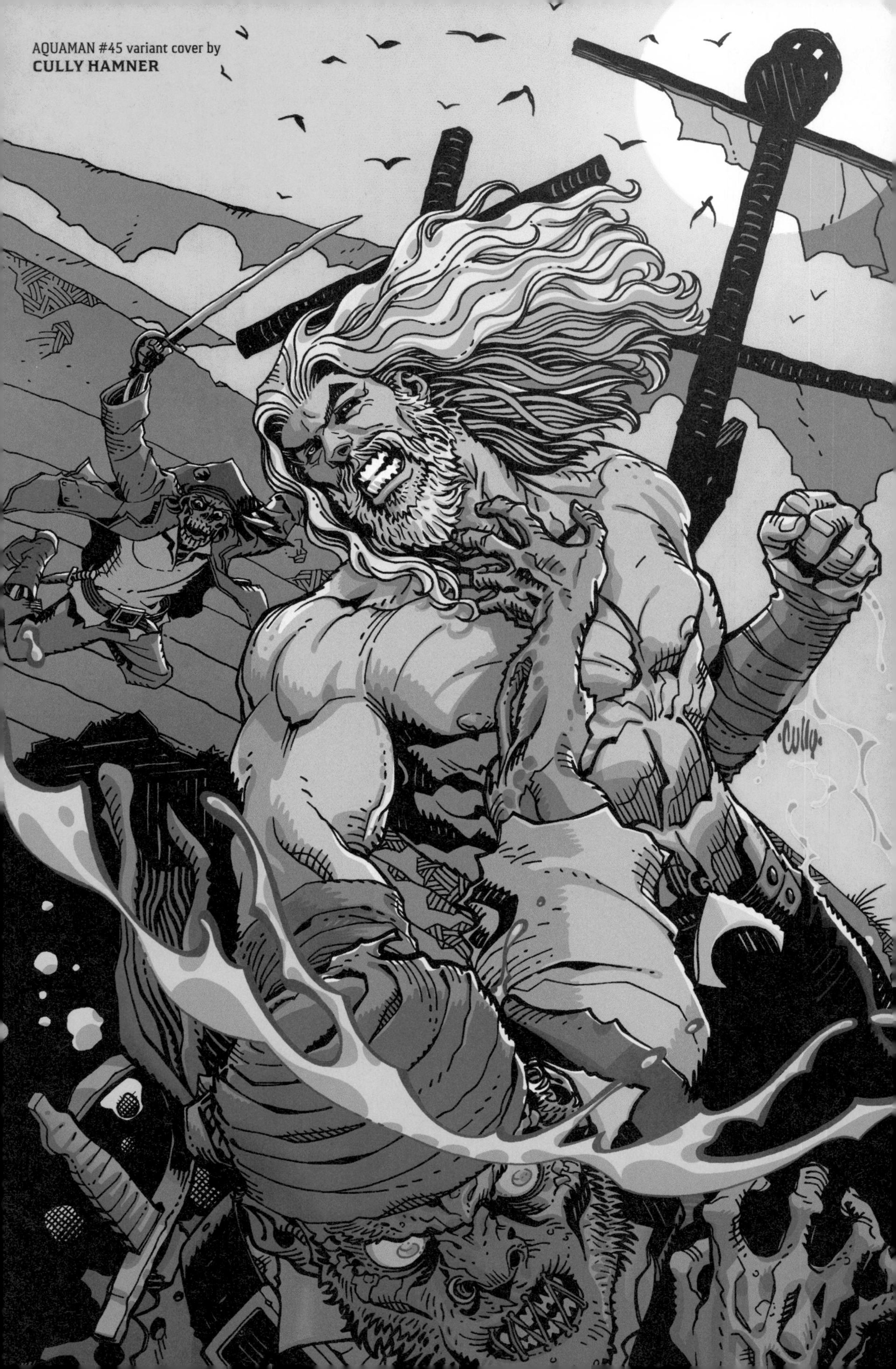
CULLY

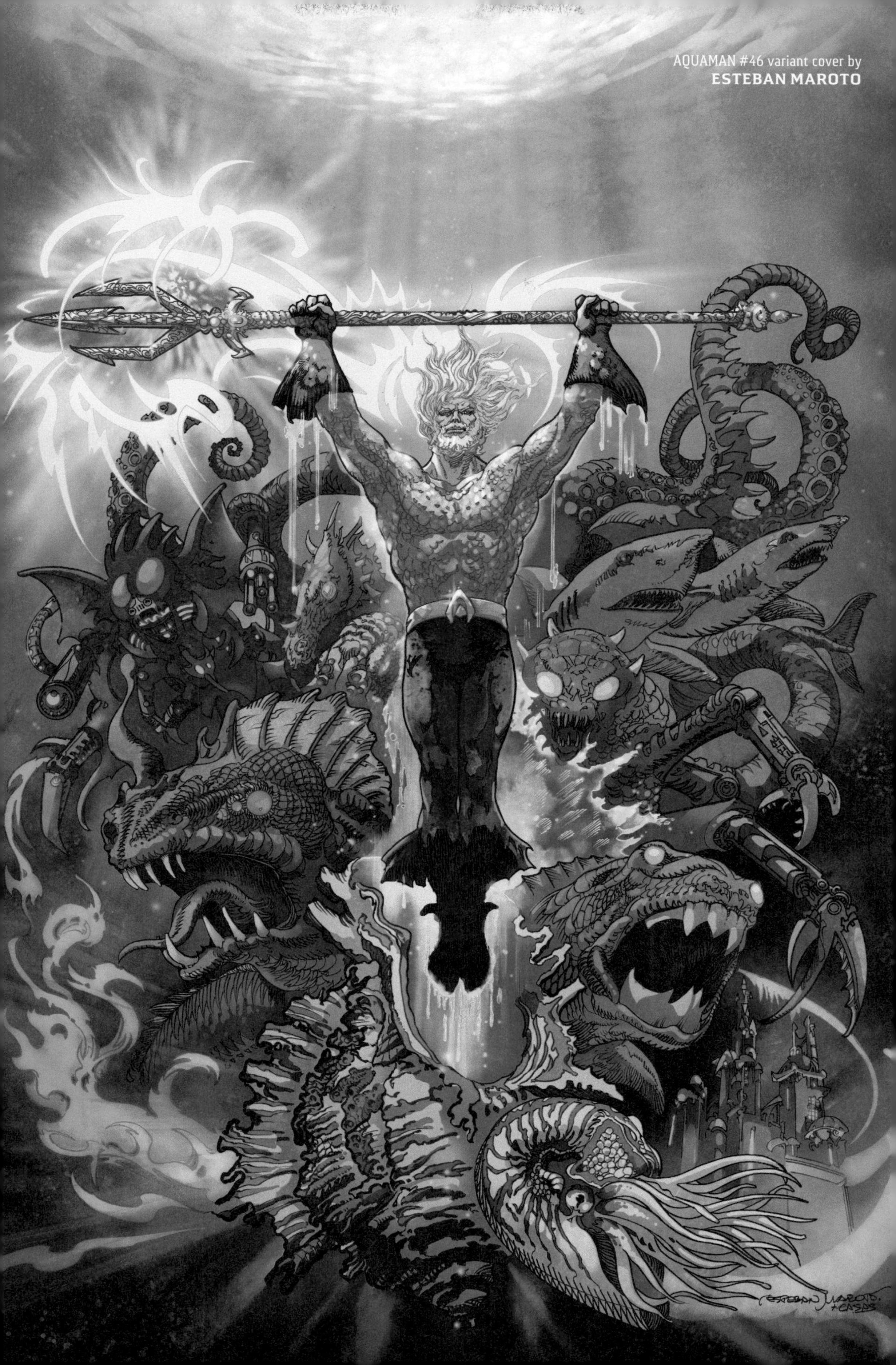

AQUAMAN #46 variant cover by
ESTEBAN MAROTO

AQUAMAN #47 variant cover by **JOSHUA MIDDLETON**

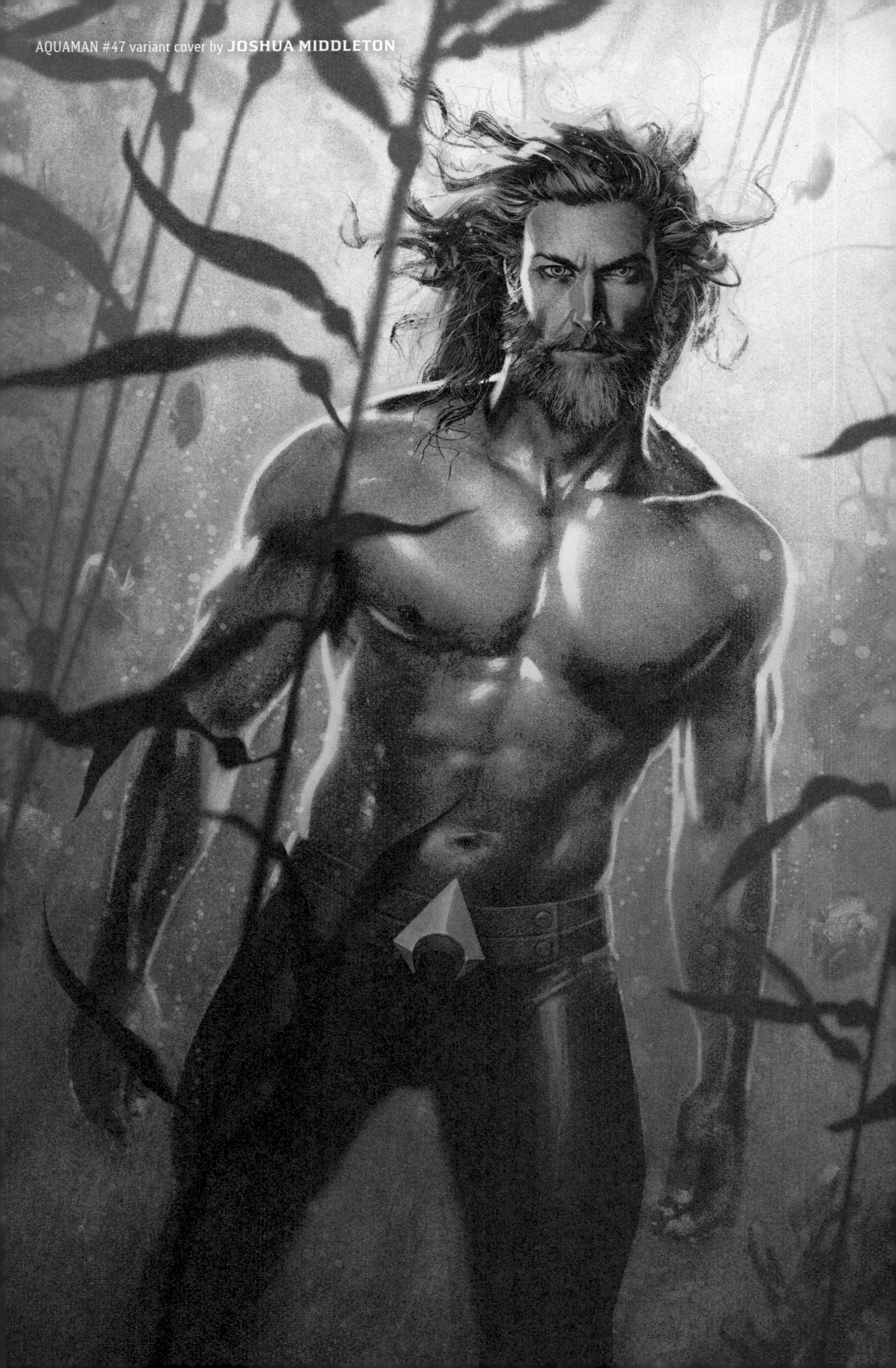

SKETCHBOOK BY **ROBSON ROCHA**

INTERIORS
PENCILLER
TITLE
INKER
ISSUE #
PAGE#
MONTH
ROBSON

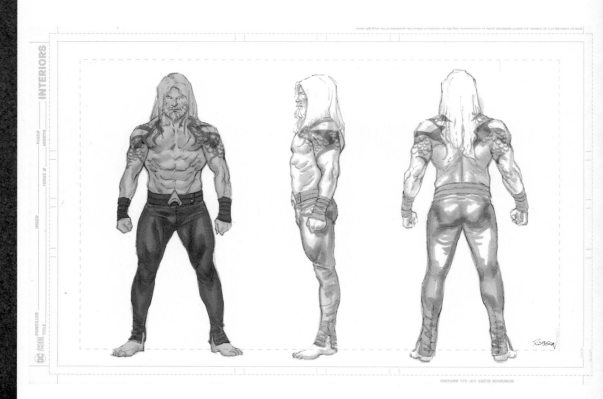

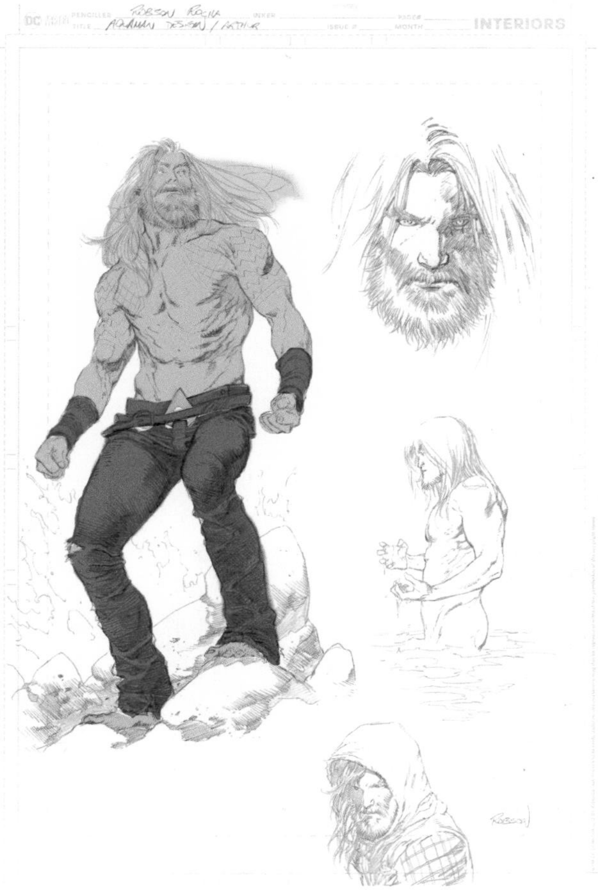
PENCILLER ROBSON ROCHA
TITLE AQUAMAN DESIGN / ARTHUR
INTERIORS
ROBSON

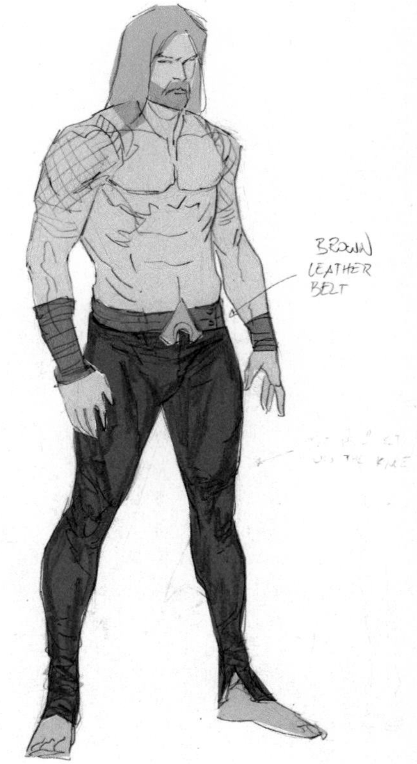
BROWN
LEATHER
BELT

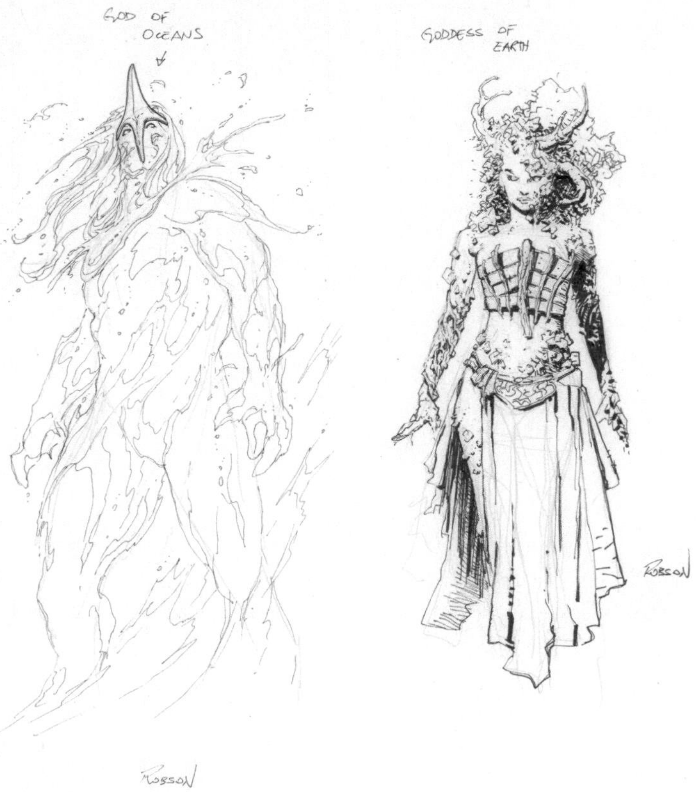
GOD OF OCEANS
GODDESS OF EARTH
ROBSON
ROBSON

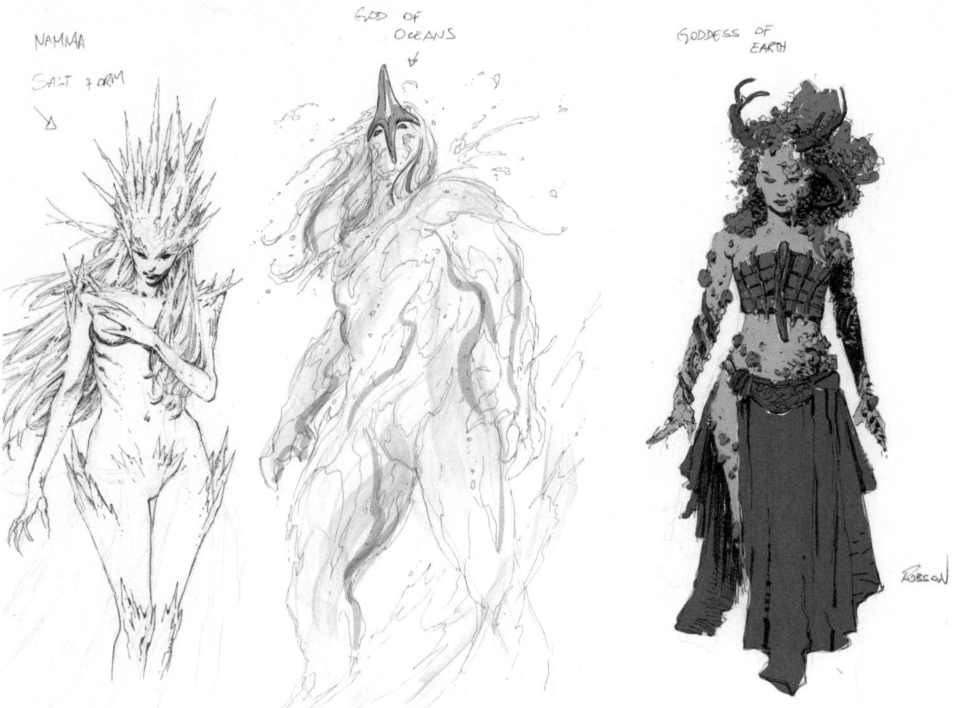
NAMMA
SALT FORM
GOD OF OCEANS
GODDESS OF EARTH
ROBSON
ROBSON

NAMMA'S DRAGON FORM

GOD OF WIND

OPEN CHEST

GODDESS OF FIRE →

GOD OF SKY

Robson

Robson

Robson

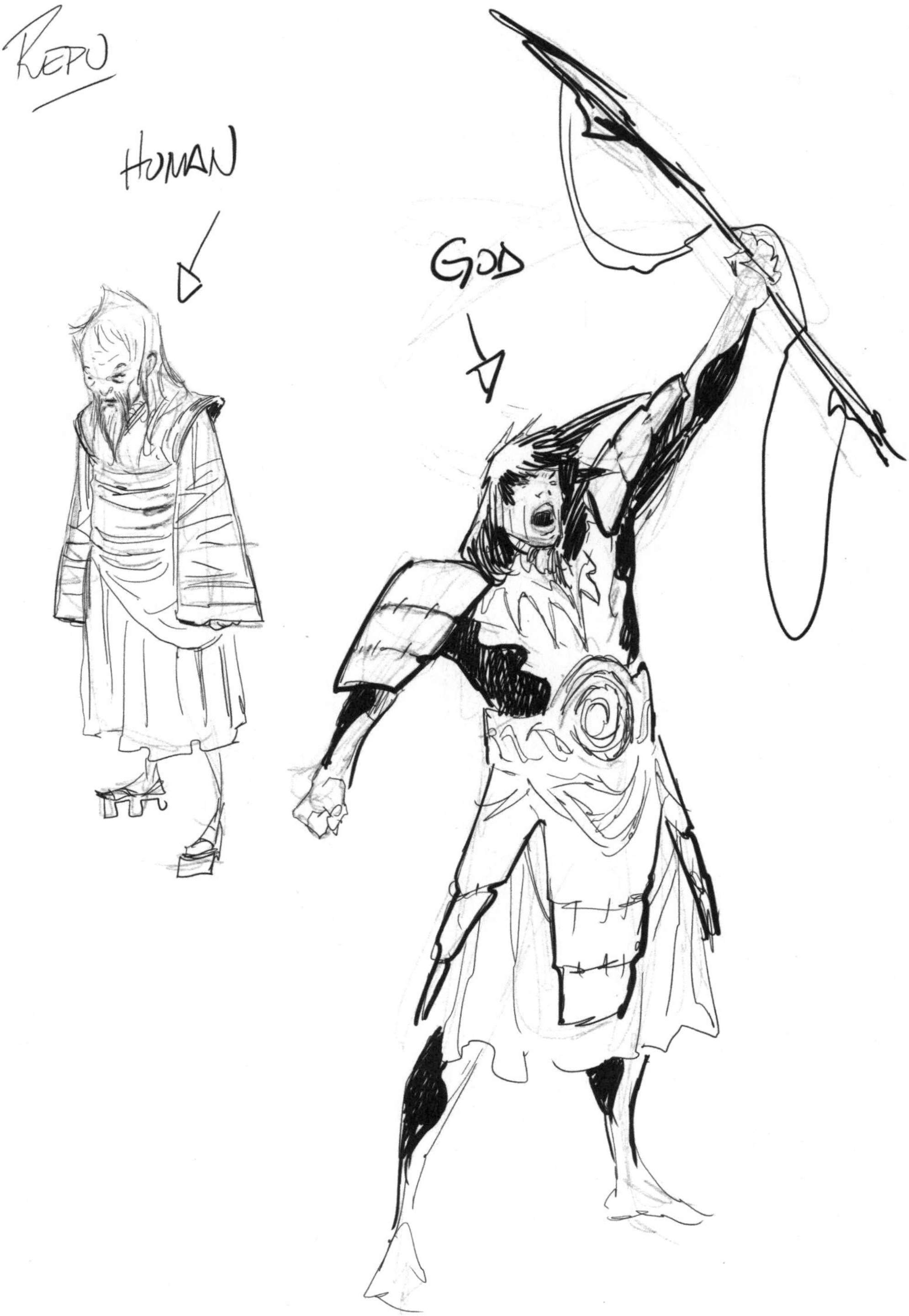
REPU
HUMAN
GOD

VARUNA
HUMAN
↙

GOD

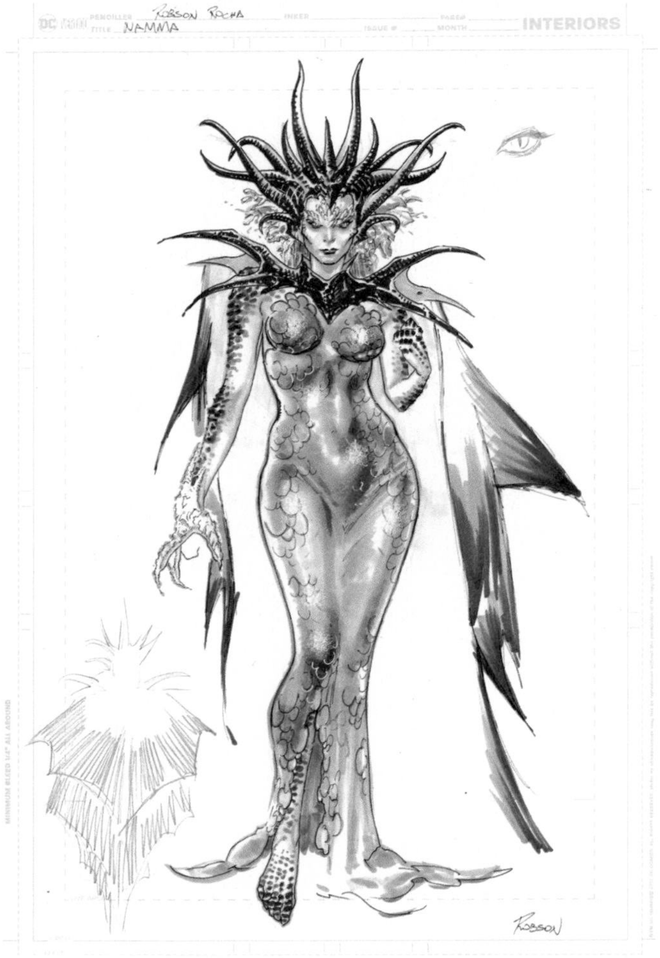
PENCILLER ROBSON ROCHA
TITLE NAMMA
INTERIORS
ROBSON

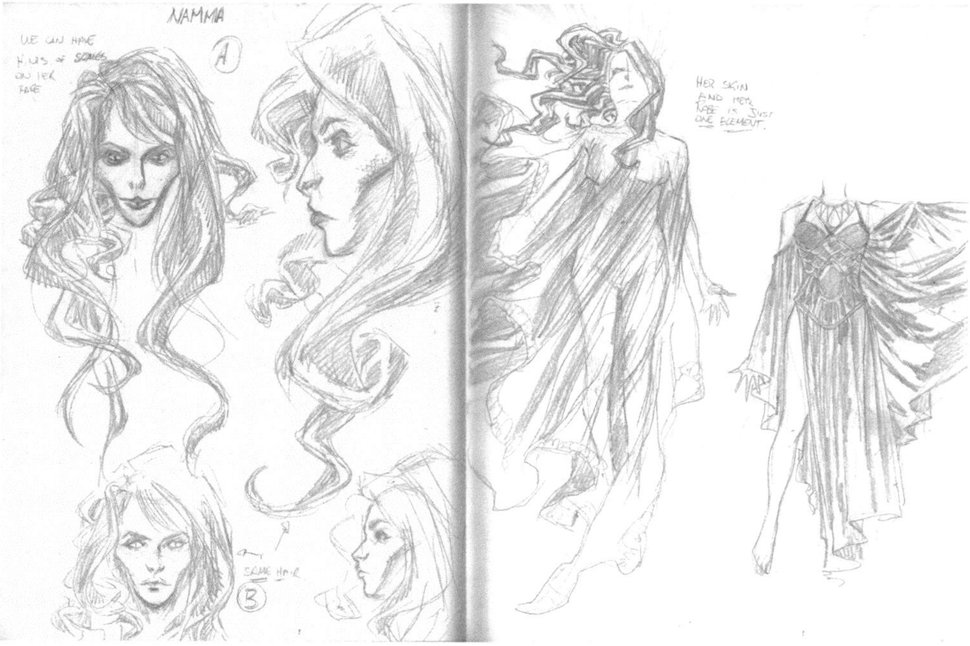
NAMMA
WE CAN HAVE HINTS OF SCALES ON HER FACE
A
HER SKIN AND HER ROBE IS JUST ONE ELEMENT.
SAME HAIR
B

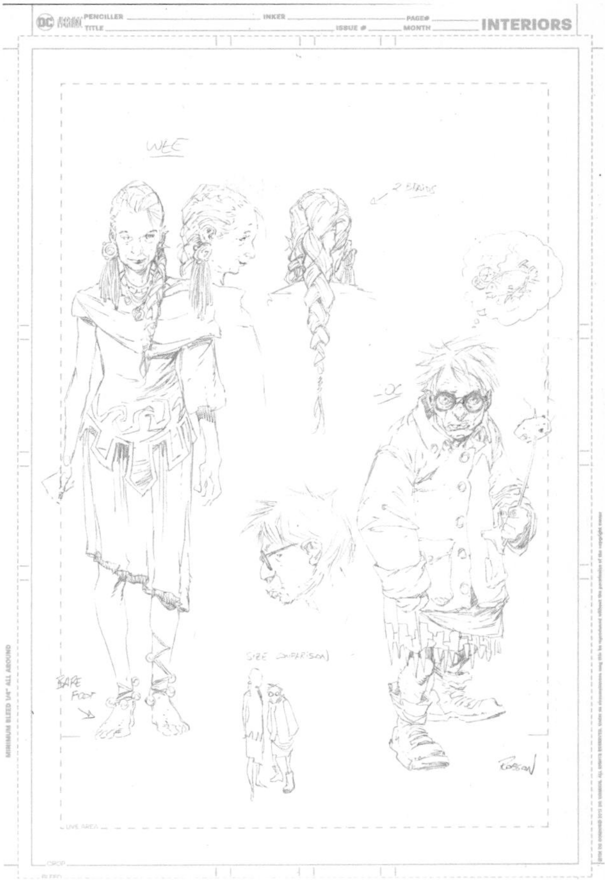
PENCILLER
INKER
PAGE#
TITLE
ISSUE #
MONTH
INTERIORS
WEE
2 BRAIDS
LOC
BARE FOOT
SIZE COMPARISON
MINIMUM BLEED 1/4" ALL AROUND
LIVE AREA
CROP
BLEED

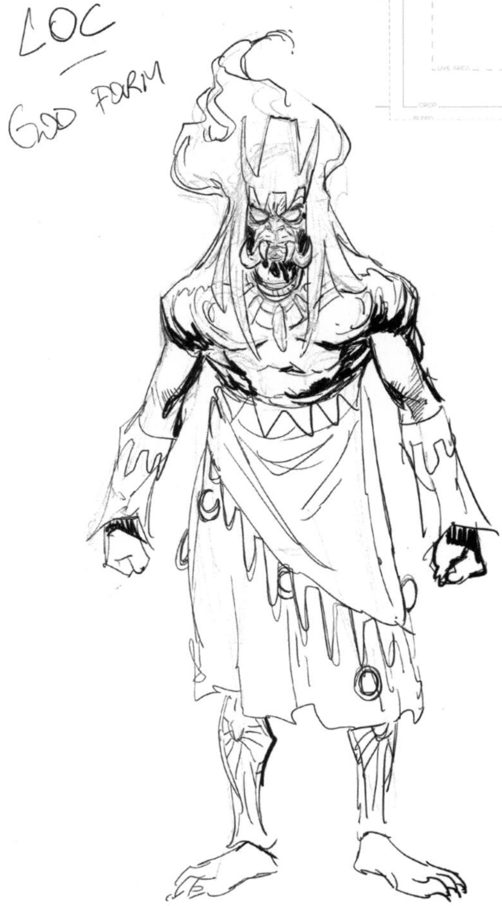
LOC
GOD FORM

PENCILLER
INKER
PAGE#
TITLE AQUAMAN CHARACTER DESIGNS
ISSUE #
MONTH
INTERIORS
TANG
THIN HAIR
SMALL AND DEEP EYES
TATTOOS SHOULD BE BLUE
KU
MINIMUM BLEED 1/4" ALL AROUND
LIVE AREA

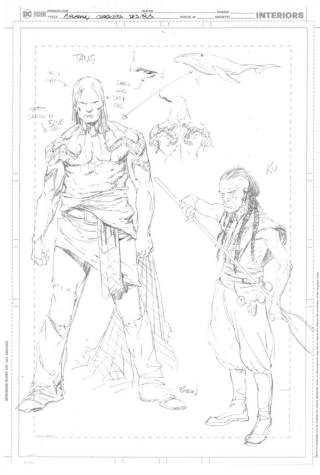

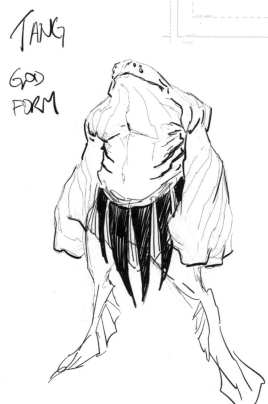

TANG
GOD FORM

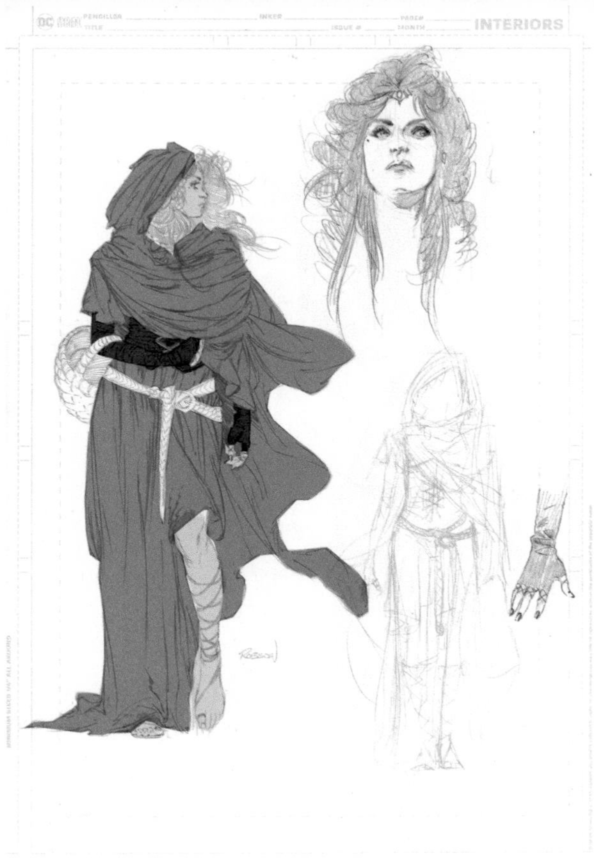
INTERIORS
ROBSON

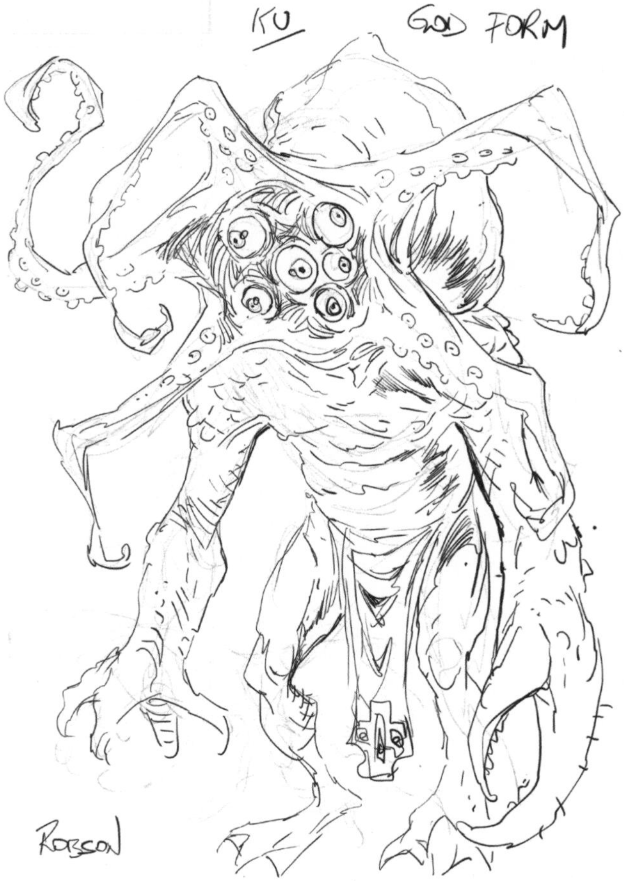
KU GOD FORM
ROBSON

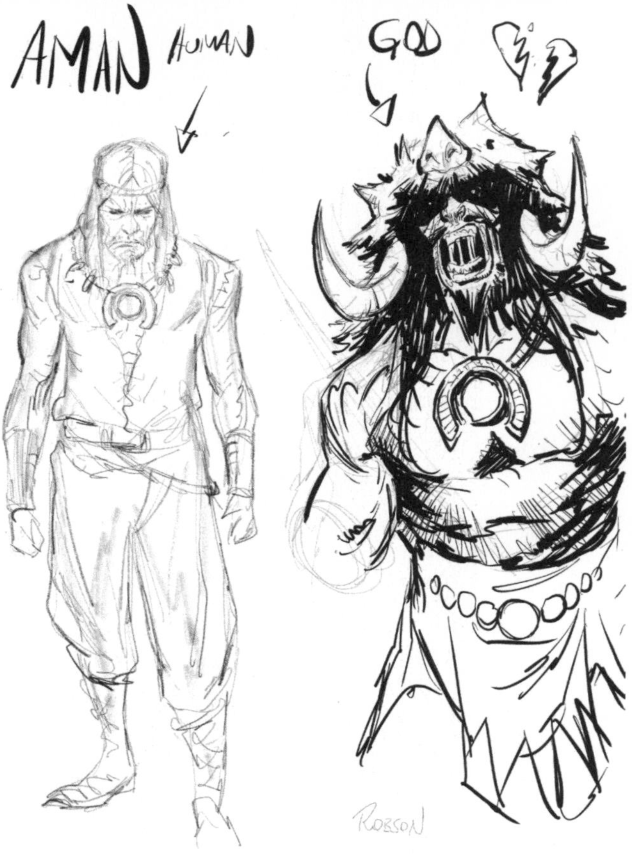
AMAN
HUMAN
GOD
ROBSON

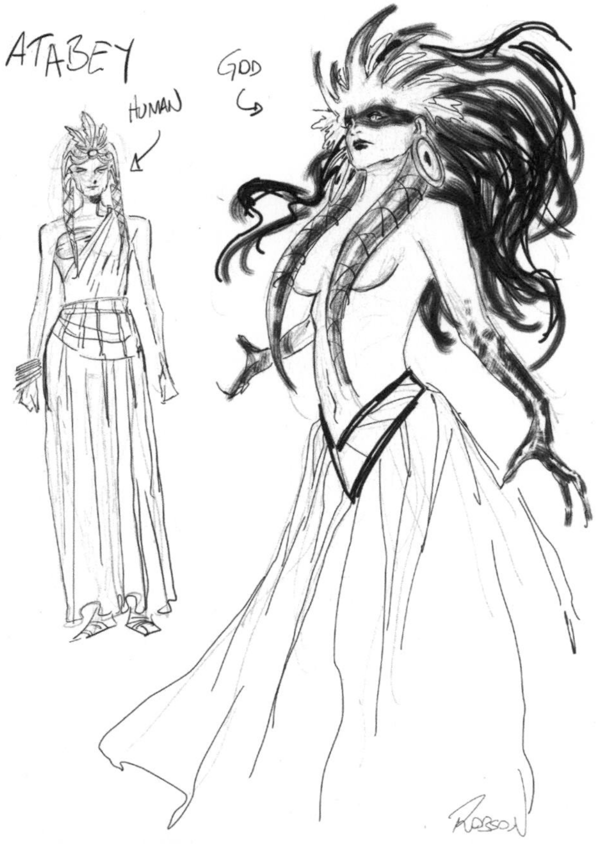
ATABEY
HUMAN
GOD
ROBSON

AGWE

HUMAN

GOD

MAC

HUMAN

GOD

Pencil art and sketch for AQUAMAN #43 cover

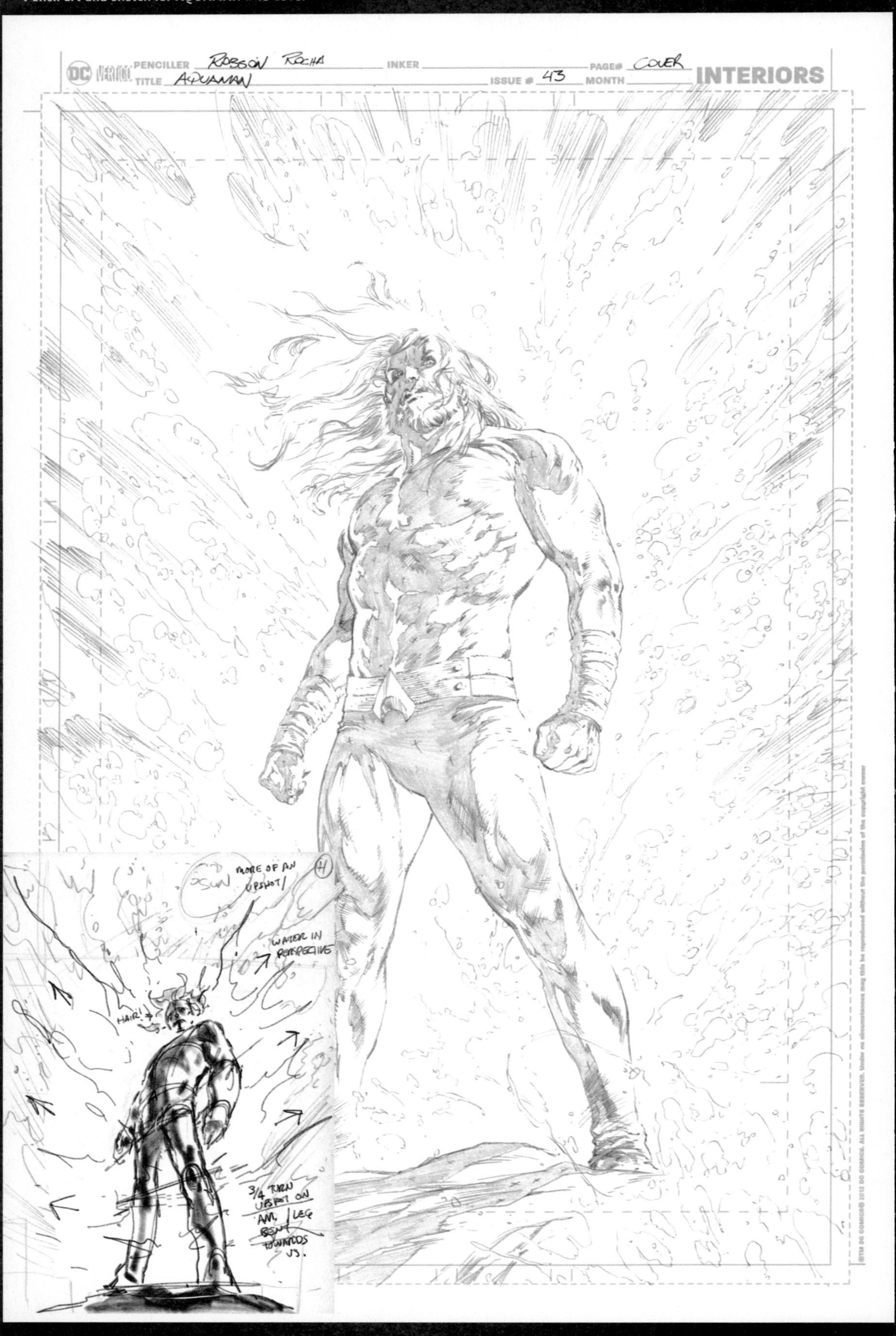

Pencil art for AQUAMAN #43 page 2

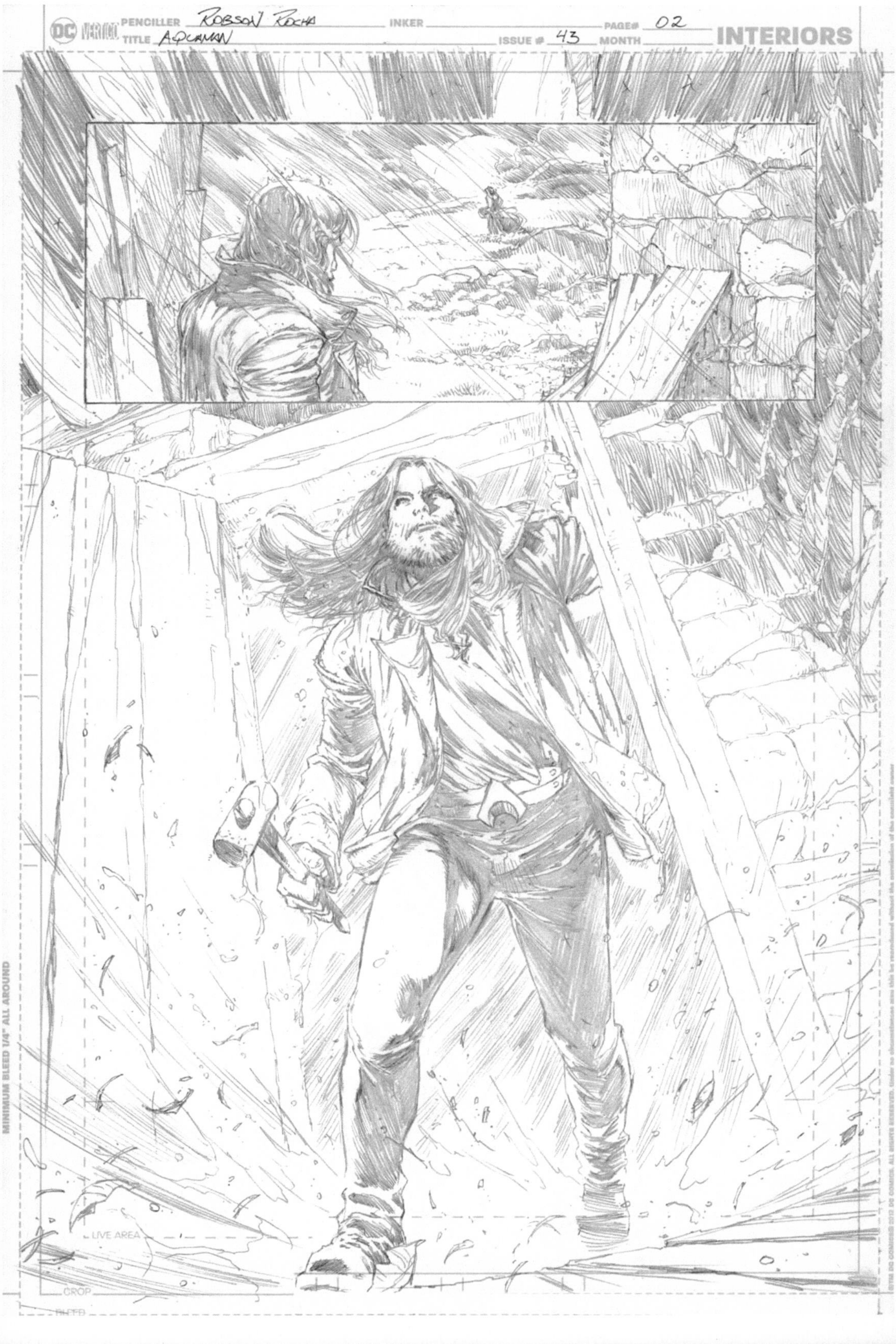
PENCILLER ROBSON ROCHA
INKER
PAGE# 02
TITLE AQUAMAN
ISSUE # 43
MONTH
INTERIORS
LIVE AREA
CROP
MINIMUM BLEED 1/4" ALL AROUND

Pencil art for AQUAMAN #43 page 5

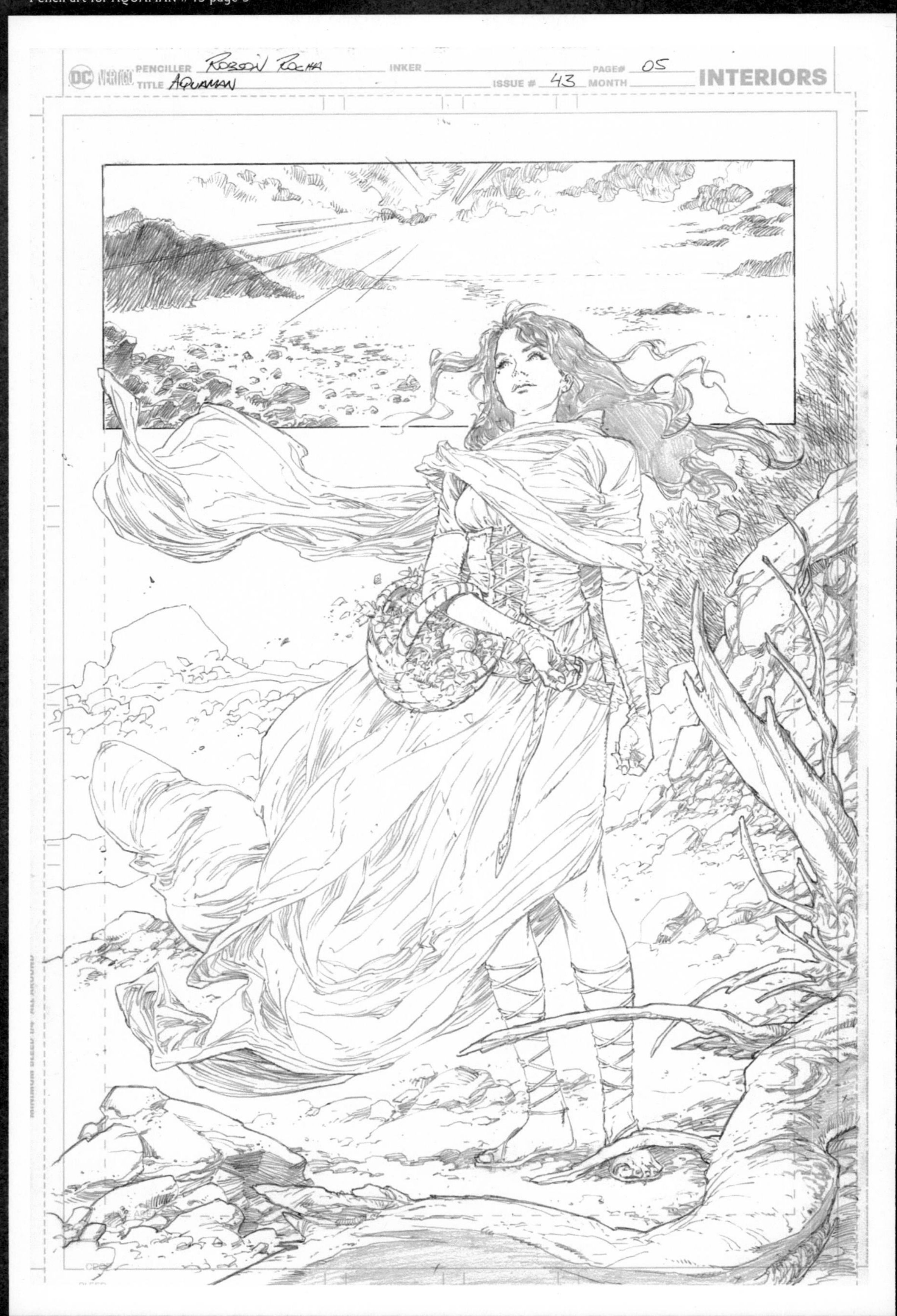

PENCILLER ROBSON ROCHA
INKER
PAGE# 05
TITLE AQUAMAN
ISSUE # 43
MONTH
INTERIORS

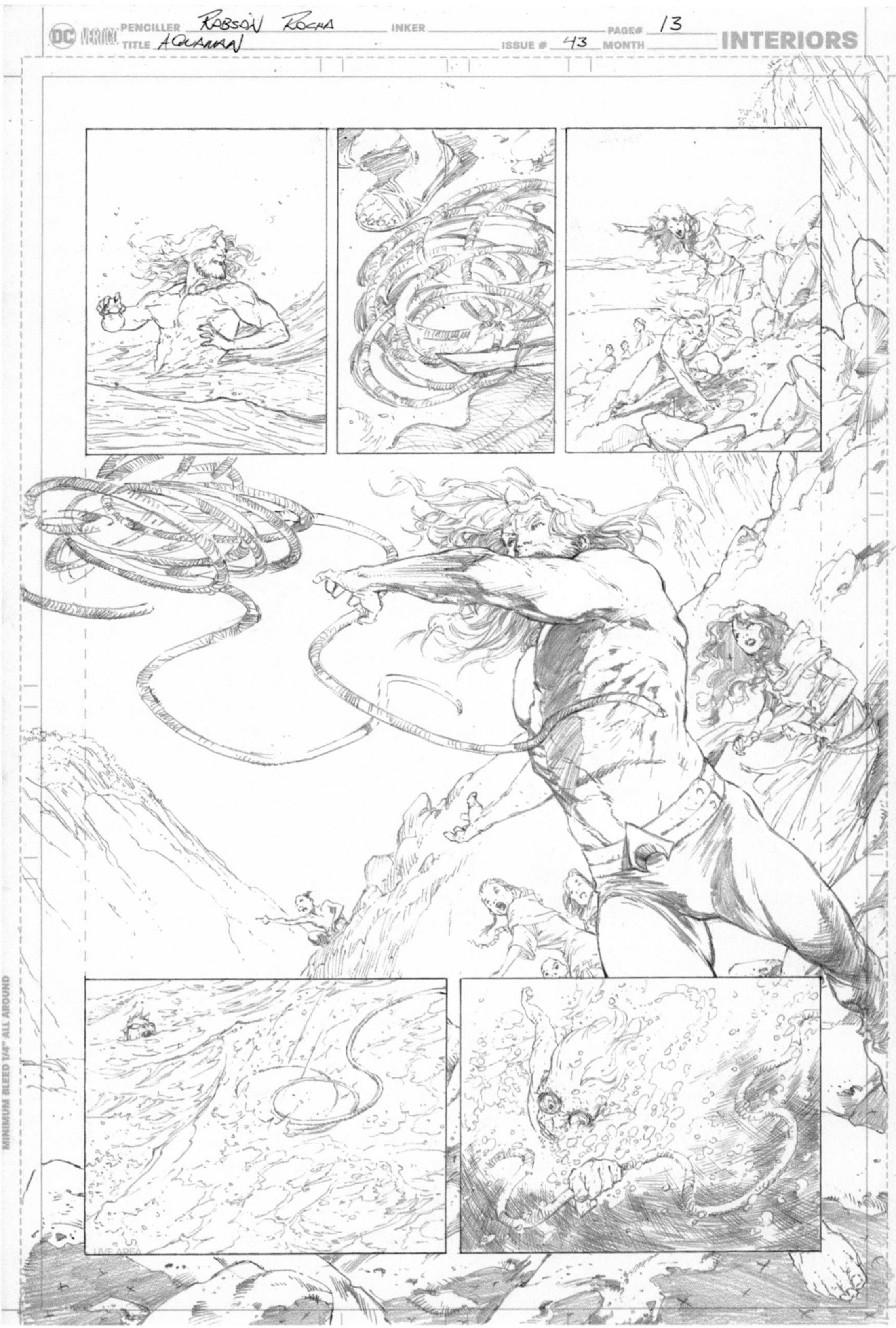

PENCILLER ROBSON ROCHA
INKER
PAGE# 13
INTERIORS
TITLE AQUAMAN
ISSUE # 43
MONTH
MINIMUM BLEED 1/4" ALL AROUND

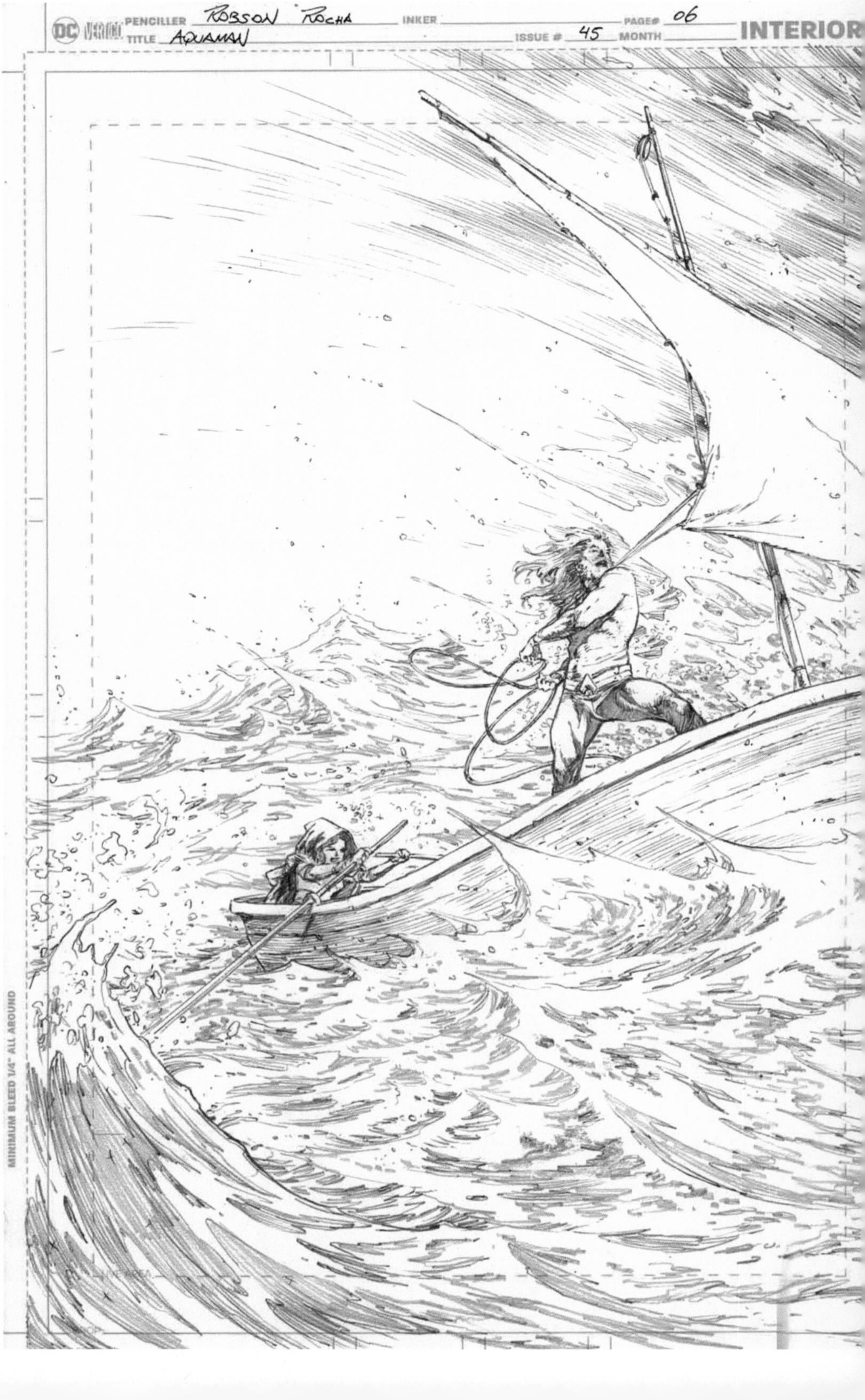
PENCILLER ROBSON ROCHA
INKER
PAGE# 06
INTERIOR
TITLE AQUAMAN
ISSUE # 45
MONTH
MINIMUM BLEED 1/4" ALL AROUND

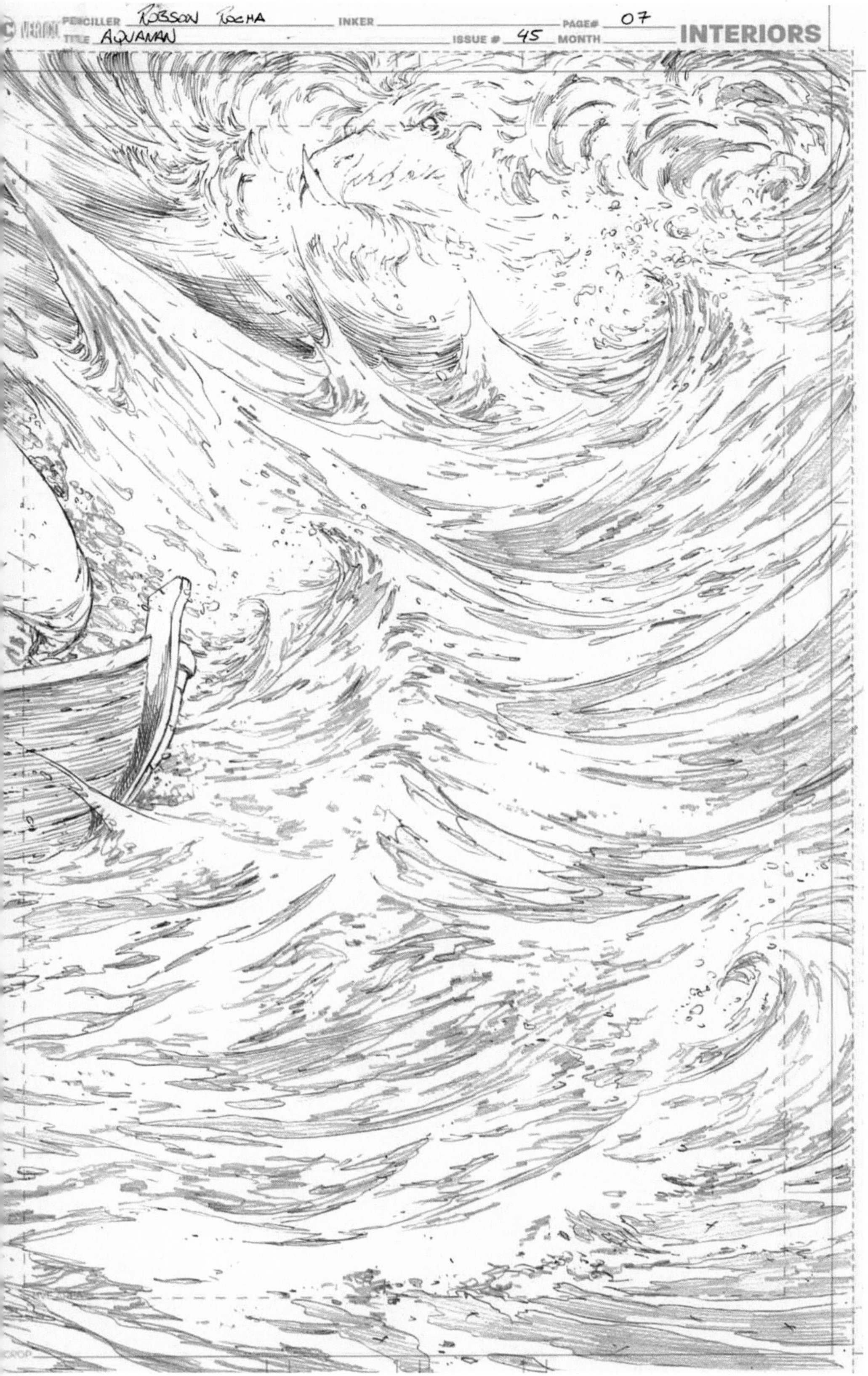
PENCILLER ROBSON ROCHA
INKER
PAGE# 07
TITLE AQUAMAN
ISSUE # 45
MONTH
INTERIORS

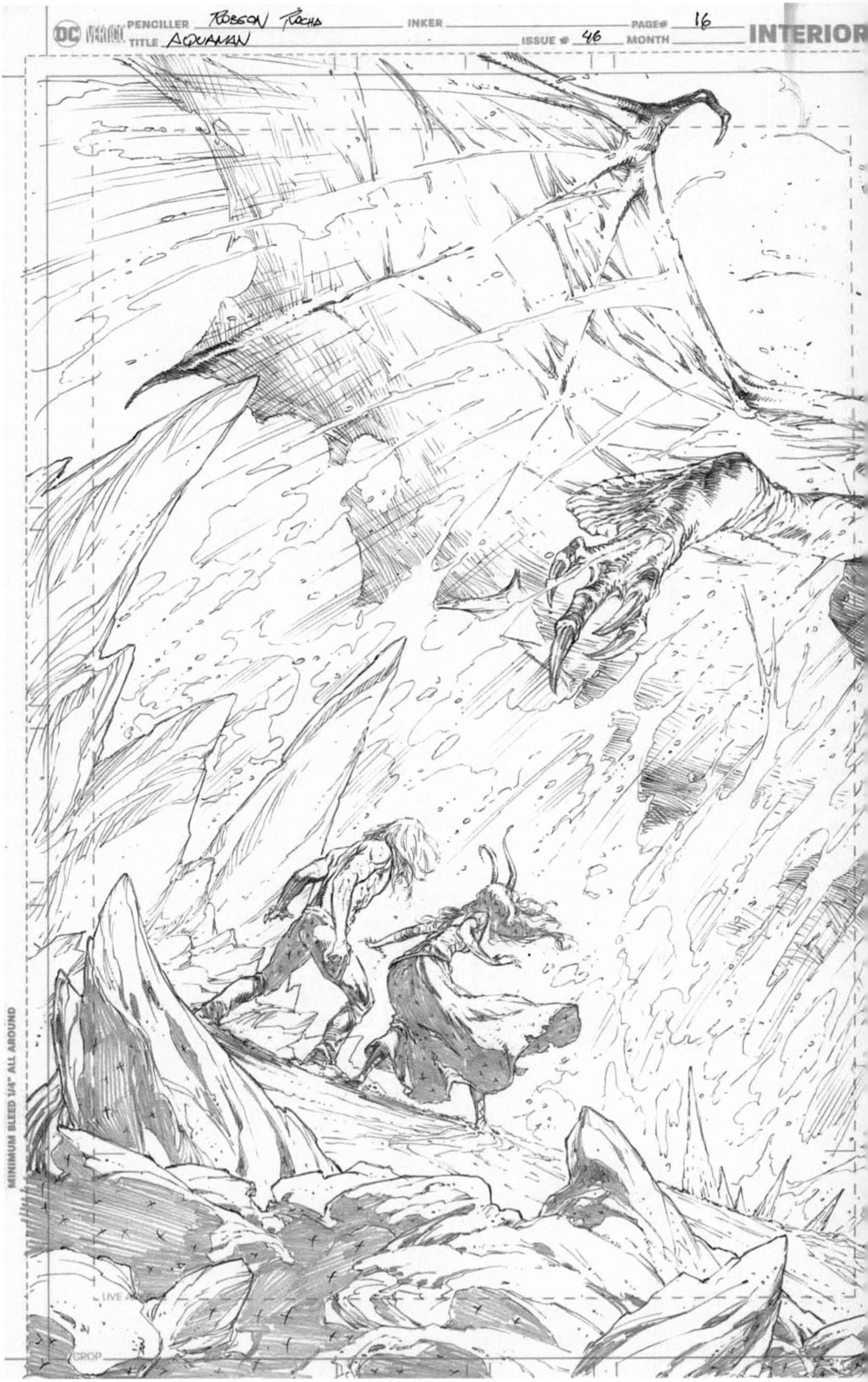
DC VERTIGO
PENCILLER ROBSON ROCHA
INKER
PAGE# 16
TITLE AQUAMAN
ISSUE # 46
MONTH
INTERIOR
MINIMUM BLEED 1/4" ALL AROUND
LIVE AREA
CROP

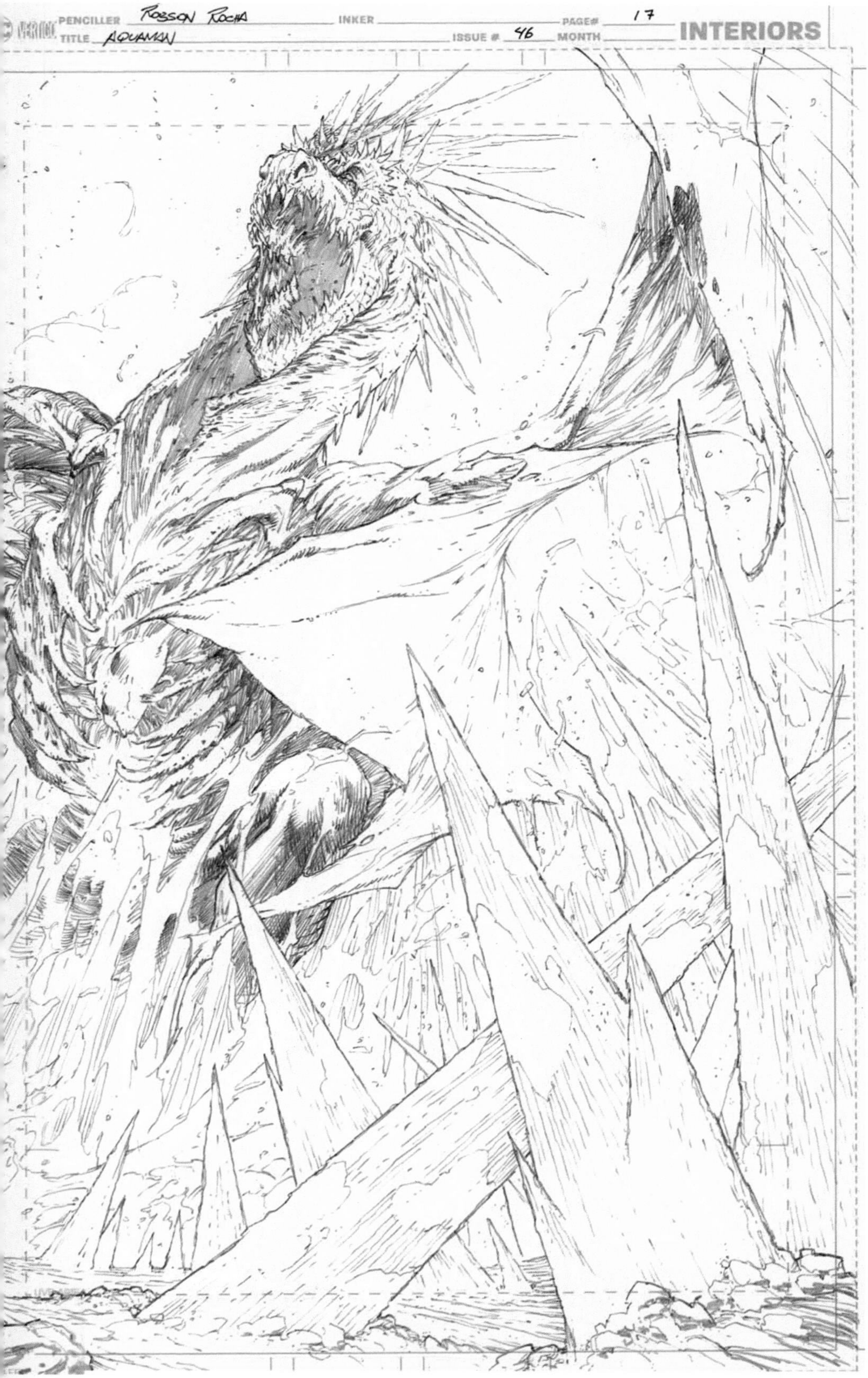
PENCILLER Robson Rocha
INKER
PAGE# 17
INTERIORS
TITLE AQUAMAN
ISSUE # 46
MONTH

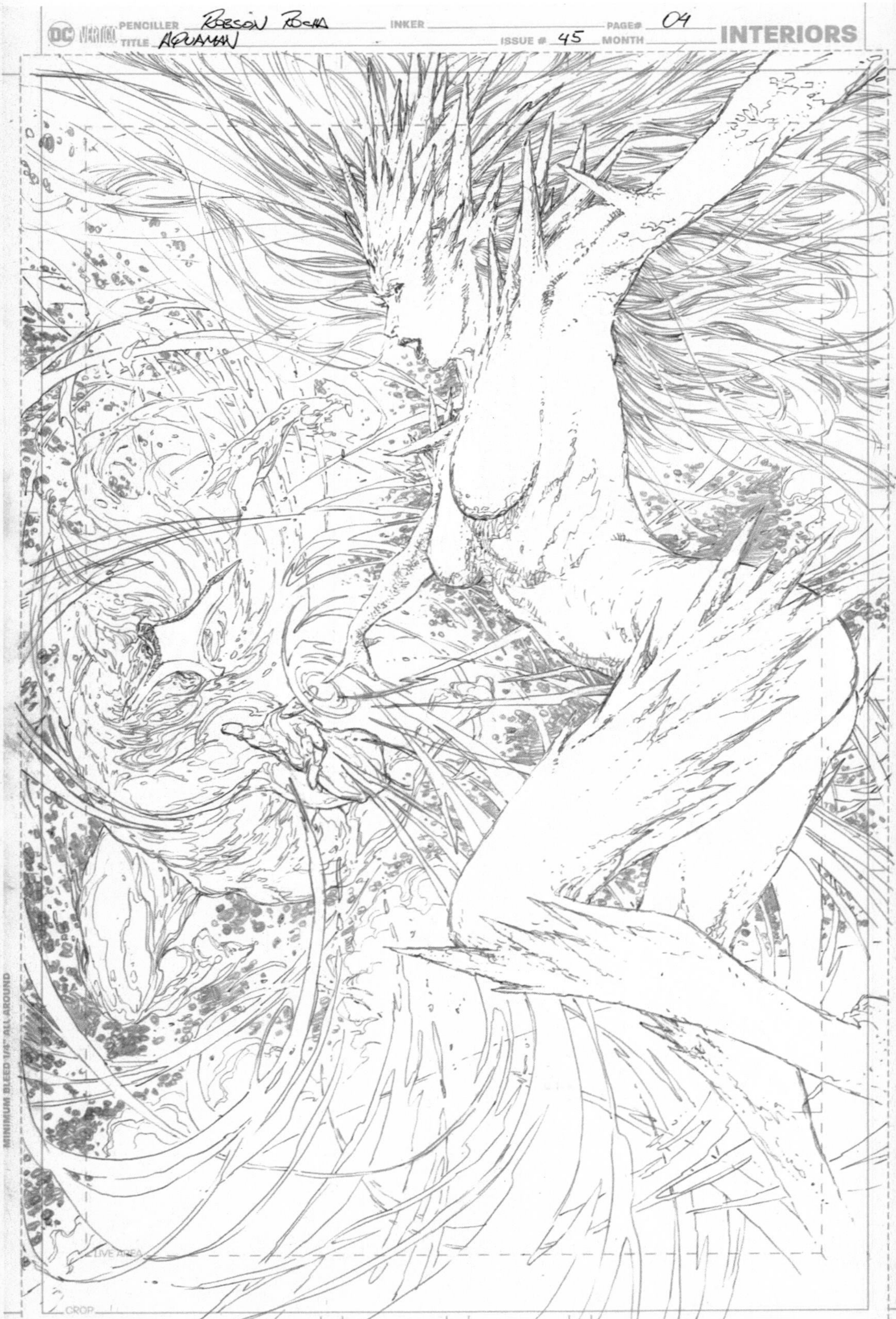
PENCILLER ROBSON ROCHA
INKER
PAGE# 04
TITLE AQUAMAN
ISSUE # 45
MONTH
INTERIORS
MINIMUM BLEED 1/4" ALL AROUND
LIVE AREA
CROP
BLEED

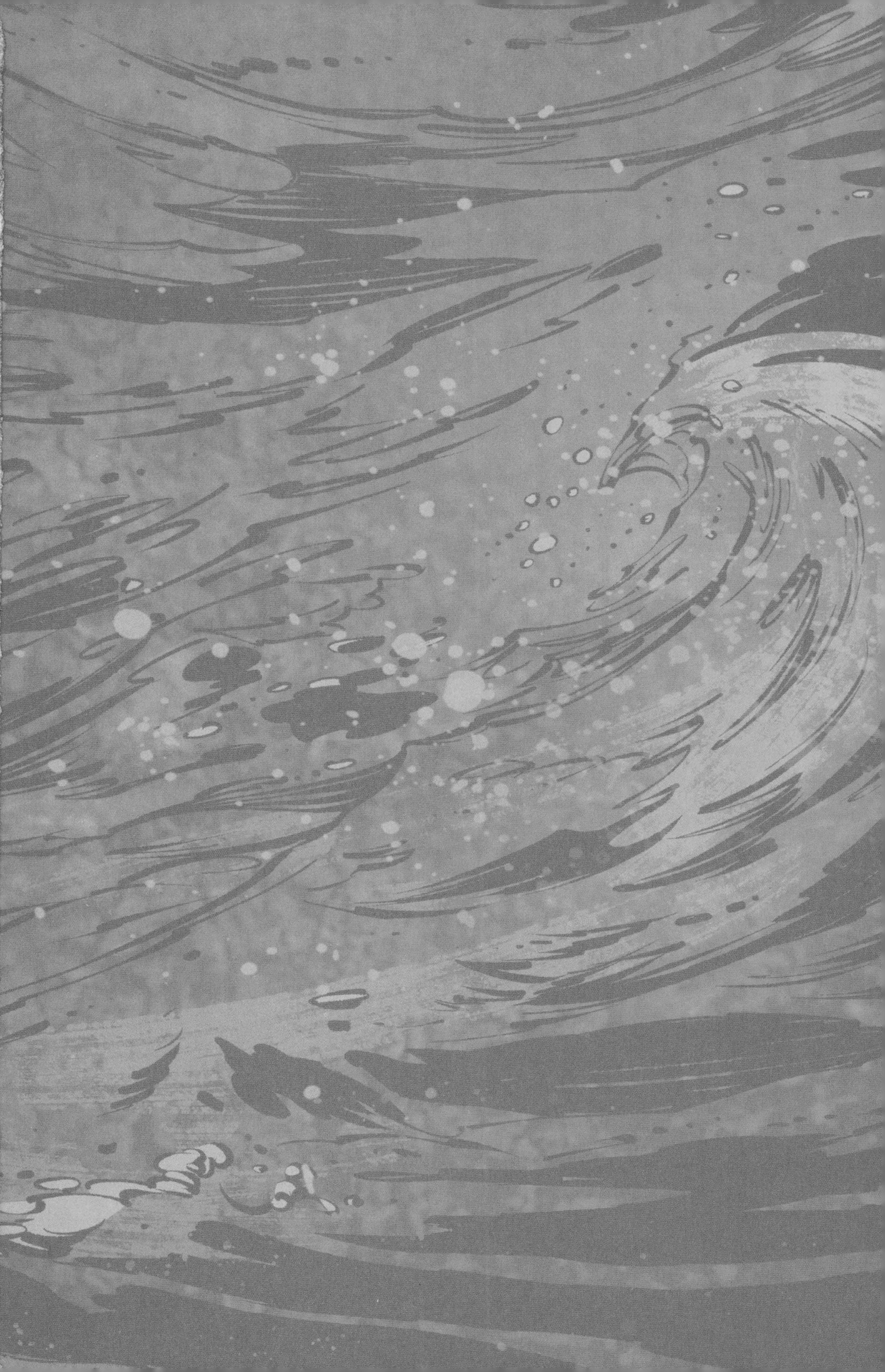

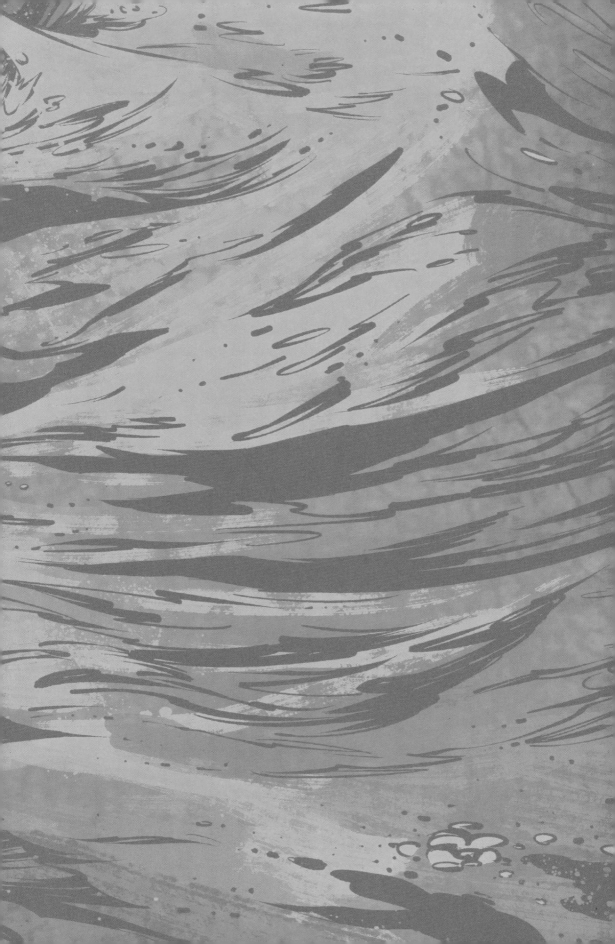